By *FRANK GOODWYN*

LONE-STAR LAND:
Twentieth-Century Texas in Perspective

LIFE ON THE KING RANCH

THE MAGIC OF LIMPING JOHN

THE DEVIL IN TEXAS

LONE-STAR LAND

LONE-STAR
Land

Twentieth-Century Texas in Perspective

by FRANK GOODWYN

Alfred A. Knopf — New York, 1955

L. C. catalog card number: 55–7850

© Frank Goodwyn, 1955

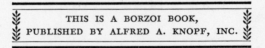

THIS IS A BORZOI BOOK,
PUBLISHED BY ALFRED A. KNOPF, INC.

FIRST EDITION

DEDICATED TO MY MOTHER

with happy recollections of our travels

together over the lone-star state

Preface

◇◆◇

THE PURPOSE of this book is to describe Texas as it is today, so that outlanders may dispose of all misconceptions about it and Texans may know what to expect of it. The method is to begin by portraying the most salient traits of the state as a whole, then to penetrate beyond the surface to the several influences acting upon it from the south, the east, the west, and the north. In each case, the region from whose direction the influence came is first described, then the nature of the influence is ascertained through those historical events whereby it is most clearly expressed.

In addition to providing useful information, the book proffers a new technique for studying societies. Today's scholarly disciplines have been built on vague and sometimes arbitrary divisions of subject matter. Geology, geography, anthropology, sociology, psychology, and the humanities tend inevitably to overlap as soon as they begin claiming relevance to the affairs of human life, for no human problem is ever purely geographical, purely social, purely psychological, purely political. . . . Exclusivistic specialization hence becomes abortive, and the best of specialists are those who know all fields but choose to emphasize a single aspect of human experience. Since the aspects themselves blend into one another so that no distinct line may be accurately drawn between them, the happiest choice for emphasis is a geographical area. Accordingly, this book embraces the geology, geography, anthropology, sociology, psychology, history, economics, and culture of Texas. Selectivity is necessarily high, and all details are eschewed except those which delineate the essential peculiarities of the chosen area.

Contents

◇◇

Illustrations

Maps

LONE-STAR LAND

I

ALTITUDES AND ATTITUDES

◇◇◇

1. The Land and the People

A COMBINATION of lucky accidents and extraordinary individuals is rapidly making Texas one of the world's most formidable concentrations of power. Located where the Gulf of Mexico meets the boundary between Anglo and Latin America and occupied by a little over eight million people, her 263,644 square miles of varied earth produce two and one half million barrels of oil per day. These, together with abundant agricultural production and vast natural gas and sulphur resources, are creating fabulous fortunes. According to the disposition of persons into whose hands they fall, the fortunes are working social changes, establishing foundations, and endowing institutes that attract fine brains from all over the world. Contending with them are a conflict-ridden state government, an adamant rural conservatism, and a fast-growing urban culture.

Of the eight million persons now living in Texas, about one and one-quarter million are of Mexican origin and almost one million are Negro. Because of the conditions under which they came, these two ethnic minorities have been categorized by the majority in such a way as to cause serious cleavages and

tensions. New Mexico, Arizona, and California have the same
Anglo-Mexican cleavages. Louisiana and the rest of the southern states have the same Anglo-Negro tensions. But Texas is
peculiar in that it combines the Mexican border situation with
the deep-south culture coming in from the east and equally
potent forces from the west and north. The socio-political
complexion of Texas is also considerably colored by the religious traditions of the populace, about one and one-third million being Roman Catholic, a little over three million being
Protestant, and one twentieth of a million being Jewish. The
remainder of the state's eight million souls, while they profess
no specific religious affiliation, are influenced both directly
and indirectly by religious traditions.

Since the breaking of Spain's dominion over Texas in
1821, people of diverse proclivities have poured into the area,
but until World War II the majority of them either were ag-
riculturally inclined or had homes in small towns dominated
by agriculture. All census records before 1950 show a vast pre-
dominance of rural over urban population. In 1850 there were
only 7,665 city dwellers in the state, while 204,927 lived in the
country. In other words, one hundred and five years ago Texas
was 96.4 per cent rural. Through the last half of the nineteenth century, both rural and urban population increased by
leaps and bounds, but still only a small fraction of the people
lived in the cities. By 1900 Texas was 82 per cent rural, with
two and one-half million people in the country as contrasted
to only a little over half a million in the cities. In 1940 the urban population was almost three million and the rural a little
over three and one-half million, but by 1950 the rural had
fallen back below the three million mark while the urban had
come up almost to five million. The Census Bureau's recent
redefinition of "urban" to include suburban districts slightly
exaggerates this latter contrast. Yet the fact remains that at
present, for the first time in history, the focus of Texas political power is within city limits.

Texas's rapid rate of population growth (20.2 per cent during the 1940–50 decade), if not described in detail, would give the impression that at present the state is being flooded by newcomers. This is not the case. While Texas gained 1,296,-370 people between 1940 and 1950, only 27,000 are attributable to the excess of immigration over emigration. Of the 254 counties in Texas, 145 lost people during this decade. Within each of these, the largest city often gained, but the most rapid population increase has been in cities of more than one hundred thousand.

The growth of Texas cities, then, is due to people moving in, not from outside the state, but from its own rapidly mechanizing farms. Much of the population increase can also be attributed to the excess of births over deaths. Thus the people of Texas are still predominantly native-born, imbued from babyhood with traditions that have come down to them, plus some readjustment, modification, and elaboration, from the days of the Texas Republic. Improved transportation has enabled them to enjoy city life and drive out every day or so during the proper seasons to work their farms with large machines. Along with their accumulation in cities comes the same romantic nostalgia for "pioneer" life, expressed in Texas literature and supposedly historical writing, which has accompanied rapid urbanization at other times in other parts of the world.

Improved transportation also causes an increased flow of money into the cities, and this in turn draws more people from the rural areas. Country folk who used to shop at local stores can now drive or fly once a week or so to the cities. Again, the city with the widest range of choice has an advantage. Meanwhile, the old home towns languish. Their stores and hotels close for want of business. Their workers go to the cities to hunt new jobs. Urbanization thus accelerates itself.

The lives of Texans are being vastly enriched by numerous new opportunities in the mushrooming cities, and life in the

half-abandoned rural regions is being just as vastly improved
with little real loss of original charm. Not only have the new
city dwellers been given access to a range of experiences never
before available; human invention under the stimulus of free
enterprise has brought hitherto unheard-of conveniences to
those who remain on the farms. Tall poles stand in double file
over the hills and plains, holding wires that convey electric
power to rural refrigerators, lights, and washing machines.
There are still a few windmills, built tall enough to catch the
wind and fill high cisterns so that the weight of the water will
cause pressure in the faucets. But most Texas farmers and
ranchers now have electric pumps, which will work on either
still or windy days, forcing water from wells into small pressure tanks on the ground. Like the steam locomotive and the
Colt revolver, the windmill is becoming obsolete. With it may
go some romantic associations, but its successors make men
less dependent on the elements than they ever were before. If
the old romance is lost, a new and greater one is announced
as the grim roar of trucks and autos forms a novel background
for the musical courtship of sparrows and cardinals. In most
spheres of activity, old and pleasant customs, refreshed rather
than replaced by the new gadgets, seem destined to persist
indefinitely. Daily when their work is done and supper eaten,
the remaining rural dwellers sit on their porches and talk
about the weather, or politics, or fine-bred stock, or oil prospects, until the sun goes down, the air loses its heat, the sunset colors lose their brilliance, and the trees lose their distinct-
ness to become black silhouettes against the sky.

Life in the small towns also retains much of its old charm
while profiting from the growth of Texas industry. Towns between one and twenty thousand retain the physical form of
their original plans, which follow two predominant patterns.
The less frequent is the long main street with a public building at each end. By far the more popular is the public square,
with places of business facing it from all four points of the

compass. If the town is a county seat, the courthouse will stand in the center of the square. The county jail may be a separate building, or it may occupy the upper floor of the courthouse. Almost always, the courthouse is the largest building in town. Often it is the only two-story structure in the vicinity, so that it towers above the others like a mother hen clucking above her baby chicks.

Most Texas towns hold yearly fairs, often accompanied by rodeos for the demonstration of cowboy talent. There are long parades in which community leaders display their gracefulness in cowboy regalia. Young drum majorettes mingle the beauty of bare legs and cavorting bodies with the music of blaring brass bands, usually trained in local schools. Business concerns view the fair as a chance to advertise their wares. Contests are held among competing farmers and ranchers for the raising of the best vegetables and livestock.

The growth of Texas cities is in many ways similar to that of other modern metropolises. As the business section spreads into the older residential areas, the wealthier dwellers move out to suburbs and commute in automobiles, leaving their former homes to stand either empty or occupied by vagrants, with decaying architectural adornments robbed of all except a few fugitive memories. Thus a bracelet of slums develops around the business sector, endangering the lives of all with contagion from filth and insect pests. As the business sector continues to encroach upon it, this slum area is congested until life in it sometimes grows hardly bearable. Crime waves sweep across it, shocking the more fortunate suburban citizens, who have often sacrified their suffrage by moving outside the city limits. The municipal government sweats blood.

But the Texas cities differ from those of other lands in that they are extremely young and are expanding at a fantastic rate, so that their growing pains are peculiarly acute. As great cities, all of them are less than a generation old. None had more than sixty thousand people in 1900. In 1950 three of them had gone above four hundred thousand. They were San Antonio (with 406,811 in South Central Texas), Houston (with 594,321 on the Gulf Coast), and Dallas (with 432,927 on the high prairies of North Central Texas). Each of these cities is now more than eight times as big as it was in 1900. This growth is largely owing to oil, of course, and to the gains that any industry can make from being near its source of fuel and raw materials. But there are also other factors.

For instance, it is simpler to build a home in a Texas city than in a northern or eastern city. Homes in such older communities as New England, especially if heated by steam, are most economically built on two floors. Land is scarce. Lots are small. Winters are cold. There has to be a basement for the furnace. Most Texas dwellings, on the other hand, are built entirely on top of the earth, and they seldom have more than one floor. There are no stairways to climb. Frame foundations rest on blocks a foot or two above the ground. City edicts sometimes forbid two-story houses in choice residential sections. These factors vary, of course, with the widely varying character of the land in different parts of the state.

◇◇

2. Altitudes

ABOUT SIXTY MILLION YEARS AGO a disturbance inside the earth caused an upward thrust of West Texas lands, cracking the ground in an irregular new-moon curve that meanders northeastward through the areas of present-day Del Rio, San Antonio, Austin, Waco, and Dallas. Through this crack, known to geologists as the Balcones fault line, oozed molten stone that soon hardened into hills of rock. The lowlands east of the fault line were enriched from era to era with more and more silt eroded from the highlands and carried by winds and rivers toward the Gulf. Thus, the coastal plain became a haven for the nourishment of life while the highlands in the west took on the bare, gaunt aspect which they still have. Only tough, tiny shrubs with shriveled limbs and forbidding thorns can grow wild on those worn stone wrinkles, whereas the flat land to the south and east teems with easily accessible agricultural wealth. Also, being near the Gulf, the eastern plains enjoy heavy rains, whereas the clouds are dissipated by the time they reach the western hills.

But the water left by rains just above the line is caught in the porous limestone and exuded through natural springs all along the crack. For this reason, and because the waterfalls descending the fault can supply power for industry, Texas's great inland cities are all located along the Balcones.

The distribution of peoples, especially since methods of communication have enabled men to choose their habitat with foresight and discrimination, is necessarily affected by these geographical features. Only about one fourth of the state's eight million inhabitants live in the high, eroded area above the fault line. The other three fourths have accumulated in the less extensive silt-filled basin to the south and east.

Moreover, the lay of the land has a selective and molding influence on the mentality of its occupants. The highlands appeal to persons who, for religious, philosophical, hygienic, or æsthetic reasons, would rather have comparative solitude, even with poverty, than be rich and enmeshed in the demands of a populous community. Their life in this more isolated region further accentuates and encourages the propensities which first made them find it attractive. Thus, like the growth of cities, the accentuation of regional traits is a self-perpetuating, self-accelerating process.

3. Attitudes

LEGALLY, Texas can divide itself into five separate states any time it wishes. There is much to be said for such a division. The altitude in Texas ranges from sea level on the Gulf Coast to six thousand feet above sea level west of the Balcones fault line, with the Guadalupe peak in the northern edge of the state's western tip rising 8,751 feet. The mean annual temperature ranges from fifty-five degrees in the north to seventy-two degrees in the south. The yearly rainfall ranges from nine inches in the western tip to fifty inches along the Gulf Coast.

The Mexican border is a unit in itself, with assets and problems all its own. East Texas and the Gulf Coast have more in common with Louisiana than with the rest of the state. West Texas has more in common with New Mexico than with southern or eastern or northern Texas. North Texas has more in common with Oklahoma than with the Mexican border. Each of these sections would be far better off with its own state government serving its own peculiar needs and desires. Besides, by dividing itself into such sections, Texas would multiply its power five times in the national senate. It would have ten senators where it now has only two. Every Texan would therefore have five times as much power in the upper house as he now has.

There are also some strong arguments against any division of this kind. Five state governments would cost five times as much in taxes as the present single government. It is possible, of course, that the new governments would give the average Texan more than five times the benefit he is getting now. Being smaller, they might function more economically. Under the present setup, in a state so large, a candidate for state office cannot come to know his constituents very intimately. He has to spend too much of his time on the road. Air travel may help offset this difficulty in the future, but the expense of a Texas political campaign would still be prohibitive to many excellent would-be candidates. The distances are so great that frequently a man's chances are determined not by his appeal to the people but by the amount of travel money he can muster.

The most potent objection to the division of Texas is a sentimental one. Many Texans have personified their state, glamorized it as a kind of living god. Others feel for it as a child feels for a lovable pet. It may be burdensome, but they would rather die than see it butchered. Of course, this sentimental symbol could remain even after political partition took place. Texans could render it homage just as Canadians and Australians render homage to the phantom British Empire. But the people of Texas would not readily trade their lusty giant for such a poor ghost.

There is more to this objection than sheer regional loyalty. If the state were divided, its citizens could no longer inflate their individual egos by identifying themselves with it. The dry farmer of the western hills above the Balcones fault line, his crops withering for want of water, could no longer picture himself as living in the nation's number-one cotton state. The drouth-stricken rancher, his cattle carrying hardly enough meat between their skin and bones to pay for their killing, could no longer impress himself and the world with the fact that his state produces more beef than any of the other forty-seven. The urban factory worker, paying dearly in sweat for every dollar of his daily wage, could no longer proclaim himself a part of the nation's largest, richest state. It is a hoary human habit for the poor to drown their pain in shouts of glee over the glory of their Cæsars.

In Texas this habit has a particularly strong hold, not only because the state was once an independent nation, demanding and receiving patriotic homage, but also because Texas has long been the target of criticisms from outlanders, against which this cult of bigness is the most readily apparent defense. Early criticisms hinged on such heated controversies as the slavery question and stemmed from such northern grievances as fever caught from Texas cattle and the region's convenience as a retreat for the destitute and sinful. Recently Texas has been victimized by journalists who have little to sell except a vaunted knowledge of "the inside story." They suggest to the reader that all authorities and scholars are fools, that all established agencies of information are full of liars, and that the only way for the public to get the truth about a community is for some true-blue reporter with a sleuthing eye to sneak in through some back door, uncover some deep, dark secret, and scamper away to the press with it. This suggestion appears, for instance, in titles like *Inside U.S.A.* and the other "Insides" of John Gunther. More recently it came out in the "Confidentials" of Mortimer and Lait, among which *U.S.A. Confidential* caused Texans considerable distress by peddling gossipy tales. Trained to single out the spectacular, yet compelled by popular demand to appear profound, such writers pick up a few freaks and give them undue dignity by labeling them as typical. The result is a distortion of the picture and an insult both to the subject and to the intelligence of the reading public. In such fictionized flights as Edna Ferber's *Giant,* the distortions are carried to an absurd degree.

More significant than these are the magazines which picture Texas as a land of greasy, bilious millionaires who live like a bunch of New World maharajas, oppressing and controlling their fellow Texans through deception and mechanized elections. One expression of this conception is a couple of articles by Theodore H. White in the *Reporter* magazine (May–June 1954) entitled "Texas, Land of Wealth and Fear." Perhaps inadvertently, because of his strong feelings on political issues, White sometimes throws the facts out of focus by using words that subtly allude to generally stigmatized concepts. For instance, he does not say that the Texas government is a political machine; in fact, he admits that Texans have "no machine in the recognizable Eastern form of patronage, spoils, and bloc-delivered votes." But then he goes on to say that Texas politics rests "on a series of autonomous self-winding groups in each community, consisting of the local aristocracy of enterprise and commercial achievement." Note the word "self-winding," which attaches to the picture the idea of the machine, though the author cannot be pinned down as saying that the machines are there. In the same manner, he speaks of the Dallas billionaire H. L. Hunt as "engineering" public opinion.

The "Big Rich" of Texas, says White, are too busy with national politics to run the state. This local job is hence left to the "Little Rich," who "see in every school-board contest, in every independent candidate who repudiates their leadership, the hand of Moscow or of the CIO bent on destroying Texas institutions." The inaccuracy here comes from lines of distinction drawn too sharply and an arbitrary grouping of entirely different individuals. Actually, both the "Big Rich" and the "Little Rich" help run Texas, to the extent that they are interested citizens. Some of them see Moscow as a booger behind every bush; some of them do not. It is true that there have been efforts to censor the holdings of Texas public libraries. There is a notorious group of self-appointed female sentinels known as the Minute Women. But these movements have mostly dwindled on exposure, and those who oppose them can often be numbered among the "Big" or "Little Rich." Certainly Texas wealth has no monopoly on the fear of Communism. It is widespread among the poor as well, and it is often justified. Nor do the "Big Rich" or the "Little Rich" hold anything like absolute power in their own communities. Time and time again they have had to back down, to compromise, to pay taxes in highly articulate pain.

Although there are no sales taxes or state income taxes in Texas and the oil business pays the bulk of governmental expenses, the average Texan is by no means well off financially. The median income in 1949 for Texas families was only $2,680 and for unrelated individuals only $871. Only a little over 3 per cent of Texas's families make $10,000 and above per year, while 36.51 per cent of the families and 76.45 per cent of the unrelated individuals get less than $2,000 per year. Painful extremes of wealth and poverty are therefore added to the extremes of altitude and climate which characterize Texas. One circumstance that keeps the economic extremes acute is the close proximity of Mexico, from which peppery winds of human influence move northward constantly.

II

PEPPERY WINDS FROM THE SOUTH

◇◇

1. *Mexican Border*

THE SOUTHERN and southwestern edge of Texas naturally has more Mexican smells—pepper spice and corn tortillas—than any of the regions farther north. Yet its three biggest cities—Brownsville, Laredo, and El Paso—have little in common other than their heavy proportion of Mexican population: about 68 per cent.

The lower Rio Grande Valley—the citrus paradise of world-wide fame—is separated from the rest of the state by a band of ranch country some forty miles wide transversing the broad upper body of the state's blade-like southern point. The King Ranch, with approximately one million acres, is in the eastern end of this band. It is a sandy, semi-arid plain, covered with scattered mottes of shrubbery, with mesquites prevailing in the west and live oaks along the coast. Running south across the ranch lands are two heavily traveled thoroughfares: highways 77 and 281. Together with the railroads that parallel them, they form the principal arteries of land commerce leading into the valley. The ground is all flat as a floor. There is no noticeable slope, even toward the Rio Grande. The valley's

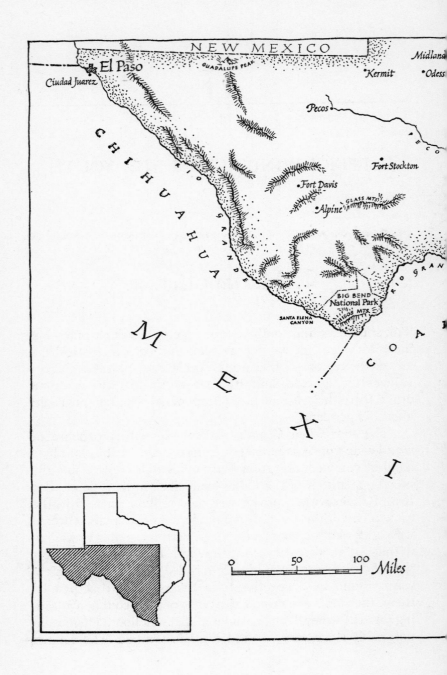

NEW MEXICO

Midland

El Paso

Ciudad Juarez

GUADALUPE PEAK

Kermit

Odess

Pecos

PECO

CHIHUAHUA

Fort Stockton

RIO

Fort Davis

GLASS MTS.

GRANDE

Alpine

RIO GRAN

BIG BEND
National Park

CHISOS MTS.

COA

SANTA ELENA
CANYON

M   E   X   I

0   50   100   Miles

beginning can be discerned only by the character of the vegetation: the irrigated fields, the orchards, the palms.

The palms of the valley are phenomenal. How they stand
against the wind on their tall, thin trunks is a mystery. The
fan palms tower far above anything else on the land. They are
often more than twice as tall as the telephone poles. Yet their
stems are extremely slender and their heads are always heavy
with green and dying leaves. Planted for miles in straight rows,
they scallop the fields and orchards, giving the land an atmosphere of semi-tropical opulence. On far horizons, where their
slim trunks are hidden from view by distance and humidity,
their fan-tousled heads look like beads strung on invisible
strings or magically suspended just above the sky's straight
rim.

The most intensely developed land in the valley is a strip
ten to fifteen miles wide extending parallel to the eastward-
flowing Rio Grande for a little over forty miles. Up the spine
of this rich strip runs Highway 83, with towns spaced on an
average of four and one-half miles apart: Harlingen, La Feria,
Mercedes, Weslaco, Donna, Alamo, San Juan, Pharr, McAllen, and Mission. These towns have large business districts and
relatively small residential sections. Their stores must serve
both their citizens and the farmers who live outside the city
limits. In recent years many of the farmers have built homes
in the towns, where they sleep with their families while they
continue to oversee their farms by day.

This string of valley towns has almost merged into a single
agricultural metropolis, with palm-lined roads blocked off like
streets and symmetrically planted orchards interspersed like
public parks among the residential sections and shopping centers: a solid farming city with a total population of approximately 350,000. Living thus in close proximity, with the same
geographical environment, the valley towns are very much
alike. All of them are dominated by the valley's most prosperous citizens, who are largely of Anglo-Saxon origin. All of

them are supported by the labor of low-paid field hands, mostly out of Mexico. All of them profit from the valley's combination of fertile alluvial soils and a year-round growing season.

Yet a few of the valley cities have features peculiar to themselves. Harlingen is the valley's chief eastern terminal. Weslaco's annual birthday celebration, held in December, is climaxed with a style show in which the city's most beautiful girls wear costumes made by the various women's clubs from the perishable crops grown in the valley. Blouses, vests, and sleeves are fashioned from parts of the grapefruit, the daisy, the chrysanthemum, the poinsettia, the prickly pear, the eggplant, the green pepper, the carrot.

San Juan has a "people's church" made up of twenty-three different denominations. Organized in 1918, when the valley did not have enough Protestants to form a whole church in one single denomination, it remains open to all to this day. The Latin element in San Juan has constructed an air-conditioned cathedral with a $20,000 pipe organ, an altar from Spain, bells from France, and tile from Mexico.

The developed strip of the valley does not reach all the way to the Rio Grande. It fades into huisache and mesquite brush about five miles north of the riverbanks. Through this brush runs the Military Highway. Its towns are populated largely by Latins: old owners whose ancestors have been here since the days of Spain's dominion; who would rather have their little *ranchos,* with a few horses and cows and a few fields, than all the fine orchards of the *sajones* (Anglo-Saxons) a few miles to the north. The unpredictable nature of the Rio Grande helps keep the *sajones* away. Heavy with silt from high mountains in the northwest, this *río bravo* (fierce river), as the Mexicans traditionally have called it, eats continuously into its banks. Sometimes its waters burst across new ground, cutting off hunks of erstwhile Texas or Mexican property, causing international contentions. Ambitious boosters have de-

cided after bitter experience that they had better leave these
close environs of the "fierce river" to the wild shrubs, the
mosquitoes, and the Mexicans.

During the harvest seasons the Latin owners along the riverbanks take their families a few miles north, or sometimes
many miles north, to work the more productive ground of the
Anglos. The Anglo's air of superiority and consequent scorn
for field labor, plus the valley's richness, draw large numbers
of destitute Mexican farm hands. In the valley's developed
strip these form a servant class, spurned by all who would
rise in the world, despised along with their language and their
ways. Alert Mexicans in the lower valley therefore learn English as soon as they can and display it at every opportunity for
the same reason that a millionaire's wife displays her diamonds.

Up the river from Mission the land soon begins growing
arid and hilly. A dazzling heterogeny of shrubs, all the more
weird because they stand in semi-desert wastes, sets in. Seventy-eight thousand acres of this bleak earth have recently
been inundated by waters caught behind Falcon Dam. This
immense reservoir is expected to save the lower valley from all
future drouths.

Laredo, being situated almost exactly between San Antonio and Monterrey, has the largest tourist and import-export
business on the Texas-Mexican border. Its Texas-Mexican attitudes are not at all like those of the lower valley, because it
has no unusually prolific soil to attract either domineering
Anglo land-buyers or submissive Mexican laborers. The Latins
living in Laredo are from old families, well established and
often well-to-do. Among them, therefore, Spanish is respect-
able, and Anglos often take pride in their ability to speak it
well.

Stretching north of Laredo is the Winter Garden area,
where artesian-well-water irrigation has made possible the cultivation of highly diversified farm and orchard products. Crys-

tal City, in the center of this area, specializes in spinach. A life-size statue of Popeye, the sailor man, appropriately stands on its public square.

Above the Winter Garden area, the Pecos River runs southeastward into the Rio Grande. The land beyond it is more mountainous than ever, and more thinly populated. I remember that when I was a child my father drove with my mother and me in a rattletrap car through these awful stretches of dust and space. I remember him sighing, almost groaning, at the lack of moisture or any circumstance favoring life. As far as we could see there was not a living thing: not a sprig of grass, nor a bird, nor a jack rabbit; only the road, a tiny white line winding through the hills; only the monster stones, the wind, the sun's glare, and the blowing sand. At last a moving speck appeared on the pale, faint thread of road. When it came half an hour closer, we could see that it was a lone man in a Model-T Ford. I remember Dad's remarking, in a tone half of disgust, half of resignation: "Yonder comes another damn fool."

Yet human ingenuity, enlightened by science and inspired by competitive private enterprise, may someday make something even of these lands. Many of the desert plants contain important medicinal and chemical compounds. Others, if irrigated, could be marvelously transformed. The *candelaria* plant covers itself with a thin wax coating as a protection against West Texas heat. Removed from the stem, this coating is now being refined at Alpine to make floor wax. The *canaigre* is rich in tannic acid with which hides can be transformed into leather.

Besides being fierce, the Rio Grande is old: older than the hills of Mexico and West Texas. Millions of years ago, when those hills first began to rise, this *río bravo* was already making its way toward the slowly retreating Gulf of Mexico. The uplifting movement of the earth, though of cataclysmic consequences, was gradual enough so that the Rio Grande could always find a way through by circumventing the more elevated places and cutting canyons among them.

A glance at the map of Texas will show the big bend that the river has to make to get around the five-thousand-foot Chisos Mountains. It veers first almost due south, then bears to the east, then turns almost due north before it can resume its southeastward course into the Gulf. In one place, as it bears east, it has chiseled a vertical wall sixteen hundred feet high. This gorge, named the Santa Elena Canyon, has grown famous for its scenic grandeur. So spectacular are the river's cuttings all along this southward aberration that in 1944 the United States government bought the pocket of Texas land formed by the water's detour and converted it into a public pleasure resort. Now called Big Bend National Park, it is widely recognized as an excellent place for seekers of vacational diversion and geological information.

But the real importance of these mountains is in what they have done to the river basin above them. By inhibiting the progress of the water, they have caused it to overflow frequently during the last fifty-eight million years. These overflows have distributed a rich topsoil over an extensive region, some seventy-five thousand acres of which are on the Texas side of the river, just above and below El Paso. The Elephant Butte Dam in New Mexico now prevents further floods and affords irrigation water for the valleys.

All rich agricultural regions are beautiful, but the El Paso valleys have a peculiar luster due partly to the brash breezes of their high altitude, partly to the blue haze shrouding the mountain peaks all around, partly to the long, straight, uniform rows of poplar and cottonwood trees that shade the walks and boundaries of the farms. There are no palms here, and cotton blooms much later here than in the lower valley. The Pima, a Far Eastern variety of cotton, is highly favored here. Its stalks are unusually tall and leafy, and a field of it in bloom has a fine blend of shades from the bluish hue of its foliage to the almost golden yellow of its blossoms. It yields less per acre than lower-valley cotton, but it brings a better price.

Huddled in the midst of these lush fields lies El Paso, following an eastward bend in the river. Viewed by night, she is a new-moon-shaped accumulation of beadlike lights, more fitful and less regularly formed than the new moon of the sky. By day she looks flimsy and small in her august environment. Her houses are mostly of smooth white stucco, pink brick, and adobe, materials contrasting sharply with the dull red of the surrounding mountains. The tall brick buildings of her business district would be called skyscrapers anywhere else. Here they appear as tiny upright prisms at the foot of promontories more than three times as high. Yet the streets of El Paso are over 3,700 feet above the sea. Her air is dry and kind to suffering lungs. There is an unusually high proportion of sunny days during her year, and storms are practically unknown in her mountain-framed pocket of fertility.

Like the other border cities, El Paso is highly colored by the culture clash between Latin and Anglo. Reverberations from this clash now pervade most of the state, but modern society along the Rio Grande has been shaped, from its beginnings in the early decades of the nineteenth century, by the peculiar viewpoints and habits which Anglo-Latin contacts tend to engender.

2. Border Backgrounds

SPANIARDS AND BRITONS had been in the western hemisphere for three centuries before they came in contract with each other along the borderland now known as Texas. Their experience on the new continents had affected them differently because they had come for different reasons and had encountered different kinds of aborigines. Spain sent her best and her strongest: her priests and her knights errant. They came, with her official blessing, on missions of conversion and exploitation. They wanted fabulous wealth to expand and enrich their Christian empire. They scorned common labor, strutted through the jungles in gaily colored silks and fluffy white ruffs, and claimed the land in the name of their Roman Catholic sovereign. When threatened with defeat, they wrote home for more support. They found thickly settled Indians whose idols they could smash with conscience-soothing eloquence; whose men were already accustomed to hard labor under an exacting native hierarchy; whose women could be easily baptized and enjoyed. There were exceptions, of course, but this was the most usual situation. The result was a haphazard mixture of beliefs and bloods, a region convulsed by bitter struggles and eventually cut up into sundry countries among which our nearest and most important neighbor is Mexico.

Voluntarily, Britain sent much less than Spain. Out of her religious broils came self-willed individuals who wanted nothing but a place where they could worship as they pleased and live by the sweat of their brows away from the Old World's iniquities and restrictions. They built log cabins, roamed the woods in buckskin, and claimed the land in their own names.

When threatened with defeat, they had no choice but to bar their doors and fight. They found wild, scattered Indians, whom they seldom tried to tame or Christianize or include in their society, and whose women, as a general rule, could not be caught without a strenuous chase. Other groups, with other aspirations, were spasmodically expelled from England and her neighbor nations. Though different, they all chafed under Old World domination and eventually joined forces to get rid of it. The result was the United States of America.

Meanwhile, Texas remained a frontier region, half-heartedly held by a few missions and settlements under the tottering Spanish despotism. The only permanently important Texas cities established by Spaniards were Laredo and San Antonio. Their persistence as centers of Hispanic culture is largely owing to the fact that they were deliberately settled by colonists who had come to live, rather than merely by missionaries who had come to save heathen souls. To be sure, these two towns had their missions and military garrisons, but their principal claim to existence lay in their secular, home-building population. San Antonio soon became the capital of the Texas province, whose name came from an Indian word meaning "Good Neighbor."

The land's full development would have been long delayed had it not been for an Anglo-American lead-miner named Moses Austin and a Dutchman named Felipe Enrique Neri de Bastrop, generally called the Baron de Bastrop. Austin went broke in Missouri in 1819 and turned west for another chance. In 1820 he arrived at San Antonio hoping to get free land from Spain and colonize Texas with families from the United States.

Free land from Spain meant more than just a chance to get rich quick. It meant bringing together people from two mammoth civilizations that had little inclination to be brought together, two globe-embracing empires which for three hundred years had been shaking the world and storming the oceans with bitter battles over God and gold: Catholic Spain and Protestant Britain.

The fact that the Anglo-Americans were now free from Britain did not make them less different from Spain. A man of Austin's background might have known that he could gain no concessions from the Spanish authorities. The governor at San Antonio refused to see him, but Baron de Bastrop, whom Austin had known in Louisiana, happened to meet him in the street. The two put their heads together.

The Baron knew both cultures from the inside, and he had a winning way. Moreover, he had a fine countenance; he was tall and beautifully proportioned, with a sandy mustache, a sweet, calm face, and a soft voice. His manners were simple, easy, and affable. These qualities enabled him to turn Austin's failure into a successful movement for the population of Texas by Anglo-Americans. He persuaded the Spaniards to let Austin bring a colony into the province.

Before the prospective settlers could be recruited from the United States, Moses Austin died. But his son Stephen brought the colony into Texas in 1821. By the time Stephen had established his village on the rich Gulf Coast, the Spanish government was overthrown. The young Austin and the old Baron faced a bewildered and unpredictable independent Mexico. But Mexican independence had been in part accomplished by liberals who wanted a representative government. In 1824 Stephen F. Austin helped them write a constitution which in many ways resembled that of the United States. Under this constitution, Baron de Bastrop was elected representative from the newly formed state of Coahuila-and-Texas, in which capacity he served until his death. He had made a contact that would reap fantastic fortunes, but not for him. He did not leave even enough money to pay for his own funeral. In the galaxy of Texas heroes, he remains a dim, almost forgotten star; a small town northeast of San Antonio bears his name.

Stephen F. Austin is better remembered. Austin was not a crusader, nor a warrior, nor the kind of genius whose brilliant achievements dazzle the world. Everything about him was unspectacular; nothing about him conformed to the popular conception of heroism. He was small in body, soft-voiced, cool toward those who strove to glorify him, patient and forgiving toward those who abused him. His regard for the wishes of others was so high that he often pled their cases against his own better judgment. He had little ambition to be famous and none to rule. Yet he was an excellent systematizer and as adept at finding possible compromises as he was willing to accept those proposed by others. There was, and still is, a demand in Texas for more of such talents as he possessed.

◇◇

3. *Border Tensions*

"EVEN IF I were God Almighty, I would yearn to be greater still." These words have been attributed to a Mexican politician named Antonio López de Santa Anna. Throughout his long, checkered career, Santa Anna expressed their sentiment in his every act, for he was more a man of action than of words.

He could use words with fine adeptness when they appeared necessary to help assuage his lust for self-aggrandizement, but it was primarily with the sword that he carved his rubric in the hall of fame. This does not mean that he had no convictions. On the contrary, he could entertain any creed that seemed politically expedient. When the Mexican liberals clamored for democracy, he was a rabid democrat. When the powerful upper classes betrayed fear of losing their special privileges, he avowed himself a stalwart guardian of the *status quo*. If approval could be garnered by starting a revolution, he would start a revolution. When the insurrections grew irksome to his rich constituents, he would hunt out and crush the rebels.

One of his favorite stunts was to get himself elected president of Mexico, leave a liberal vice-president in charge of the government, and retire to his plantation home for a rest. When the vice-president's rash acts had tried the patience of the conservatives, Santa Anna would return, take a firm hold on the ship of state, and quietly correct his assistant's errors. Thus he would earn the applause of the conservatives without losing the goodwill of the liberals, acquired through the vice-president's ill-starred reforms.

In this manner Santa Anna maintained precarious authority during the year 1833. Eight times he tested public opinion by retiring and letting his vice-president take the rap for those steps toward democracy which are always such a relief to the downtrodden and such a heartache to the mighty. Eight times he returned to reap the praise popularly reserved for wisdom. Then in 1834, when the privileged had grown sufficiently vexed with representative government, he proclaimed himself dictator of Mexico and abolished the constitution that Stephen F. Austin of Texas had helped write ten years before.

This brought protests, especially from Texas. Several prominent Mexican liberals soon went there to join the objectors. Meetings were held condemning the newly elevated dictator's land policy. Austin took a list of complaints to Mexico. The new government clapped him into prison and kept him there almost a year, making him a martyr in Texan eyes.

Reaffirming the Mexican constitution of 1824, a contingent of Texas volunteers joined an adventurer from Kentucky named Benjamin Rush Milam to drive the dictator's garrison from San Antonio. They succeeded at the cost of Milam's life and occupied the Alamo, a stone fortress originally built as a mission, with walls three feet thick and a graceful arc on a symmetrical elevation above the front door.

The loss of the Alamo may have struck many Mexicans as a blow, but for Santa Anna it was an opportunity to elevate himself still higher in Mexican eyes. At the head of a large force, he marched across the Rio Grande to reduce the northern rebels. His first major target was San Antonio.

Three alternatives were open to the Texans in the Alamo when they heard the news of Santa Anna's approach. First, they could withdraw, saving their lives without losing their honor, for they were so overwhelmingly outnumbered that any experienced military man would have advised retreat. Second, they could surrender on condition that the enemy treat them as prisoners of war after the custom of civilized nations. Third, they could remain in the Alamo and kill as many Mexican soldiers as possible before they fell themselves. This last course would be suicide, for the superior Mexican force would surely slay them all in the end, but in the struggle for Texas liberty it was a highly useful kind of suicide. Protected by the fortress, they could seriously weaken Santa Anna's army before the thick walls could be scaled.

Thus, the choice before the Texans in the Alamo was clear-cut: years of peace for the gratification of life's appetites versus a violent early death for the sake of others. Most of them were young, fresh from a society in which the fight for survival conflicted with religious admonitions about the sinfulness of killing. Unless they decided to retreat or surrender, no rewards awaited them except the thrill of battle followed by destruction to the body and possibly the spirit. Yet they chose the third course, voluntarily giving their lives so that their fellows might have a better chance at freedom from Santa Anna's dictatorship, and the sense of sacrifice made their fight sacred.

This is why the Alamo, standing in the center of San Antonio's business section, is remembered as a military fortress rather than as a religious mission. This is why the names and portraits of the fighters who died in it, rather than those of the priests who built it, now decorate its walls. This is why the story of its fall, rather than that of its erection, is taught in Texas schools as a classic example of disinterested charity. This is why the pupils of these schools come to love so profoundly the land for which those unselfish lives were paid. This is one of several important reasons why the pride of Texans astonishes the citizens of other states.

Having stormed the Alamo and burned the corpses of its 145 defenders in early March 1836, Santa Anna turned eastward, for the highest concentration of settlements was on the coastal plain. In the edge of the rolling country southeast of San Antonio was another mission fortress held by Texans: La Bahía, near the present town of Goliad. Just as the fall of the Alamo exalted the Texas side in the eyes of those who admire self-sacrificing valor, the episode at Goliad increased the opprobrium on Santa Anna's side. The men at La Bahía faced the same three alternatives that had been open to those at the Alamo. They chose the second course, surrendering in return for assurance from Santa Anna's over-optimistic representative that they would be treated well. After they had given up their personal rifles, their five hundred spare muskets, and their nine brass cannon, they were marched into the woods and shot. Of the original Texan force at Goliad, 342 fell before the firing squads on March 27, 1836. Twenty were spared in response to the entreaties of a Mexican officer's wife named Francisca Alvarez. Twenty-eight escaped from under the guns.

All this gave meaning to the battle cry chosen by the newly elected Commander in Chief of the Texas forces, General Sam Houston: "Remember the Alamo; Remember Goliad!" Using it, Houston lured Santa Anna up the coast to San Jacinto, defeated him, and sent him to confer with President Andrew Jackson on the cession of Texas to the United States.

But the fight did not stop when the sound of cannon died.

Into the second decade of the twentieth century there were bandit raids along the Rio Grande, aimed at regaining for Mexico at least the southern tip of Texas. Although they did not attain this end, these raids helped keep alive a resentment that has been handed down, in the face of two important counterforces, to the present generation.

The first counterforce was economic. It began in the early twentieth century, when the discovery of oil changed the value of land owned by both Mexican- and Anglo-Texans. Until that time the two groups had been separated by coinciding religious, linguistic, and economic lines of demarcation. The Mexicans were Roman Catholic, the Anglos Protestant. The Mexicans spoke Spanish, the Anglos English. The Mexicans were poor, the Anglos comparatively well off. This last line resulted partly from Anglo-American military victories and partly from the larger reservoir of wealth provided by the United States. Mexico had originally been rich in good soil, gold, and silver, but a one-crop corn economy and three hundred years of Spanish imperialism had impoverished her. Yankee investors could buy up all productive agricultural lands in Texas, leaving the farmers of Mexican extraction in the more arid areas. With a few notable exceptions, this is what they did.

Then oil was struck in the semi-deserts east of Laredo. People of Mexican background, who had long lived humbly on the sallow hills, suddenly became oil millionaires. Some of their Anglo neighbors now shake their hands in congratulation. Others, though inwardly miffed, see political advantage in currying their favor. Still others, mostly of the older generation, cannot reconcile themselves to the new circumstances. They are dying hard deaths.

The second counterforce was political. It came with the Good Neighbor Policy and the Second World War. For a hundred years Anglo-Texans had been remembering the Alamo, identifying themselves with its heroes, their Spanish-speaking neighbors with its villains. Customarily, they acted on the memory in dealing with Latin Americans who had nothing to do with Santa Anna and the type of opportunistic chicanery whereby he had at times seized dictatorial power.

Then, to stop Hitler, the American Army took Texans of every extraction and gave them equal opportunities. Trained according to their individual proclivities, they fought bravely. On returning, Latin Texans found the custom of discriminating against their people both repugnant and inconsistent with the principles for which they had risked their lives. They protested against being excluded from restaurants, theaters, roller-skating rinks, and swimming pools merely because they were "Mexican." They resented the system of segregation in Texas public schools, where children of Mexican background were often relegated to separate buildings with inferior instructional and sanitary equipment.

Meanwhile, the drafting of American citizens into the military had caused a drastic labor shortage that could be relieved only by importing troops of workers from Mexico. Also, Mexico was supplying the United States with large quantities of strategic war materials—principally lead, copper, mica, zinc, and rubber. Hence, her friendship was essential to the defense of the free world. Discrimination against people of Mexican origin became an offense not only against democratic philosophy but also against the immediate war effort.

The office of the Co-ordinator of Inter-American Affairs, created by Franklin D. Roosevelt in 1940, was well equipped for awakening Texas to the need of a change in her attitude toward Mexicans. But its scope was nationwide. Something had to be done by Texas specifically to improve her relations with Mexico.

Accordingly, the governor of Texas appointed a Good Neighbor Commission in 1943. It consists of nine businessmen and political leaders of both Anglo and Latin extraction, who serve without pay. The purpose of the Commission is to "devise and put into effect methods by which inter-American understanding and goodwill may be promoted, and inter-American relations advanced, without resort to punitive measures or the application of civil or criminal sanction." The state legislature appropriates enough money to hire an executive secretary and a stenographic staff for the Commission. However, the national Co-ordinator's office has been abolished and the state Commission has become involved in problems of foreign trade. More permanent and effective than either of these governmental agencies are two spontaneous organizations of Latins which began in Texas and spread into other states with Mexican population: the League of United Latin American Citizens and the American G.I. Forum.

The former, known as Lulac, grew from a merger of three Texas groups interested in combatting discrimination. Formed in 1929, it is composed largely of successful middle-class Latin Americans who wish to retain and consolidate the gains they have made as full-fledged United States citizens. Proud of their achievements, they maintain a stanch conservative position in politics, insisting that their less successful fellow Latins "discharge their duties before they assert their rights as citizens. . . ." Lulac members are taught to "defend the rights of all people." They believe in educating their people according to "the best American principles and standards." While this means learning English, it does not necessitate the rejection of the members' Latin heritage. Through the schools and through legal action, Lulac has done much to improve the qualifications and status of Texas's Spanish-speaking citizens. Local Lulac councils also give scholarships to Latin high-school graduates of exceptional ability, distribute Christmas gifts to the underprivileged, and engage in other charities, raising the necessary funds through dances and bingo parties.

The American G.I. Forum was called into existence by what has come to be considered a shameful discriminatory act against the dead. In the spring of 1949 a Texas town re-

fused to bury one of its war heroes because his name, Félix
Longoria, revealed Mexican ancestry. After volunteering for a
Philippine patrol, Longoria had been killed in a battle against
the Japanese. His corpse was shipped back to his Texas wife,
but the local undertaker feared that the "whites" would object
to its being honored with funeral services in his chapel.

However, Texas Senator Lyndon B. Johnson wired Longoria's widow that she could lay the body in the Arlington
National Cemetery. Also, an eloquent Corpus Christi veteran
of the Medical Corps named Hector P. García organized a
group of ex-servicemen, which he called the G.I. Forum, and,
raised $3,000 to transport Mrs. Longoria and her family to
Arlington for the funeral. The Texas undertaker subsequently
testified to a legislative committee that he had only "discouraged" the use of his chapel because of "serious trouble" between the hero's widow and his parents.

Today the G.I. Forum is a highly integrated network of
some two hundred active local groups. All their meetings are
open to the public and begin with a pledge of allegiance to the
flag of the United States. The local units are of three kinds:
first, the Forums proper, consisting primarily of G.I.'s; second,
the Auxiliaries, made up of veterans' wives and other female
relatives; third, the Junior Forums, for persons under twenty-
one whose fathers were in the war. Membership is open to
both Latins and Anglos, but most of the members are Latin.
The Local Forums keep vigil over their respective communities and report all discriminatory practices to their state chairman, who co-operates with them in obtaining justice.

Providing a scientific basis for the work of the Good
Neighbor Commission, Lulac, and the G.I. Forum is the
Study of Spanish-Speaking People under the tutelage of Dr.
George I. Sanchez at the University of Texas. Assisted by
scholars in economics, sociology, and other studies that throw
light on the Texas-Mexican problem, he is investigating its
many phases systematically. The resulting papers are published by the University of Texas Press.

Through these media, and through court action, segregation of Latins has been almost entirely eliminated from the public schools of Texas. The economic and social aspects of the problem have also been carefully investigated, and indications are that by far the majority of Texans, especially in the cities, now want equal opportunities and a high standard of living for Mexicans as well as Anglos. By and large, both the opportunities and the standard are being rapidly accomplished.

By way of directing the reorientation of these groups, no man has done more than Thomas S. Sutherland, a brawny Texan who speaks English and Spanish with equal fluency and can be as much at home in a millionaire's mansion as in a peon's jacal. He was field representative for the Co-ordinator of Inter-American Affairs when that office was set up by Roosevelt. It was at his suggestion and under his supervision that the Good Neighbor Commission first came into existence. With a farm near the state capital and a counseling service near the campus of the state university, he has now broadened his work to include all groups from all nations.

Tending to undo Texas's accomplishments in Mexican relations is an apparently endless stream of illegal immigrants out of Mexico's poverty-stricken heart. Since they enter secretly, swimming the Rio Grande instead of crossing the international bridges, these immigrants are called "wetbacks." A study by Lyle Saunders and Olen Leonard, published by Sanchez in 1951, reveals that most wetbacks would prefer to live in Mexico. "*Es mi tierra* (it is my land)," they say. They come to the United States because it is the only way left for them to support their families.

From all unbiased points of view, the wetback is a pitiful figure. Exiled from his homeland by the threat of starvation, unselfishly hoping to mitigate the woes of his less venturesome relatives by sending them a few dollars each week or month, he is willing to work for as little as twenty cents an hour. Almost anything you give him is an improvement over his original condition. Being undernourished from babyhood, he is often weak and listless and has little resistance against prolonged physical exertion. To those who know nothing about the real reasons for his inefficiency, his appearance seems to corroborate the traditional myth of Mexican inferiority. This jeopardizes the position of the native Latin Texans, especially in these critical times when they are just beginning to get full-fledged social equality with all other American citizens.

For this reason, Latin American workers born in Texas strongly oppose the admission of immigrant day laborers from Mexico. Because they lower the wage standard, labor unions also resent their presence. Health authorities point out that they bring all manner of contagious diseases and spread them among the native population. They take or send their earnings into Mexico, where the money is lost from the Texas economy.

But farmers and ranchers, of either Anglo or Latin background, welcome wetbacks into their most remote nooks of safety. So do some industrialists who have secluded workrooms and are on the lookout for cheap labor. Merchants in Spanish-speaking neighborhoods also befriend the wetback, partly because his immediate purchases help business, partly because he is in a sense a fellow countryman.

The Immigration Service is caught between its duty to enforce the national law and the threat of political pressure from local employers who dislike being deprived of low-paid Mexicans. The national law is not very helpful because, while it forbids the entrance of wetbacks, it does not prohibit their being hired. Only the alien—never the farmer or the rancher or the industrialist who employs him—can be punished. In addition to being legally immune, the employer of wetbacks is often a power in the community: a man of influence, prestige, and wealth. He may be a city alderman, or a county commissioner, or a member of the state legislature, or an elected official of even higher dignity. These circumstances, coupled with the huge surplus of aliens to be apprehended, encourage

the immigration officers to concentrate their attention on un-
employed wetbacks along the public roads.

Yet farms and ranches and industrial establishments are
sometimes raided. Saunders and Leonard tell of one border
patrolman in the prosperous, palm-festooned lower Rio
Grande Valley who stopped a farmer with three wetbacks in
a truck loaded with fertilizer. The farmer complained that if
the wetbacks were taken at once, he would have nobody to
unload his truck. The patrolman agreed to wait until the hauling was finished. When the fertilizer was properly distributed,
he called at the farm and deported the wetbacks who had
done the work. Thus he got his duty discharged without of-
fending the farmer.

Such practices put the wetback entirely at the mercy of
his Texan employers. Once within the walls or fences of a
factory, ranch, or farm, he has no recourse to appeal, no bargaining power, no protection of any kind. He cannot even
move from one farm or ranch or workshop to another without
risking capture. If he expresses dissatisfaction with the treatment he receives, his employer can merely expel him, where-
upon he will be caught by the officers and taken back to face
worse privation in Mexico. This makes him in one respect
more hapless than the slaves of old: his temporary Texas mas-
ters need take no pains to preserve or nourish his vagabond
body beyond its immediate term of usefulness. Even if he
works well, he can hope for security only while there is work
for him to do. Once the tasks are accomplished, he may be
ejected and deported.

Legally, any wetback apprehended is subject to a sentence
of from sixty days to one year in federal prison. But customarily the sentence is suspended or the prisoner is allowed to return to Mexico "voluntarily." The tremendous volume of ap-
prehensions renders formal trials impossible. Wetbacks deported in Texas during the fiscal year 1953 numbered 875,318.
This figure comes nowhere near revealing the actual number

of wetbacks who entered the country. It only shows the maximum capacity of the badly understaffed Immigration Service,
which was forced by lack of manpower to limit its arrests in
the lower Rio Grande Valley to one thousand per day.

The year 1953 was unusual because the Rio Grande went
dry in the early spring and no river water flowed for over two
months. Wetbacks were no longer wet. They merely walked
across the sun-parched river bed, while the drouth made their
services on farms unnecessary.

The governments of Mexico and the United States have
worked out a system whereby Mexicans can enter legally to do
farm work. Until recently the procedure was complex and involved long waits at processing stations. In the spring of 1954
it was improved, but processed laborers were not much in demand north of the river. Texas farmers naturally want the
cheapest labor they can get, and a legalized laborer, however
paltry his pay, has recourse to governmental protection. This
makes him less desirable, from a short-sighted economic point
of view, than the helpless wetback.

In the summer of 1954 the Border Patrol undertook the
most drastic "wetback roundup" ever known so far. Unlike
the former timid moves, it was bold and thorough. Whole
farms were raided, and the wetbacks were marched into
Mexico sometimes many miles up the river from the place of
their secret immigration. As a consequence, the contracting of
legal laborers, known as *braceros*, was accelerated. Unfortunately, large numbers of these *braceros*, being unschooled in
the responsibilities attendant on such arrangements, bolted
their contracts. This aggravated an already unpopular situation, for the whole economy of the Mexican border has been
adjusted to the low cost of wetbacks, and readjustments are
often painful. Moreover, the problem is tied in with traditions
entering the state over its eastern boundary.

III

STRONG WINDS FROM THE EAST

◇◇

1. *Timberlands and Farms*

THE ENTIRE eastern pocket of Texas, from Red River south to the Gulf Coast, is rich both economically and æsthetically. As soon as one crosses the state line from Louisiana, the wholesome health of a wealthy area becomes apparent in the landscape itself. The dilapidated shacks so characteristic of the old south are seldom seen. Houses of lumber have a freshly painted look. The brick and stucco homes of the more opulent stand in modest half-seclusion amidst cool groves of pine, gum, oak, and cypress trees. The rolling terrain is conducive to distant vistas, even in the most wooded spots. The hills are just wide and sloping enough, and the trees just low enough, so that miles of highway can be seen ahead. The grass along the highways is mowed close. Blooming shrubbery is often planted in rows along both sides of the road. Deep valleys for the enjoyment of slow-passing farm days are protected from the sun, but not from the damp Gulf breeze, by piny woods. The branches of the pine trees often do not begin until the trunks have shot a long way above the roofs of the houses.

Except in the comparatively new iron and oil fields of the

region's northeastern corner, East Texas has long been dominated by the lumber industry. Lumbering began in Texas as
an extractive enterprise. No thought was paid to the nursing
of young trees or the nourishment of maturing groves. Whole
forests were destroyed, their stumps left to sprout misshapen
runts. But lumbering has now become highly refined and
scientific. Old stumps have been removed and used for tur-
pentine and paper. Depleted farms have been planted in carefully planned new forests. Consequently, between 1934 and
1946 there was an over-all reduction of only three per cent in
the volume of growing Texas timber.

Long experience now enables lumbermen to get the maximum in value from any given tree. Trees are cut so that splitting from the impact of the fall is eliminated. Crooked trees
are sawed in lengths which minimize the crook as much as
possible. Modern mills, especially in the larger plants, have
reached a high stage of precision.

A big East Texas sawmill is a spectacular establishment.
In contrast to the tranquillity prevailing outside the wide tin
shed, and in the forests and in the millpond, where logs float
by the hundreds in turgid water, the interior of the mill is a
hive of high-speed movement. Large carriages, ridden and
guided by seasoned operators, hold the logs in clamps as they
are ripped by rotary saws. With the bark still on them, the
strips rush like living crocodiles down long runways, carried
by bands, to be sidetracked by expert classifiers. The screech
of smaller saws mingles with the roar of the great log-cutters
in a rough but exhilarating rhythm.

But the human side of East Texas lumbering still suffers
from immaturity. Negroes manipulate the logs in the ponds,
riding them, standing on them, and poking them about with
long poles, while whites hold jobs of higher dignity. East Texas
sawmills are strictly non-union, and communities around lumbering concerns betray a deeply ingrained feudal organization.
Large-scale ownership of timberlands is more prevalent in

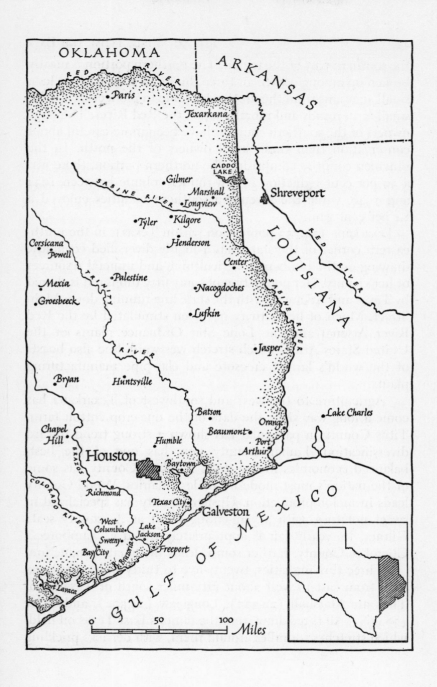

OKLAHOMA

ARKANSAS

RED RIVER

Paris

Texarkana

CADDO LAKE

SABINE RIVER

Gilmer

Marshall
Longview

Shreveport

LOUISIANA

RED RIVER

Tyler Kilgore

Henderson

Corsicana
Powell

Center

SABINE RIVER

Mexia
Groesbeck

Palestine

TRINITY

Nacogdoches

Lufkin

RIVER

Jasper

Bryan

Huntsville

Batson

Lake Charles

Chapel
Hill

BRAZOS R.

Houston

Beaumont Orange

Port
Arthur

Humble

Baytown

COLORADO RIVER

Richmond

Texas City

West
Columbia
Sweeny
Bay City

Lake
Jackson

Freeport

BRAZOS R.

Galveston

GULF OF MEXICO

Port Lavaca

0   50   100   Miles

the southern part of the region. The northern portion is mostly broken up among owners of three thousand acres each or less: small agrarians from the north who came in pioneer days, with small-farm minds and morals, across the Red River. The large owners of the southern counties have been more careful about conservation than these small owners of the north. In the nineteen counties comprising the northern portion, there was a 39 per cent reduction in saw-timber volume between 1934 and 1946, while the seventeen southern counties enjoyed a 14 per cent gain.

Texarkana (24,753 population within Texas), in the northeastern corner of the state, has a highly diversified economy, drawing on the lumbering, agricultural, and mineral resources of her vicinity. Her population of some fifty thousand is shared by Texas and Arkansas, with the state line running down Main Street. Much of her activity has been stimulated by the Red River Arsenal and the Lone Star Ordnance plants of the United States Army, which stretch westward. She also boasts of the world's largest creosote and clay-pipe manufacturing plants.

Agriculture to the west and southwest of Texarkana has come a long way since the days of the one-crop cotton farm. Titus County in particular has shown a strong trend toward diversification. Lamar County now has one of the best-balanced economies in the state. Hopkins County has some of the nation's most modern Grade A dairies. Wood County leads in melon-production. Upshar County has specialized in sweet potatoes, with a yam-curing plant at its county seat: Gilmer. Its yearly fair is appropriately called a "yamboree." Cherokee County, farther south, leads in tomato-production.

Three thriving cities, twenty-five to thirty miles apart, extend from east to west about fifty miles south of Texarkana. They are Marshall (22,327), Longview (24,502), and Tyler (38,968). All three draw from the famous East Texas oil field, which stretches for miles around them, with derricks prickling the pine-covered hills, sometimes as thick as quills on a porcupine. All three have multitudinous manufacturing plants, some of which draw on iron beds to the north. All three have excellent public-school systems and locally supported colleges. All three enjoy the music of the East Texas Regional Symphony Orchestra, whose headquarters are in Tyler, and the retreats of Caddo Lake, which lies under jungles and low-hanging moss some twenty miles northeast of Marshall.

The aggressive community spirit of Tyler's citizens has made it one of the state's most prosperous smaller cities. Its rose-growing industry has become nationally famous. The roses are raised like cotton, in whole fields, but whereas cotton rows are uniformly white when ripe, Tyler's rose rows run a wide range of hues. One row will be pink, another orange, another a deep wine red, another yellow. Two thirds of the nation's field-grown rosebushes originate within fifty miles of Tyler. About six hundred carloads, averaging fifteen thousand plants to the car, are shipped from Tyler each year, going to the forty-eight United States and some twenty-five foreign countries.

The industry is revitalized yearly by a rose carnival, when the land's most beautiful girls deck their bodies in blossoms often worth a dollar apiece, to march or ride rose-covered floats, accompanied by more than thirty school bands, in a parade approximately two miles long. Spectators come by the hundreds of thousands from all over the world. In 1950 there were nearly 250,000 visitors. Flocks of teen-age girls, lavishly loaded with roses by the armful, pass out rare buds to pedestrians. Other young women, adorned like dolls, toss bouquets into passing automobiles. Low-flying airplanes and helicopters shower the crowds with rose petals from above.

Tyler's rose specialization is not of the exclusive and hence abortive kind. While the emphasis is on the ornamental shrub, 122 bankers, businessmen, and farmers of the Tyler area have set up the East Texas Agricultural Council, with a budget of $14,000 a year, to help farmers use their land to its utmost capacity. Similarly the Tyler Industrial Foundation, with an original fund of $200,000, encourages new industries by judicious financing and by providing ideal plant locations and structures. Another notable consequence of this city's co-operative zeal is Camp Tyler, where the school children go by turns, a week at a time. Adjoining it is a model farm where they can learn all phases of diversified agriculture through actual contact with the land and its problems.

South of Tyler and her neighbor cities, oil derricks are as thick as trees in a forest, covering hill after hill. There are piny woods, but the twenty-four thousand producing wells of the vast East Texas field dominate the landscape for over fifty miles from north to south and ten miles from east to west. Huddled under the lush oak, gum, and pine forests, with their solid shade and their low-hanging moss, farm-owners can get forty-hour-a-week jobs in town, drive to work every day, and continue their agricultural pursuits with the help of their families. Wage-earners of this type have come to be known in East Texas as "drugstore farmers." Their lucrative arrange-ments conspire with Texas labor laws and deeply ingrained traditions to keep unionization down.

South of the East Texas oil field, the slopes grow gentler and the roads wind with broader curves. The lanes are wide and neatly cleared. The pavement is flanked with smoothly mowed grass and long rows of crepe myrtle following its bends with measured ease. The day's brightness runs an infinite series of degrees from the bare sun's heat against shimmering willow leaves to the deep, cool shadows underneath. Enclosed in roofs of foliage and walls of moss are numberless natural rooms where growth and decay are always taking place at the same time. The towns are proud of their forest-shadowed se-clusion, their good salaries voluntarily paid, their remoteness from the big city's sins, their tranquil solitude.

Lufkin (15,135), about two hundred miles south of Tex-

arkana, has a public-spirited citizen named William F. Hanks.
He has created a five-minute cartoon movie on the blessings
of life in Lufkin. It features a dog who buys a newspaper from
a newsboy hawking: "Extra! Extra! Read all about Lufkin!"
After reading the paper, the dog catches the Lufkin Special to
the city therein described. Once established in Lufkin, he lives
happily on fat checks ever after.

Jasper (4,403), sixty miles southeast of Lufkin, has the
central offices of Morgan & Lindsay, a retailing chain with over
seventy variety stores in Texas, Louisiana, Arkansas, and Mississippi. Says Bronson Morgan, the chain's graying president:
"We've got everything in Jasper that the big cities have, except what we don't want." Orange (21,174), where the Sabine
approaches the Gulf of Mexico, supplements her large industrial payroll with ten million dollars annually in salaries from
the United States Navy to 3,700 civilians and service workers.
Hardin County, adjoining Orange County's northwest corner,
has 3,500 part-time farmers and only 500 full-time farmers.
Beaumont (94,014) and Houston (596,163), in the southern
edge of the timberlands, add seaport facilities to the snugness
and abundance of East Texas. Down the coast from them, the
highways run straight as arrows for miles and miles. The steer-
ing wheels in automobiles can remain so still that the drivers'
arms might as well be paralyzed. The roar of motors grows
monotonous.

Without having to slow down or move a muscle, you pass
rice fields billowing softly in the salt sea breeze. Their green
is richly brilliant: almost yellow, varying in depth as the sun
and wind play across it. Flying low over these fields are small
airplanes, emitting clouds of spray to eradicate pests and
weeds. Much of the rice-farming, particularly the planting
and spraying, is now done by plane, so that germination and
growth are not disturbed by footsteps or tractor wheels. The
plowing and harvesting, of course, are done by large, earthbound machines.

But the rice fields are not continuous like those of other agricultural products in other areas. Normally a farmer will grow rice on only one third of his land each year and let the other two thirds lie fallow. A different third will be planted every year, and cattle will be grazed on the acreage not currently under rice. Thus cattle and rice go together, and the upper Gulf Coast is notable for both.

Except for the owners of oil and sulphur enterprises, rice-farmers are the richest people in the region. They drive shining new cars to Florida and Canada for their vacations. In their own communities they build beautiful churches, usually Protestant, and support roomy, up-to-date schools. There are also some Catholic churches. These draw the famous Acadians of Longfellow's *Evangeline*, who are locally known as "Cajuns" and still speak a French dialect.

Some of the world's finest pine forests grow on the plain between Beaumont and Houston. Though the land is flat and the atmosphere humid, the tree heads stand high and dry. Long-leaf pine needles hang in big, soft clusters, spreading outward like the beams of a bright star. Even where the trees stand close together, with dwarf fan palms thick around their roots, there is plenty of room for the sun to penetrate their branches and illuminate the underbrush, for pine foliage is never so dense as that of the oak, gum, and pecan groves that grow around the river beds. Sunlight is diffused into numerous new degrees of brilliance rather than blocked by pine timber.

Both inside the forests and on the open plain, there is a glossiness about the Beaumont-Houston country: an exuberance that only a combination of rich soil and relatively heavy periodic rainfall can cause. All the plants, even the weeds, have a thriving vigor about them. The sensation of vast breadth and rapid growth, nourished by abundance, is everywhere.

While modern industry has added much to the face of East Texas and the Gulf Coast, these areas were first settled at a time when the principal pursuit in the land was cotton-raising. For this reason, the social structure in these regions still follows lines of cleavage set in the days when cotton was king and the biggest men were those with the biggest cotton fields. Like the Texas-Mexican clash of the southern border, cotton-raising has now spread throughout the state, and its impact on Texas life is everywhere apparent, but its human consequences have been most incisive in the east and southeast.

◇◇

2. Pioneers and Gentlemen

BECAUSE THE SILT-FILLED SOUTHEAST has the best farm land, Stephen F. Austin's first Anglo-American colony settled below the Balcones fault line along the Brazos and Colorado rivers. The Brazos enters the Gulf of Mexico just southwest of Houston, and the Colorado a few miles farther west.

Austin and many of the other colonizers who followed him had resolved to keep the new land pure and clean. They were themselves high-minded citizens displaced by the economic depressions of the 1820's and 1830's, and they wanted a place where the mistakes of the United States would not be repeated. They required evidence of good moral character from all who aspired to own Texas land.

Despite these precautions, much good ground was soon inhabited by ruffians whom the United States government had made uncomfortable for well-justified reasons. Some were criminals who sought the wilderness as a slight improvement over a genuinely deserved life in prison. Others were drones who had come to escape their creditors. Their only ambition was to live as long as possible with as little work as possible.

On the whole, the remoteness of civilization and the dif-

ficulties of transportation forced both sinner and saint into a
humdrum, rhythmic existence which followed willy-nilly the
fluctuations of the weather. Survival itself largely depended on
the hardihood derived from high moral principles and frugal
habits.

This was the kind of society that Stephen F. Austin had in
mind when he helped write the constitution of 1824 for the
liberal Mexican government. These were the people for whose
protection and ethical betterment the stringent clauses of that
fine instrument were intended. These were the families for
whom the fighters of the Alamo, defending the constitution,
laid down their lives.

About one thing in particular this constitution was pain-
fully specific: slavery. It forbade the sale and purchase of slaves
and stated that the children of slaves, if born within Mexico's
domain, should be free when they reached their fourteenth
year. These free children were to receive a good education and
an opportunity to advance in whatever line of work they chose.

This was painful because many of Austin's settlers, and an
even larger percentage of those brought by subsequent colonizers, came from southern states where Negro slavery was the
order of the day. The Brazos and Colorado river valleys could
be reached in three days by boat from the mouth of the Mississippi. The almost equally fructiferous valleys of the Trinity
and the Sabine, farther east, could be as easily reached by land
from Arkansas and Louisiana. The Sabine River, which served
as the boundary between Louisiana and Texas, became a
favorite haven for slaveholding speculators, who furtively
fenced off plantations on the Texas side. When the danger
of Mexican legislation against slavery became too great, they
spirited their slaves across the river into Louisiana. To the
Brazos and the Colorado came bolder ones who hoped that
the seclusion of deep forests and canebrakes would protect
their slave-worked fields from any sudden enforcement of the
Mexican law. To circumvent the letter of that law, some of

Young citrus trees surround the landscaped grounds of an estate north of Weslaco in the Lower Rio Grande Valley.

Santa Elena Canyon in Big Bend National Park, with perpendicular walls rising more than 1,500 feet above the Rio Grande (Chihuahua, Mexico, on the left; Texas on the right).

these immigrants nominally freed their slaves, then put them under ninety-nine-year "apprenticeships."

In the United States a combination of pressures encouraged the emigration of slaveholding planters into Texas. The soil of the Atlantic seaboard had been impoverished by the exploitive methods of these planters. They had to have new land. Yet the Missouri Compromise, effective since 1820, forbade the further extension of slavery within the states. The rich Gulf Coast of Texas was the only place left for them to go.

Stephen F. Austin recognized what these pressures meant for Texas and soon came to see that a forthright enforcement of the Mexican anti-slave laws must gravely inhibit the coming of southern gentlemen, whose money he considered indispensable in developing the new country. Hence, although a Pennsylvanian and personally opposed to slavery, he used his influence to exempt Texas from the full force of the Mexican law.

When Texas threw off the Mexican yoke in 1836 to become an independent nation, this feeling of need for wealthy southerners had grown strong enough to inject itself into the constitution of the young republic, so that this instrument annulled all the anti-slavery legislation of the previous Mexican regime and made Texas a safe place for slaveholders. The door was flung wide open for the influx of planters from the southern states to the highly productive Texas coastal prairie. Before long they had great tracts along the Colorado and Brazos river basins.

These planters were very different from the small pioneer farmers who were pouring into the northern timberlands of East Texas. The pioneer farmer lived behind his plow, or at the handle of his hoe, or beside his wagon harvesting his own cotton and corn. He did little trading, for he had no surplus possessions even for barter. He never speculated, for he had no money to spare. He raised what he ate and ate what he raised. He made bread from his corn, grinding it himself on a hand mill or having it ground in town. When he came to the colonial village, he rode the same wagon in which he loaded hay and corn. His wife and daughters spun his clothes out of the cotton patch. They were not ladies, but mere women.

The planter, on the other hand, was not a farmer at all; he scorned being called a farmer. He lived not in the field, but at his desk in a wing of his spacious home or at the trading posts and seaports. He traveled in buggies or carriages with easy-riding springs. Unlike the farmer, he had no intimate contact with the land; his only interest in it was for the dollars and cents that could be got from it. His life was tuned to the genteel tradition which had been preserved since feudal times and brought over from the Old World's nobility. His training and position led him, often subconsciously, often in word and deed, to fancy himself a knight in shining armor, born and bred for war, leadership, fine arts, and luxury. Productive work was beneath his dignity. It had to be done by his "niggers." His wife and daughters were ladies, with numerous black hands at their beck and call.

His attitude toward his "niggers" often involved the same paternalism with which medieval lords treated their serfs. He housed them in little log villages to the rear of his lumber mansion. He was their great white god, their chief source of happiness and pain. Sometimes he lent them to his neighbors. Sometimes he rented them out for a good price. If his sensibilities prevented his dealing with them directly, he hired an overseer to work them.

During the nine-year life of the independent Texas Republic (1836–45) both farmers and planters continued going to Texas in large numbers. Because the Gulf Coast offered such easy ingress and commerce over the water from Louisiana, and because the open coast country required no expensive clearing, planters accumulated in southeastern Texas, while pioneers hewed small openings and built log cabins in the northeastern piny woods. This is why lumbering, agriculture, and petroleum-extraction are still undertaken on a large scale along the coast, whereas in Northeast Texas these same enterprises are pursued by small owners. The small owners of the northeast have more sympathy for one another and more need for sympathy than do the big concerns of the Gulf Coast. Hence the civic spirit which prevails around Tyler. Hence also the contrasting indifference to community movements which is still found on the coast.

The old-south plantation-owners of the early days had an advantage over the pioneers and soon began to set the standards of the whole Texas Republic. The small farmer could not effectively compete against these gentlemen. They built their own cotton gins and grain mills, whereas the small farmer had to have his "money crop" handled by some commercial gin or mill. The big plantation-owners' mass production made it possible for them to demand a good price for their product. The small farmer had to take what he could get. Thus, the farmer's only hope for economic betterment seemed to lie in becoming a planter. The possession of Negro slaves became an emblem of success, a source of personal pride. A man's merits were measured primarily by the number of "darkies" on his place. Today these attitudes have been transferred to Texas industry. Slavery as an institution is gone, but the standards it engendered still prevail, coloring Texas thought, Texas education, and Texas politics.

Corn and sugar cane were tried by the planters, but the river bottoms of Texas seemed best fitted for the growing of cotton. Hence, the economy, politics, and diplomacy of the Texas Republic were dominated throughout its nine years of existence by the exigencies of cotton-production and marketing. The invention of the cotton gin and the development of the textile industries in Britain and the northeastern United States had made cotton king. Good soil, a mild climate, the right amount of rainfall, and a pro-slavery constitution made Texas its favorite kingdom.

The machine age had enabled the northern states and England to transform cotton into huge quantities of fabrics by hiring a few experts to operate the mills, but the care of cotton in the fields persistently defied mechanization. Its seed had to be carefully distributed in rows measured by the human eye. When the plants were a few inches high, they had to be "chopped"—that is, thinned with a hoe, to prevent their growing too thick and choking one another out. The chopper chose the healthier plants for preservation and hoed up the others. No machine could do this. When the chosen plants had matured and their bulbs had opened to disclose "bolls" of white lint, only human hands could harvest it, one boll at a time. Hundreds of such hands were needed if the cotton was to be produced as fast as it could be consumed by the northern and British mills.

Manufacturers in Britain and the northern United States, who had their mechanical slaves at work, railed at the southern planter for using unpaid Negroes in the field. Northern laborers, disliking to compete against wageless blacks, joined the cry for the abolition of slavery in the south. Northern churchmen saw in slavery a violation of Christian principles, and northern laymen of normal sensibilities were keyed to intense disgust with tales of brutality perpetrated by southerners upon their black bondsmen.

Being peculiarly suited to cotton-raising and beyond the political control of northern idealists, Texas soon became a center of attention in the struggle over slavery. Immediately after she won her independence from Mexico, an election was called to name officers for the newborn republic. In addition to choosing leaders, the voters were asked whether or not they wished to be annexed to the United States. They voted 3,277 to 91 in favor of annexation. Accordingly, on August 4, 1837, the republic asked to join the Union.

Northern abolitionists were outraged. A new slave state would sway the balance of power in favor of the south. This was a nefarious plot by southerners to extend their odious institution in violation of the Missouri Compromise. Texas had been "dismembered from Mexico by a band of robbers." Now the land of the free was expected to clasp this "den of scorpions" to her bosom.

But the question also had its commercial aspect. Again, cotton-raising was the pivot on which the controversy turned. An independent Texas might at any time place a prohibitive tariff on her cotton exports. In such an event, whence would the northern fabric mills be fed? Moreover, if taken within the tariff wall of the United States, Texas would become a highly rewarding market for northern manufacturers. If left outside that wall, she might find it profitable to trade elsewhere.

Closely akin to these considerations, but more important to farsighted leaders, was the military aspect of the question. Great Britain's economy, like that of the northern states, was geared to the manufacture of cotton goods. If left independent, Texas would be free to trade with this competitor and erstwhile enemy of the United States and make agreements which might jeopardize the latter's safety. Texas would be an excellent springboard from which Britain could invade the United States over the vague, poorly defended western frontier. If Texas was annexed to the Union, however, the steep mountains along the upper Rio Grande would form a strong natural barrier against foreign aggression.

There was another consideration, less widely published but probably more decisive than the issues of slavery, commerce, and military defense. Many powerful northern speculators had acquired certificates to Texas land by purchase and as collateral for money lent to the war-debt-ridden Texas government. The future value of this land could be more fully assured if Texas was annexed and the United States government, with its more affluent treasury, was established there.

As time passed, these economic and military tensions became more acute, until by 1841, with the Texas government more perilously in debt than ever before, the annexation controversy burst forth full blast. Throughout the early forties it raged, until finally, in 1845, Texas became one of the United States.

Now the southern planters could exploit the Brazos and Colorado river valleys with more assurance than ever. The rate of immigration became fantastic. A state census taken in 1847 revealed a total population in Texas of 143,205, of whom 39,000 were Negro slaves. Three years later, in 1850, the total population had soared to 212,592, with 58,161 slaves. In both these counts, the percentage of slaves is 27.3. By 1860 the total population had almost trebled (604,215) and the percentage of slaves had risen to 30.2, with 182,566 in bondage. Near the mouths of the Brazos and the Colorado, where access from the Gulf was easiest for the southern immigrant and cotton could be shipped out in mass quantities, there were as many as four slaves for every free individual. Wharton County, on the lower Colorado, had only 646 whites holding sway over 2,734 blacks.

Up these two rivers, and also up the Trinity and the Sabine, the plantation system spread as far as the Balcones fault line, where the cities of Austin, Waco, and Dallas were beginning to thrive from the natural springs and the water power of the streams as they descended the fault, Austin on the Colorado, Waco on the Brazos, and Dallas on the Trinity. Beyond these cities the percentage of slaves in the population suddenly dropped, because cotton could not prosper in the eroded "hill country." Almost 40 per cent of the people in Travis County, where Austin stands, were slaves in 1860, but Burnet County, which adjoins it on the northwest, was only 9 per cent slave. The highlands of the latter were peopled by 2,252 freemen devoted mostly to cattle-ranching. The same was generally true of the counties farther up the streams.

Thus, the lay of the land had already set the tone of the

society. Below the fault line was an extension of the "deep south." Above it was the "wild west." Since the southerners outnumbered the westerners, and since the westerners were not much concerned one way or the other about slavery, Texas joined the Confederacy in the War between the States.

The southern planter's attitude was not softened by the triumph of the north and the woes of reconstruction. If changed at all, it was hardened and fortified with hatred. Edmund Jackson Davis, the carpetbag governor who kept the state under martial law from 1869 to 1873, was dubbed "Edmund the First." Some of the big plantations went out of business. Others persisted, paying their Negroes a small wage. Still others permitted the freedmen to work the land as tenants, paying either a fixed rental or a percentage of the crop returns. In all cases the Negroes continued doing the manual work, and their monetary rewards were small.

In the cities this condition is being fast obliterated, but in the small towns and farm communities, particularly along the Brazos, it persists to this day, protected largely by the Negroes' ignorance. Education among them is kept at a low ebb, and their activities are limited to the hard labor of the fields. Many of their children pick cotton through the early part of the school year, so that when school opens in September only a few attend. Later, when the cotton season is over, they flood the schoolhouses. In one Brazos bottom Negro school there are two rooms for each grade: a regular room and a "cotton-pickin' room." Until 1954 segregation was practiced generally in the public schools, and the colored schools of many small Texas communities were far inferior to their white schools in facilities and buildings. In the cities, wealthy southerners have poured large quantities of money into Negro school plants in the hope that the fine buildings would dampen the Negro's desire to attend white schools. Even though the courts have ruled that Negroes must be integrated with the whites in public schools, much Texas money still flows into such institutions as Texas Southern University, where beautiful modernistic buildings lure the colored. Situated in the southeastern part of Houston, Texas Southern has a current enrollment of twenty-five hundred exclusively Negro students. It is run by an interracial board with a Negro chairman. Five of the board members are white; four are Negro.

The recent Supreme Court decision will accelerate the already rapid process of urbanization in Texas. When the time for integration comes, white families now living in small towns will move to the city, where they can send their children either to a private segregated school or to a public school in a purely white district. Enrollment in private schools may also be expected to increase in Texas as a natural consequence of the southerner's resistance against integration. Small communities in the Brazos and Colorado river valleys, which now have a heavy percentage of Negro population, may become purely Negro settlements.

As yet, however, the whites in these small towns continue to maintain their medieval tradition of chivalry. Instead of shining armor, they wear white shirts and cheap Panama hats. Much of their time, especially when they pass middle age, is spent sitting on street benches, chatting about the weather, their crops, and their "niggers," displaying the leisure-class membership which they have inherited together with their blessed complexions.

Even so, for two good reasons the weaning from slavery left less lasting wounds in Texas than in the other southern states. First, Texas was tucked away in the west, safe from the immediate devastations of the Civil War. Second, her proximity to Mexico gave her at once a market during the war and a new source of cheap labor. The northern forces successfully blockaded the coast, but there was no way to prevent river boats on the Rio Grande from taking Texas cotton into Mexico at the fantastic price of a dollar a pound. Although often confiscated by the Confederate government for its own use, this cotton eased the financial blows attendant on emancipation.

Before the war, cotton-raising had spread to the Guadalupe River, which flows southeastward about fifty miles southwest of the Colorado. After the war, it continued spreading southwestward into the valleys of the San Antonio and the Nueces, which flow between the Guadalupe and the Rio Grande. Here, low-paid Mexican labor took the place of slavery. Today the assignment of agricultural tasks along these streams remains about the same as it was at its inception, with a large Latin American labor class spreading northward beyond the Guadalupe River Valley. The planters of the Brazos and Colorado have their "niggers"; those of the San Antonio, Nueces, and Rio Grande have their "meskins." The towns along the former streams have a high percentage of Negro population; those of the latter are congested with Mexican slums. Those of the Guadalupe have both Mexicans and Negroes at the bottom of the social and economic scale.

Although actually very different in origin and training from the Negro, the Mexican peon easily fills the Negro's role in the planter's mind. Since slavery was repugnant to Mexico's national outlook, Mexican landowners of southwest Texas and northern Mexico often harbored runaway blacks before emancipation. To the planter, who made no distinction between peons and landowners, it seemed that if Mexicans protected Negroes they must be of the same stamp. Moreover, the Indian and Spanish tint of the peon's skin made him resemble the Negro. Both Mexicans and Negroes were from southern climes. In their original habitat, they had been of miserable condition. Both were unable to achieve in their homelands a government like that of the United States. Both were therefore underendowed with initiative and critical acumen. Both were better fitted for the cotton field than for participation in a self-governed society.

So reasoned the bargain-hunting farmers as they spread

into South and West Texas to establish over the Mexican peon a dominion similar to that maintained over the East Texas Negro. Not all of these farmers were from the older communities of the Brazos and the Colorado. Many came directly from the northern states. Although their ancestors had been averse to Negro slavery, they had no scruples about low-paid Mexican labor. Under the prevailing economic, social, and cultural pressures, they fell perforce into the conscience-mollifying philosophy which their native Texan competitors applied to both Negroes and Mexicans.

We are now in a position to understand more fully why the Texas farmer is unwilling to avail himself of the legal arrangement for hiring Mexican field hands. This arrangement is based on an international agreement between the United States and Mexico. It provides for a temporary period of work under contract in the United States on the part of Mexican peons. It requires that these peons be paid the "prevailing wage" of the region. This wage, being ascertained from the employers' testimony, is modest. Nevertheless, its existence represents a controlling agency from outside the farmer's domain.

Meanwhile the wetback, having no legal status, is more completely within the farmer's little autonomous principality. He costs almost nothing and can be kept as long as the farmer sees fit. Therefore, he can be made to take the place formerly occupied by serfs and slaves, whereas the contract laborer cannot.

In 1950 the President of the United States sent a migratory-labor commission to Texas to inquire, among other things, why wetbacks were still being used instead of the legal contract labor. The farmers testifying to this commission pointed out that under the international agreement the labor contract was for a limited period, its absolute maximum being eighteen months. This limit had been set because the harvest season was limited and the work of harvesting required no particular skill. Yet the commission was told that employers could not "train" crop-gatherers in so short a time. Besides, the farmers went on, the arrangement required that they put in their applications for field workers several months before the harvest season, and the size of the harvest was unpredictable. Another objection: the employer was compelled to guarantee the worker an opportunity to labor during at least three fourths of the work days embraced by the contract. The result was, said the farm-owners, that they could not fire an inefficient worker.

All the timeworn adjectives formerly used on Negro slaves were now applied to the Mexicans. They were described as being accustomed to the hot sun, low altitude, and intense humidity of Texas's Gulf Coast cotton fields. This despite the fact that approximately 60 per cent of them are from Mexico's mountainous interior, where the average yearly temperatures range from fifty-eight to sixty-seven degrees Fahrenheit, the altitude is between five thousand and eight thousand feet, and the annual rainfall averages 22.5 inches. The Mexicans were said to know nothing of thrift. They had no ambition to set aside savings for a rainy day. If left to arrange their own lives, they would work only long enough to earn a minimum subsistence, then loaf the balance of the time. Conditioned by numerous generations of hopelessness, many peons have displayed these traits. The farmers argued that, unless supervised by one who "understood" him, any Mexican would shirk his proper tasks. Also, Mexicans were fond of traveling. Witness their long treks northward in the harvest seasons!

Under the farm-owner's protection, the wetback's energies were more advantageously directed. The commission was edified with idyllic pictures of contentment among wetbacks on Texas farms, with pleasing details about how they were given medical attention, baseball diamonds, and spiritual ministrations at the church of their choice, which was usually Catholic. All this in the face of the fact that the vast majority of wetbacks are migrants, forced to pass from farm to farm as the harvest season progresses northward. What the farmers obviously want is to choose a few from the passing horde and keep them the year round under a gentle overlordship which resembles, at least in some respects, a vanished but venerated system.

Out of deference to the changing times, the recently popular idea of the fittest's survival is added. The Mexican's laziness and improvidence are attributed mainly to his inexperience. He is merely a few stages behind the farm-owners in the upward progress of intellectual and social evolution. He is a "raw" person, "almost one step away from Indian living." Texas farmers provide him a "training ground" where, if his fitness persists, he may someday become a tractor-driver. Thus, the "stoop labor" of the fields—that is, the harvesting by hand of cotton and similar products—is viewed as a mere passing phase, from which the worthy aspirant soon is graduated into more pleasant and nobler activities.

As a matter of fact, some wetbacks have bettered themselves considerably. They come with almost no knowledge of how to use a hoe or live in a house with wooden floors. After a few years they become adept at some specialty, educate themselves, and take out naturalization papers. The chances of their doing so on the wages now paid them in the fields are extremely small, however. In any case, the farmer runs no risk of losing his stoop labor, since every exceptional wetback who leaves the fields for a better job is followed by dozens of others fresh from Mexico.

Of course these farmers, testifying under fire to a federal commission in an open hearing, were making out as good a case as they could under the circumstances. They belonged to a relatively enlightened period and were putting their best feet forward. Sixteen years earlier Paul Schuster Taylor made a thorough firsthand study of Mexican-Anglo labor relations in the neighborhood of Corpus Christi. Mexicans, he found, had been treated very much like Negro slaves. One white man told him: "If niggers or Mexicans get smart-alecky with you, you have just got to knock them down and they will stay in their place." Another said: "My brother used to beat the mean ones with a shovel and make them work. . . . If you have to cold-cock one out of forty or fifty, that isn't many." Another: "One Mexican got smart and didn't want to do what I told him, so I hit him over the head with a six-shooter and cut his scalp. He worked for me two years after that." One farmer was rather proud of his record, having "hit only three Mexicans in eight years." Taylor found that such practices were dying out in 1934.

The commissary system, by which Mexicans were forced to pay inflated prices at farm stores, was still in vogue, however, and the Anglo farmers showed no desire to serve as a "training ground" where talented Mexicans could get ahead in the world. One said: "The Mexicans own cars; that is one thing that causes trouble. They are independent and always wanting something better." Another said: "I wouldn't have a Mexican with a car." Another: "It is best to get the Mexicans in trucks. If they have their own cars, they travel every week to see where the cotton is. If they have no way to move about, it is better."

But all Texas farmers do not hold these attitudes. Northeast Texas and the Red River Valley still contain many who maintain the pious agrarian traditions of their pioneer ancestors and predecessors. Like the planters, these forerunners were driven from the United States by a combination of pressures between 1821 and Texas's annexation to the Union. Their westward spread into the territories was hampered by a tightening of the United States land policy about the time Stephen F. Austin initiated the Anglo-American colonization of Texas. Northern capital did not want a rapid movement of pioneers into the west because it would lower the eastern labor supply and force manufacturers to raise wages. Nor did south-

ern leaders want the west filled with freedom-revering farmers.
Yet there was nothing to prevent these farmers from crossing
the Red River into Texas, where plenty of land could be had
for the taking and the authorities had no incentive to be un-
generous.

◇◇◇

3. Germans, Czechs, and
Scandinavians

BESIDES THE ANGLO AGRARIANS, there are many communities
of German, Czech, and Scandinavian descent whose ancestors
were attracted to Texas during her nine years as an independent republic. Having come directly from countries where slavery did not prevail, they show no disposition to depend on
servile labor, be it either Negro or Mexican.

Germans began coming about the time of Texas's fight for
independence, establishing their settlements in the Brazos and
Colorado river valleys, apart from those of the American pioneers and southern planters. While the planters carried on
their traditions of Old World chivalry, the Germans, being
largely of the lower class in Europe, kept up their customs of
Old World peasantry. They used no slaves, but they worked
their women in the fields. Conditioned by untold generations
to wresting a livelihood from small plots of German earth,
they fenced off modest bits of the vast Texas coastal plain and
began cultivating them intensively. Instead of relying on cotton alone, they grew a variety of vegetables and fruits. Although not numerous enough to sway the nascent government's policies, they set a fine example and demonstrated that
involuntary servitude was not essential to the development of

the new country. Even in the face of the planter's mass production, they soon began to prosper and gain a high reputation for industriousness, punctuality, and thrift. Anent their economy, a proverb has arisen among non-German Texas farmers: "We sell what we can't eat; the Germans eat what they can't sell."

Germans were also among the first to attempt settlements above the Balcones fault line. The venture was an unintentional result of blunders stumbled into by a bunch of dreaming Prussian nobles. In 1842 these hopeful bluebloods organized a Society for the Protection of German Immigrants in Texas. This organization aspired to form in America a "new German fatherland" which would improve the condition of the German working classes by giving them a new start in life. It would also open new markets for German industries and develop maritime commerce. Texas was selected as the most suitable place for this "fatherland" because of its "healthful climate, fertility of soil, abundance of products, and ease of communication with Europe." This last feature was due not only to the ports of the Gulf Coast, but also to the absence of those tariff barriers which characterized the borders of the United States. Besides, there was more hope of the Germans' having a voice in the politics of the younger, smaller Texas Republic.

The most dynamic spirit in the German organization was Prince Carl of Solms-Braunfels, a robust nobleman with forthright, keenly critical eyes, a high-bridge nose, black hair brushed slick, and a long handlebar mustache. Appointed Commissioner General by the Society, he went to Texas in 1844 to supervise the creation of German colonies. He took with him a high pedigree, an extravagant share of aristocratic bigotry, much youthful enthusiasm, and an appalling lack of business judgment. He was first cousin to Queen Victoria of England and Wilhelm I of Germany. On his arrival in Texas, he was thirty-three years old. While the southern planters'

emblems of superiority had been reduced to cotton suits and
large bow ties, Prince Carl brought with him the full-fledged
regalia of the Middle Ages: sword, epaulets, and insignia. He
rode around the country with a retinue of attendants similarly
dressed: an architect, a cook, and a professional hunter. Ob-
servantly fingering his mustache, he broadcast his opinions on
Negro slavery: his surprise that these Americans, "whose land
is the freest in the world, whose laws and institutions are the
best planned in the world, do not find it odious that these unfortunate Negroes, after being mixed with the blood of whites
until the fifth generation, should be cast under the yoke of
slavery, which would be degrading to an animal." Needless to
say, these comments did not endear Prince Carl to the planters
of the Brazos and Colorado valleys.

Twice the Prince bargained for grants of land. Twice he
learned too late that the persons with whom he had dealt did
not really own the land they were selling him. Finally he
bought a segment of rugged hills on the Guadalupe River,
just above the Balcones fault line. Its only promising feature
was a waterfall near the junction of the Guadalupe with one
of its tributaries.

But the Prince was satisfied. The water, flowing over the
bare rocks, was clear as crystal, and the stunted oaks on the
hills looked beautiful to him. Here was a veritable Eden, an
ideal place for the new fatherland. Followed by his train of
specialists, he rode blissfully across the three hundred miles of
rich coastal prairie into the inclement hills, chose a spot for
his settlement near the waterfall, and christened it New
Braunfels in memory of his European castle. For himself he
built a pretentious although clumsy house of logs and called
it the Sophienburg in honor of his most favored lady love.

Behind him, landing in Galveston, were thousands of German peasants. Having no ready means of transportation, they
camped on the coast among mosquitoes and swamp-nurtured
fevers. Unaccustomed to the climate, undernourished, and

wasted by the hard sea voyage, they died so fast that the living had not time to bury their dead kindred. Mothers were doomed to watch their children die crying for food when there was no food, for warmth when there was no warmth.

Finding these scenes unpleasant, Prince Carl resigned and went home to Europe. His successor, John Otto Meusebach, contracted with a freight-wagon company to help deliver the immigrants to their promised land, but the company failed to fulfill the contract because of the war between the United States and Mexico. To increase the immigrants' misery further, a series of unusually violent thunderstorms flooded the country. The continuous rains swelled the streams beyond their banks. Hundreds of families, unable to endure their sufferings on the coast, set out on foot for New Braunfels, leaving a trail of dead bodies behind. In their wake came hordes of buzzards and coyotes to clean the bones of the dead and dying. For many a famished straggler, the highest remaining hope was to be completely dead before the vultures began their work.

New Braunfels was not large enough to accommodate all the people sent by the Society. Meusebach therefore obtained another tract some sixty miles northwest of New Braunfels and established Fredericksburg. Thus thrust into the rugged highlands, used as a buffer between the exuberant lowlands and the Indian-infested frontier, abused throughout the Civil War because of their aversion to slaveholding, these two German settlements drew vitality from their peril, forgave their persecutors, and worked with a zeal that overcame all adversities. Today they are neat, attractive, thriving little cities. Fredericksburg, because of the less responsive soil of its vicinity, has gravitated more to ranching than to farming. In politics it has always been conservative; unlike the rest of Texas, it regularly votes Republican. New Braunfels has a spinning and weaving industry. Its fine fabrics have made it famous.

From these bases, and from the earlier settlements in the lowlands, German farmers have spread throughout the state. Their places can be recognized by their thorough and systematic cultivation. By picking their own cotton and wielding their own hoes, they have grown wealthy.

The Czechs of Texas have come to thrive in the same way, except that they had no organization of European nobles to inject them prematurely into the highlands. They settled in tightly knit communities among the American farmers, mostly on the strip of black prairie that curves like a butcher-knife blade down the eastern side of the Balcones fault line, from the Red River to the environs of San Antonio. With the advent of irrigation, the Czechs have slowly spread westward and northward until now they are nearing the Panhandle. Swedes and Norwegians, in smaller numbers, have scattered over the state, also bringing to Texas soil the frugal farming methods developed from their experience in the Old World.

The present generation of Germans, Czechs, and Scandinavians has learned English, but many of the older individuals talk it brokenly or not at all, and the mother tongue is still used in their homes. They also retain many of their original folk fests and dances. While education and the machine age have changed the face of their farm life, their energy continues unabated. Nowadays the young women have trim figures and display them with all the brazen pride of Long Island bathing beauties, wearing shorts under the bare sun. But their leg sinews control the pedals of their husbands' tractors as they rip up the earth, six or more furrows at a time.

4. New Horizons on the Farm

THE INTRODUCTION of heavy machinery on the farm, to the extent that it displaces human labor, removes the apparent need, even among the descendants of southern planters, for large numbers of low-paid workers. The ever-accelerating velocity of this trend has been prodigious. In 1950, with 86 per cent of Texas's land under cultivation, 232,328 tractors were in use, as compared with only 98,923 in 1940. In 1930 there had been only 37,348, in 1920 only 9,048. By using tractors and other modern farm machinery, a farm-owner can cultivate more land with less help from hired hands, tenants, and share croppers than ever before. One effect of this is to reduce the farm population without reducing the acreage of the fields. Another is to enable the small owner to expand his holdings, so that while the average size of the farm increases, the total number of farms in the state goes down. Whereas in 1935 there were 501,017 separately managed farms in Texas, in 1950 there were only 331,567. The average size of the Texas farm has almost doubled during the last three decades, rising from 261.5 acres in 1920 to 438.5 acres in 1950. This rise is all the more striking when one considers that throughout the thirty years many big cattle ranches, considered "farms" by the census bureau, were being broken up into smaller plots for cultivation. If this process of ranch-to-farm conversion were eliminated from the figures, a still greater increase in average acreage among original farms would be revealed. Of these larger farms, 228,372 are now operated by their owners, in contrast to only 190,575 owner-operated farms in 1930.

Of course, the extent to which mechanization can eliminate the stoop labor of the fields is limited by the nature of the crop being produced. Cotton having been the principal Texas money crop for over a hundred years, its mechanization would change the picture more than that of any other product, and considerable progress has recently been made in this direction. Mechanical cotton-choppers have been devised, but they are not yet used extensively.

Far more widely used is the mechanical "cotton-stripper" for harvesting. It cuts the cotton, boll and all, from its stem. In 1950 there were 9,923 strippers at work on Texas farms. Since they get burrs and other parts of the plant along with the cotton, it has to be cleaned at the gin, and the quality of the lint is often reduced.

This hazard is removed by the more elaborate mechanical cotton-picker, particularly if the plants are first relieved of their leaves by frost or a chemical spray. There are several types of these pickers. They force the plant's branches together and tear the lint from the bolls by means of tiny spindles combined with air suction to lift it like huge grains of freshly popped popcorn into a glass container or a truck bed. One model picks two rows at a time, moving through the field at two miles per hour with the driver seated at the wheel in front of the glass container. With it, one man can do the work of eighty hand pickers, covering about one and one half acres per hour.

One trouble with most cotton-picking machines is that they fail to get the cotton that has fallen to the ground. However, most cotton fields can be picked twice, since some bolls mature earlier than others. Farmers often hire hand pickers to do the first picking, cleaning the cotton off the ground. Then, when the younger bolls open, a machine is used for the second picking.

Since in this case the mechanization is only partial, its effect has been to aggravate rather than remove the feudal pattern of the cotton farm. The large owner may now have fewer workers under him, but these are no less dependent on him than before, especially if they are Negroes or Mexicans. On the contrary, his opulence makes him all the more formidable. The competition of synthetic fabrics, by reducing the cotton market and forcing the farmer to raise more highly mechanizable crops instead, may eventually help break the pattern, but for the time being, cotton is still Texas's principal crop, and Texas leads all other states in its production. With all its new techniques, the human side of cotton-farming remains basically the same.

The small grains—rice, wheat, and milo maize—have in recent years become extremely popular where climate permits. Rice is limited to the upper Gulf Coast and wheat to the north, whereas milo maize and similar grain sorghums are more widely distributed over the state.

The increasing popularity of these and other crops is partly due to a more prudent concern for the soil which the Texas farm-owner began evincing soon after the Civil War. Since that time, while his relationship with his "hired hands," when there are any, remains medieval, his attitude toward the land and its fruits has radically changed.

The original settlers, coming mostly from cotton and corn states, with some experience in wheat culture where the weather permitted, had little interest in raising anything else. From the wheat and corn they got bread and feed for their cows, oxen, horses, and mules; from the cotton they got clothes, first by spinning and weaving it themselves, later by selling it and buying what they needed. They were too busy contending with Indians, Mexicans, and "runaway niggers" to visualize a limit to the possibilities of the earth from which they drew their sustenance. The land was so vast and productive that they regarded it as a kind of God-given bonanza, an everlasting fountain of life.

Then, toward the end of the nineteenth century, the fields began to weaken under repeated extractions of the same crops.

The Brazos bottom domains gradually fell into grand decay. In less than fifty years Texas farm-operators frittered away large quantities of the alluvial matter that had been accumulating for more than fifty million years. In their ignorance, they subsequently began to fear that old age was creeping into the heart of the agricultural giant that had vanquished Mexico, tantalized Britain, and successfully wooed the United States despite her squeamishness about slaveholding. Experts in botany and soils were called to the rescue.

On April 17, 1871, the state legislature set aside $200,000 to create the Agricultural and Mechanical College of Texas, currently known as A. and M. Its purpose was "to offer white male students, at the lowest possible cost, a liberal and practical education." Mechanics and military tactics were included in its curriculum, but its principal interest was agricultural science. The campus of 2,416 acres was located near Bryan, in the heart of the Southeast Texas farming region, five miles north of the Brazos River, about halfway between Waco and the Gulf. It soon became a meeting-place for the numerous farmers' organizations that were beginning to mushroom over the country as a result of the increasing need for organized protection against impoverishment.

A still more striking indication of the new trend was a state fair held in Houston just one month and six days after the creation of A. and M. The fair grounds comprised an eighty-acre tract at the north end of Main Street. On May 23, 1871, these grounds were alive with tents and flying flags. The central building, in the shape of a Maltese cross, displayed a bewildering variety of Texas-grown vegetables, fruits, and melons. One farmer had brought seventy different kinds, all grown on Galveston Island. The local newspaper boasted of cucumbers two feet long. Power Hall, to the right of the fair grounds entrance, teemed with steam engines, mowers, reapers, rotary harrows, and recently improved cotton gins.

Horace Greeley was the speaker of the day. Before the

Civil War he had been hated in the south for his abolitionism, but now he was as widely loved for his denunciation of those who wanted to keep on fighting the war after it had ended. On a quest for southern support in the forthcoming presidential race, he had crossed the Gulf from New Orleans for a brief visit in Texas. Having grown up on New England farms, where land was dear and had to be nursed with care, he was amazed at the vastness and extravagance that characterized Texas farming. From a grandstand draped with red, white, and blue cloth, he addressed a crowd of ten thousand. His white hair and whiskers were like cotton lint, framing a pink-cheeked face at the summit of a stocky sixty-one-year-old frame. But he knew farming and showed it.

"It is far easier," he warned, "to maintain the productive capacity of a farm than to restore it. Rotation may not positively enrich a farm; it will at least retard and postpone its impoverishment." The response of the crowd, declares the local news reporter, was deafening.

But the fair and Greeley's ovation were little more than gestures in a new direction. The fruits, melons, and vegetables that so gaily decked the fair grounds had not actually penetrated to the average Texas dinner table. The Texas people's habits were tuned to times when one had to make the best of meager provisions: when gold coins sometimes had to be chopped into slugs to serve as buckshot against Indians, when only Indian corn and the wild hogs that ate it could be found for food. Hence, with few exceptions, they still limited their diet to corn bread, bacon, beef, and potatoes.

So glaring was the contrast between the fair-grounds display and the actual nutrition of the people that Greeley wrote back to the *Tribune:* "She [Texas] is in urgent need of twenty thousand more schoolteachers and fifty thousand instructed cooks. It is a grief to see beef that might be broiled into tender and juicy steaks fried or stewed into such repulsive, indigestible messes as I have encountered at all but her two best hotels.

It is a crying shame for a region where the peach, the grape, the pear, the strawberry, &c. grow so luxuriantly and bear so bounteously, to be living almost entirely on meat, bread, and coffee. In Labrador or Alaska, such a 'hog and hominy' diet would be faulty; under this fervid sun, it is atrocious."

Not custom alone, but economic conditions as well, retarded the trend toward diversification. Cotton could bring more money for the same land and labor than any other crop. It could be shipped for miles on slow boats or wagons; if kept dry, it was never in danger of spoiling. Texas farmers, especially those who were in debt, needed to be sure of their returns. They could not afford to take chances with untried, perishable products. The result was that while the diversification of vegetables and fruits increased year by year, cotton kept its place at the top.

By 1881 Texas was being advertised as a bonanza land for oats, sugar cane, tobacco, flowers, and all kinds of fruits, nuts, and vegetables. Pecans had been found growing wild along Texas rivers by the first European explorers. Before 1900 many a fine pecan tree was cut to make way for cotton plantations. Since then the remaining pecan groves have come to be respected for the way they can reward respectful owners.

Today, in addition to her bumper cotton crops, Texas produces annually an average of more than ten million bushels of corn, more than forty-six million of wheat, and more than six million of rice. The truck crop is likewise prodigious. In 1950 Texas orchards yielded 1,209,511 bushels of peaches, 363,768 of pears, 141,936 of prunes and plums, and 96,020 of apples. From Texas trees, wild and cultivated, came over ten billion pounds of pecans, and from Texas vines, mostly tame, came over a billion pounds of grapes. There are several varieties of wild Texas grape, but their sour taste makes them unmarketable. In this same year of 1950 the lower Rio Grande Valley produced almost 82,000 tons of oranges and over 185,-000 tons of grapefruit.

Yet a surprising number of Texas farm families still stick to their ancient diet: bacon, beans, biscuits, and corn bread, with beef and potatoes at noon. When dieticians upbraid them, they buy vitamin pills.

Mexican laborers, who cannot understand the dietician, are the least likely to take advantage of the land's agricultural versatility. Their tortilla, a corn cake traditionally patted by hand until almost as thin as paper and cooked with very little grease over a slow fire, is now fashioned in "tortilla factories" with heated bands and roller presses. For these Mexicans, the world's supreme luxury is a tiny wild pepper whose potency the uninitiated cannot endure without tears. The frijole bean is considered as essential as the air they breathe. Beans, corn, water, and air are for them the fountain of life. All else is vanity.

The power of these venerable habits is well illustrated by an incident I witnessed personally in the South Texas ranch country around 1932. By a brakeman's oversight, the rear half of a freight train loaded with grapefruit got separated from its front half. The front half merrily steamed a mile or so ahead and stopped at a village inhabited mostly by ranch Mexicans. When the rear half overtook it, the crash hurled two of the cars, like giant dominoes, into the air. When they came back down, their walls were shattered and their contents rolled out over the prairie. Here was grapefruit galore, aglitter in the bare sun, free for the taking.

Not wanting it to rot in the sun and draw flies, the Mexicans gathered it and carried it to their homes in gunny sacks. Nobody would take it off their hands, so they ate it. The shock was too great for their alimentary organs. Some of them told me afterward that they had never before been so sick. Even those who had followed the harvests were indisposed for days. Their hands had picked hundreds of citrus fruits, but this was the first time their stomachs had been bothered by them. Such accidents show the hold which tradition has even on the physical man. Here is one more reason why the fruit- and vegetable-growers from the north, who have poured into Texas during the last seventy-five years, so readily fall into the old Texan's habit of regarding the Mexican as a kind of subhuman species. The idea will long have value as a rationalization, for no machine has yet threatened to replace the human—or subhuman—hand in gathering fruit from trees.

The gradual deterioration of Texas crops could not be offset by diversification alone. A finer art than crop-rotation was the improvement of specific products by selective plant-breeding. For this purpose, and also for the study of insect pests, the Texas Agricultural Experiment Station system was set up in 1888, with a central station at A. and M. and branch stations in the different soil areas of the state. Administered from A. and M., the system consists principally of trained scientists who publish their discoveries in government bulletins and co-operate with farmers and agricultural organizations in capitalizing on them. For instance, as cotton spread northwest above the fault line and south into the areas of less rainfall, the average length of the lint, known as the "staple," was reduced. Much experimentation at the stations has been devoted to achieving a longer staple and more accurately classifying the lint.

Recent researches have uncovered hitherto unknown virtues not only in the length, but also in the strength, of Texas cotton. As the Bureau of Cotton Economics Research puts it: "There is no area in the world where man conspires with nature to grow so many kinds of cotton in abundance." It is almost as if an all-wise Providence had designated Texas as a spot for cotton-raising and adjusted the seasons accordingly. In the spring and early summer, as cotton plants begin to bloom, the rainfall slacks off, causing them to struggle for water and so produce a stronger fiber than that of regions where rainfall is plentiful the year around.

The climatic diversity of the state's several regions is reflected in the character of its cotton. East Texas and the Gulf Coast produce an average staple a little below an inch in length and of a relatively low grade and tensile strength. The Rio Grande Valley produces a longer staple, the longest, with the highest tensile strength, being grown in the Trans-Pecos and El Paso areas. The Panhandle and Northwest Texas produce the shortest staple of all, with a strength roughly the same as that of the East Texas and Gulf Coast cotton. This wide variety is now beginning to bring numerous new textile mills to Texas.

The complexity of the cotton picture in present-day Texas is kept from complete confusion by an organized, state-supported cotton-research program under the auspices of A. and M., Texas Technological College at Lubbock, and the University of Texas. The A. and M. researchers specialize in the art of growing cotton: seed-selection, breeding for desired fiber qualities, soil-conservation, fertilizers, and cultivation. Texas Technological College deals with the spinning and weaving end of the industry. The university deals with cotton economics: commercial problems and marketing adjustments.

With a little more attention, Texas farmers could further improve their products, but their attitudes toward the older crops were set in pioneer times, and it is difficult to re-educate them. They follow in their fathers' footsteps, proceeding on the assumption that farming is not an art, but a mere routine of chores, that all you have to do to raise a crop is break the ground and drop the seed. They still aim at quantity rather than quality, and the whole community suffers as a result. They swamp the market with low-grade commodities which cannot have much demand in a competitive economy. The small returns and staggering cost of harvesting large heaps of produce make it impossible for them to pay their laborers good wages. The low pay causes poverty, filth, and disease among their workers. This in turn lowers the living-standards of the entire area, for buying-power shrinks and insects carry pestilence from slum to mansion.

Recently initiated varieties of farm produce, for which Texans do not have long-established habits of cultivation, are raised with more of an eye to quality. Notable among these are the citrus fruits of the lower Rio Grande Valley and the truck crops that have been popularized in recent years.

Recent immigrants from Europe, also, being unhampered by the state's century-old habits of cultivation, are particularly amenable to new methods. Outstanding among them is Faithon P. Lucas, a Greek who has transformed 1,223 acres of depleted soil near Dallas to a prolific diversified farm supplying his B & B Café customers without any intervention from profit-consuming middle men. Milk, eggs, and all desired varieties of vegetables come fresh from the Lucas farm to the Lucas restaurant tables in Dallas every morning. Inscribed on the B & B menu is the following declaration by Lucas himself:

"Top soil is the source of all life. It is the duty of every good citizen to conserve what's there and to rebuild what others destroyed."

The problem of adjusting Texas crops to the markets of the world has also been a source of much concern to Texas farmers. To help contend with this and similar problems, the State Bureau of Agriculture, a branch of the Department of Insurance, Statistics, and History, was established in 1887. In 1907 this was replaced by the Department of Agriculture, under a Commissioner of Agriculture who held office through direct vote of the people. For a while there was considerable confusion over the division of duties between the Department of Agriculture and the A. and M. Experiment Station system. Then in 1921 Governor Pat M. Neff clearly defined the proper sphere of each: "All activities which pertain to the educational aspect and to the knowledge of agriculture should be, as a matter of economy in energy and money, lodged in and confined to the Agricultural and Mechanical College; and all those agencies protective of agricultural interests, which are administrative in nature and which involve the police power of the state, should be vested in the Department of Agriculture." The problem of marketing has since been left mainly in the hands of private farmers' organizations.

The handling of the land, like the handling of its fruits, has been radically changed by the threat of eventual exhaustion. Here again, new practices were retarded by habits set in pioneer times. The original settlers were at the mercy of high winds, unpredictable rains, and whimsical streams. Nature and chance had ruled Texas so long, with such inexorable power, that man's control of nature seemed incomprehensible.

To destroy this preconception, A. and M. College began an educational program in 1910. Terracing was the first effort at saving the fields from water erosion. By 1930, between six million and seven million acres of farm land were terraced. In 1939 the Texas legislature authorized the United States Soil Conservation Service to set up districts for administering its programs in Texas. Systematic planting of bushes and trees to hold the soil has now been added to terracing. Farmers now plow their rows on a level around the hills and contours, rather than up and down the slopes, so that the water will be held by the furrows rather than carried to the streams. Despite these measures, Texas streams still carry around eighty million tons of Texas earth into the Gulf each year. This is a very rough average, for the variations are enormous. The salvation of this soil is now generally recognized to be entirely in the hands of Texas farmers.

The problem of obtaining water, not only for farm-irrigation but also for human consumption and industry, is now becoming acute in Texas. The large reservoirs of underground water with which the state was originally blessed are beginning to go dry. Natural springs are disappearing. Many of the once fabulous artesian wells no longer flow. A committee of engineers, financed through the good offices of Senator Lyndon B. Johnson, has now come forth with a plan for connecting all Texas streams, from the Sabine to the Rio Grande, with a continuous inland canal. The wisdom of this scheme can be appreciated when one considers that the annual flow of Texas rivers is sixty-three million acre-feet, of which only nine million are now being used. An acre-foot is enough water to cover an acre of ground to the depth of one foot. If the fifty-four million acre-feet of river water which now flow unused into the Gulf can be caught and controlled, the state's water worries will be over.

A spectacular consequence of the new diversification is the recent boom in poultry-raising. Central and South Texas have gone in heavily for broiler-production, and the north central area, particularly at Ennis (7,817) and Waxahachie (11,196), just south of Dallas, specialize in supplying large hatcheries with fertile eggs.

But the real chicken capital of Texas—indeed, of the entire southwest—is Center (4,318), an East Texas town just a few miles from the Sabine. East Texas, whose soil has long needed those chemicals found in poultry manure, specializes in broilers, and Center has become its principal processing city. Center's processing establishments turn out approximately ten million broilers, ready to cook, each year: almost thirty thousand per day.

In addition to the A. and M. Experiment Station system, three important private establishments are now dedicated to the improvement of Texas agriculture. They are the Texas Research Foundation at Renner, near the northern outskirts of Dallas; the Luling Foundation in South Central Texas; and Rio Farms in the lower Rio Grande Valley. The Texas Research Foundation is sustained by donations from businessmen, mostly of Dallas. Staffed by high-caliber scientists, it has worked out a number of crop-rotation programs designed to restore the depleted blacklands. Since grazing is an important part of these rotations, much experimentation has gone into the development of better range grasses.

The Luling Foundation owes its existence to Edgar B. Davis, discoverer of the Luling oil field. Established in 1927 with a million-dollar donation from Mr. Davis, it stresses simple methods within the limited means of small farmers. Demonstrations are given to show farmers the proper use of fertilizers, good seed, and good equipment.

Designed to refresh man and land at once is Rio Farms, a self-supporting institution of applied agriculture at Monte Alto in the lower Rio Grande Valley, where low-income farmers are admitted as tenants and trained along with their families over a period of five years, after which their improved circumstances and knowledge enable them, in the majority of cases, to buy their own farms and run them profitably. Farmers of all racial strains are eligible, but no bachelors are taken, and the families usually have small children. Prospective tenants are interviewed together with their wives before acceptance. Available to the chosen ones are 102 farm units, each with a modern house and about 110 tillable acres. These units are as nearly as possible the same in size and quality. Having decided on one of them, a tenant may not change to another during his five-year stay. Tenancy is rotated, so that about twenty new farmers come in each year. No man may remain more than five years, nor may a former tenant return for a second term. After their departure, the tenants purchase homes or rent elsewhere; none of the land on Rio Farms is for sale.

During their five years, farmers work under the direction of experts. The institution undertakes experiments whose results redound to the benefit not only of the whole valley, but also of the entire agricultural world. They co-operate with A. and M. and other institutions in trying new crosses and plant environments. Competitions are held in the care of livestock and the growing of high-quality produce. The wives and children have contests in dressmaking and similar domestic activities. Style shows are held, featuring homemade clothes. Classes are given, accounts kept, progress watched.

The central office of Rio Farms is a broad, low, air-conditioned building on a wide knoll. In its reception room are racks bearing pamphlets for the tenants on how to keep a home free from insects, how to keep a bathroom sanitary, how to wax and care for floors, how to keep rugs and carpets clean, how to crochet beautiful bedspreads and chair sets, how to make clothes from cotton bags, how to plan high-protein menus, how to feed a milk cow. The results of previous Rio Farms experiments are published in booklets and distributed. Also, there is an archive where clippings on subjects of importance to farmers are kept in alphabetically arranged filing-boxes for use at any time.

In addition to the 102 farm units, Rio Farms has an experimental and demonstrational core with a central tract of land and seven departments covering three major fields: citrus, other crops, and livestock. By participating in the activities of these departments, tenants get the instruction which they subsequently apply to their respective units. Their degree of success with these units is the measure of their aptitudes and progress. Each tenant has a contract with Rio Farms, under which he pays, from the sale of crops grown on his unit, a specified rental per acre. All he can make above this rental and his family expenses is saved to pay for a farm of his own after he has finished his five years. During the last four years, few tenants have failed to meet these requirements because of personal unfitness.

Yet Rio Farms is not dependent for its support either on government or on voluntary donations. With rentals from tenants and proceeds from the sale of crops grown on the experimental and demonstrational core, it maintains a staff of technical experts. All income is put back into the business. The Rio Farms affairs are run by a seven-man board of di-

Downtown El Paso, looking north toward the Franklin Mountains.

Midland.

Virgin longleaf timber in East Texas. The 35-inch tree, nearly 100 feet high, is being measured in Bronson State Park, near Sabine National Forest

*Mechanical cotton-harvester or stripper in operation
in West Texas; it is 98 per cent efficient.*

Cowboys selecting horses from the remuda. Waggoner Estate Ranch near Vernon.

Cowboys moving white-faced Herefords toward the cutting chute. Waggoner Estate Ranch near Vernon.

rectors, all local residents and recognized business and professional men. They receive no pay. A general manager, hired by the board and paid from the institution's earnings, holds regular meetings with the directors.

Rio Farms was chartered by the State of Texas on December 8, 1941, the day after Pearl Harbor. Its initiation was made possible by a loan of $1,288,350 from the Farm Security Administration. On February 7, 1945, this loan was repaid in full, and the institution has since been out of debt.

IV

BLEAK WINDS FROM THE WEST

◇◇

1. The Longhorn

THE VASTNESS of the southwestern landscape is emphasized by the gradualness of its transitions. As you pass from east to west across Texas, the masses of moss hanging from gigantic oaks gradually become scarce. Gradually the trees scatter, and the growing gaps between them add a sense of expansion to the sight of land and sky. Fields of maize and grain around frail-looking but primly painted lumber homes suggest happy living. Their appearance is so gradual that no traveler can find the exact point of their beginning. The land, though absolutely flat along the coast, soon begins imperceptibly to roll. At first the slopes are so gentle that valleys are apparent only in the recurrence of huge, moss-hung oaks with wild grapevines draped over their foliage. Instead of blocking visibility, the low hills only lengthen it. To catch the breeze above them, windmills are built on higher towers than along the coast, yet they seem hardly larger than toothpicks in the distance. Cattle graze on miles of green forage. Though scattered as the patches of shrubbery, they can be seen by the hundreds at a glance.

Before the earth's undulations are high enough to be called hills, you can see them cutting waves in the horizon, far enough away to share a thin, transparent slice of the sky's blue. Giant oaks, looking like tiny spots of darker blue, dot this slightly curved horizon. Farmhouses, appearing as bead-like blocks of white, freckle the blue. Roads wind like threads of gray between them. Yet all this is on a generally level expanse of land.

As you cross the Balcones fault line, the softness of geologically recent formations gives way to the severity of cliffs and crags. To the north, around Dallas and Fort Worth, this is a slow change. Prosperous farms are cradled between the promontories. The houses and barns among them gradually become less numerous, and stretches of virgin wood grow more frequent.

Near Austin, the fault line is much more distinct. East of this capital city extend wide, rich farm lands over mild inclines. When the sky is cloudy, patches of sunlight roam at random across them. Three or four such patches are often visible at once. On bright days the shadows of clouds drift uniformly with the wind, temporarily deepening the green, yellow, and red of the fields.

West of Austin lies what is locally known as the hill country, covered with squat, thick-growing oak and cedar trees whose dark leaves provide a dull relief from the sun's glare. The heavens are often empty here, the sun severe. Not much comfort can be derived from the coo of turtledoves, the chirp of other wild birds, and the spots of brighter green—mesquite, hackberry, laurel, and granjeno—dispersed like live bubbles amidst the general roll of cedars and oaks.

South and west of San Antonio stretches the brush country. Its hills have a weirdness, a kind of magic, that all other Texas landscapes lack. There is a fairy-tale atmosphere, a seeming mendacity fraught with bizarre paradoxes, in their innumberable suggestions. White as chalk and wide at the base, they have deep gulleys which betray a hoary age. The variety of their wild shrubs is spellbinding. A soft, ash-colored bush called the cenizo hints at snow and silver, though snow seldom falls on these sun-parched crags, and precious little silver, false or genuine, has ever been directly or indirectly got from them. There is a brown-leafed shrub with an odor like strong medicine. Tea from it, drunk by young women, is said to make them have large families. There are cactus plants of such diverse shapes that an imaginative observer can find all sorts of goblins and unearthly beings among them. The hue of leaves runs from a lush near-blue to a brilliance bordering on yellow.

Whatever their form or color, most of these growths are armed with ugly, threatening thorns. The trees—even those lone oaks that tower far above the shrubs and cacti—are gnarled, knotted, and often so twisted as to suggest deformity. Their bark is as rough and hard as the white stones from which they grow, and like those stones they show evidence of rough times—of a loneliness and suffering too deep and ancient for any man to know, much less to appreciate emotionally. They appear to belong in another world, which was here for ages before the advent of men; a world whose memories are too many for humanity to grasp, whose ways and laws are so strange that the human spirit may come among them only as an intruder and human standards must fail to evaluate them properly.

As you turn either westward or northwestward from the brush country, the oaks and mesquites show increasing signs of struggle for life's needs. There begins to be a famished, frantic look about their erratic branches, as if they were scrambling for something that they could not find. They begin to be sparse, so that some of the hills have bald summits ridged with broad dry creeks that look like narrow pathways.

As the hills become larger, the trees become smaller, until even the oaks get to be little more than bushes. The earth seems crumpled and broken. The magnitude of its wrinkles in contrast with the size of its plants is the main trait that makes these western wastelands awe-inspiring. Now the softness of the Gulf Coast is entirely gone. Rough rock surfaces and abrupt bluffs are everywhere. The steepening slopes are either pocked with runt mesquites or specked with a dark-leafed weed which normally seems scorched. The whiteness of naked stones and the dullness of all vegetation find relief only in the sky-blue haze of distance that veils the higher mountains.

Whirlwinds stalk like giant ghosts over the land below the hills. Through the whole visible world, those whirlwinds are the only things in motion. Sometimes a dozen or more may be seen at a glance. Most of them tower to the clouds, yet no two are exactly alike. Some are broad and violent. Others are thin threads of white connecting earth and sky. Beyond their half-transparent substance lie the mountaintops and clouds. The land is always blowing away. The shrubs cling desperately to little mounds of sand kept intact by their roots alone. All the surrounding soil, down to the more solid crusts of rock and clay, is swept off by the roaming winds.

But vastness and bleakness are not the only striking features of these mighty hills. Another is that they all seem to have their heads cut off. They rise to a great height, then suddenly break to a flat top. They are like cones with their points sheered from them by some gigantic knife whose sweep was so even that all summits were severed to exactly the same level. But to observe this is to perceive only part of the truth. The full truth begins dawning slowly as you notice that these flat hilltops, in addition to having the same elevation, are composed of the same material: a layer of boulders which fit together with the compactness, though not the uniformity, of bricks in a man-built wall. Not only does this layer of boulders cap all the hills at equal altitudes; it has the same thickness on them all. Such regularity cannot be accidental.

Its cause is revealed by the realization that these are not

exactly hills. Their tops are not really peaks, but surviving islands from a once-solid stretch of land. The compact boulders
of that land's surface were worn away in places by the violent
winds of past millennia. Great holes were dug out through the
ages. These eventually grew into craters and joined one another, so that the high ground between them was cut into
scraps. The scraps were then worn smaller. The boulders
around their edges fell into the ever-broadening craters. By the
time of man's arrival, the network of merged craters had
grown more extensive than the remnants of the older earth's
crust. Hence, houses and highways were built in the bottoms
of the craters, and the bits of earth remaining above were
looked upon as hilltops. They are of unvaried height and
thickness because they were originally all one unbroken floor
of boulders, packed close together by the traffic of prehistoric
life.

The materials of that ancient floor first began being
formed about six hundred million years ago. At that remote
time the lay of the land was not the same as it is now. The
lowlands were high and the highlands low. Instead of the dry
hills that rise into today's West Texas sky, enormous inland
seas extended from the area of San Antonio to that of El Paso
and beyond for unknown distances. Instead of the flat plains
that now skirt the Gulf of Mexico, mountains towered over
the locale of East Texas, mingling their peaks with the steamy
mists of an atmosphere too new for life. The highest living
forms were worms and sponges deep in the earth and sea. The
mountains had no name, for there was no one to name them,
but proof of their existence is found in Llano County, up the
Colorado River from Austin, where graphite, feldspar, and
granite are derived from their remains. Modern geologists
therefore identify them as the Llanoria land mass.

Llanoria is the parent continent of North America, and
hence of Texas. It is the ancient heap of earth upon which the
outlines of the latter have been etched during the last six hun-

dred million years or so. Like any good parent, it has left its young ones an enviable heritage, and the area since named Texas is one of its most favored children. Nor can we understand the child without knowing at least a little of the parent.

As continental cataclysms followed one another, Llanoria's worms and sponges gave way to fish, scorpions, and ferns, whose bodies and fibers died to form deposits of oil and coal. Snails were also common. They developed shells of sundry shapes: curled, horned, and spangled with quills like a porcupine. One kind was a disk-shaped white coil with red lines radiating in waves from its center or following its circular contours. It often grew to the size of a man's head. The first true fish were in fresh water. Many of their descendants produced air-breathing amphibians, some of which later reverted to sea life and gave birth to an abundance of lung fish. After fish came insects. There were gigantic dragonflies and cockroaches. Then thick-leafed plants appeared.

By this time Llanoria had grown old. Her mountains were no more. Erosion from boisterous winds had worn them down to a lowland hardly more than a few feet above the level of the western sea. Streams, running west rather than east as our present rivers flow, had cut deep canyons, which in turn had eaten away the ancient hills.

Then, about two hundred million years ago, Llanoria's crust was rumpled into what is now known as the Appalachian Mountain system. By the time these new mountains were formed, Llanoria's fish and amphibians had evolved into reptiles, which grew larger from generation to generation until some became sea serpents. Others became flying dragons and yet others became dinosaurs that thundered over the crumpled lands with the tonnage of a modern locomotive and just enough brains to fill a teacup.

The largest of these was a vegetarian lizard called the brontosaurus, with four elephantine feet beyond which stretched, to the front and rear, a snake-like neck and tail. It

ranged from forty to seventy feet long, and its back humped
up to a height of ten to fourteen feet.

Slightly smaller but far more horrible was the tyrannosaurus, which stood twenty feet high on its hind legs. Although its front limbs were hardly larger than a man's arm—
tiny instruments of no practical value—it could sway almost
horizontally forward at will, for its tail was big enough to
balance its upper body. Its jaws were three feet long and it had
three- to six-inch double-edged teeth. Many of the grass-eaters
developed turtle backs armed with horns and scales for protection against this two-legged terror.

Contrary to popular belief, these monsters were not a passing whim of nature which failed to survive the cataclysms of
the ages because of their small brains and clumsy forms. Humanity will do well if it lasts one per cent as long as they did.
They lived through a period one hundred and forty times the
total span of man's residence on the earth so far. They came
into existence about two hundred million years ago, and they
lasted until around sixty million years ago, whereas man has
hardly been on earth more than one million years. Of course,
many different species evolved during the era of the dinosaurs,
and the younger mammal family, including man, has now
overshadowed the older reptile family to which the dinosaurs
belonged, but the career of the latter alone was fantastically
long, and they certainly left the land in a condition very different from the state in which they found it.

The boulders of the flat West Texas hilltops were formed
of pulverized dinosaur bones and lime dust from Llanoria's
worn-out mountains. Thrice were those boulders submerged
under deep seas, to be coated with sediments and compressed
by the water's weight. Thrice they rose again, to have their
blankets of silt trampled by the big reptiles, which were then
at the peak of their career on earth. Seeming lofty to those
who now travel the road hundreds of feet below, those heaps
of chalk-white stone are all that is left of the earth over which

the brontosaurus, the tyrannosaurus, and hordes of other
giant lizards roved more than fifty million years before humanity appeared.

But this is true only in the far and windy west. In Central
Texas the surface of the land is still the surface upon which
the dinosaurs lived. Whereas today along the Gulf Coast this
layer of lime and chalk descends deep beneath more recent accumulations, and whereas to the west and north it has been
whittled into hills by the wind, it remains at the top of an immense territory stretching through the center of Texas, blend-
ing into the coastal prairies below the Balcones fault line,
spreading far into the highlands above it. This area is uniquely
Texan. Nowhere else have the remnants of the dinosaur era
impressed themselves so indelibly on present-day life. By furnishing nourishment to edible vegetables that now grow in the
region, these remnants exert an impact on animal health
which, being difficult to measure, is seldom appreciated. They
are a vital ingredient in the strip of black waxy ground running
south from the Red River, passing east of Dallas, Waco,
Austin, and San Antonio. They feed the cliff-shadowed farms
and ranches around Fort Worth, the runt cedars of the hill
country, and the dazzlingly kaleidoscopic growths of the brush
country. They supply the hardy but often drouth-stricken
shrubs of West Texas. They are particularly rich in those minerals from which bones, teeth, and horns are formed.

In 1521, just three hundred years before Stephen F. Austin's first settlers came to Texas, Spaniards began bringing their
livestock to the North American mainland. Wherever they
went, they left cows, bulls, horses, and hogs to shift for themselves among the virgin woods or on the prairies. Sometimes
the more rebellious animals got away from them and, because
of the land's strangeness and the sundry lusts which harried
the Spaniards from place to place, could not be recaptured.
Sometimes, when a Spanish explorer was traveling a long way,

hounded by hunger or in a hurry to find what lay beyond his range of vision, he left his straggling beasts behind for want of means to sustain them. Sometimes stock was set free deliberately to provide food for subsequent explorers.

Descendants of the hogs thus liberated still root up shrubs along the riverbanks of Texas and other southern states. Because of their thin spines, they are called razorbacks. Although claimed by the owners on whose land they roam, they are as free as they were when first set at large by the Spaniards. The horses, known as mustangs, wandered in droves over the continent until a few decades ago.

One strain of the Spanish cattle had been bred for centuries with bullfights in mind. Through innumerable generations before their arrival in America, their ancestors had been selected for well-formed, gracefully curved horns and high combative spirit. Consequently, they throve without man's help wherever they happened to escape. When they began grazing across Texas, where the remains of saw-toothed sea serpents and heavily armored reptilian monsters were within easy reach of grass and shrubbery roots, they developed bigger bones and longer horns than their breed had ever possessed before.

Texas contained not only the materials but also the demand for mighty horns. In high mesquite limbs there was tender mistletoe that had to be hooked down before it could be eaten. When grass was scarce, tufts could be found in secluded spots by brushing away brambles with a sweep of the horns. The calf whose mother had the best horns to fight off wolves, bears, and panthers stood a better chance of living than any other.

By the time Austin's colony began bringing agriculture to the Gulf Coast, many of these wild cattle were wandering over Texas prairies and hills. From the farms they lured the heavier British breeds brought by the settlers. With these breeds they mixed, gaining in size and stamina.

West Texas has never had a monopoly on cattle-raising. In fact, the first Anglo-American to herd Spanish cattle in Texas was James Taylor White, who set up a ranch along the upper Gulf Coast about 1819. White is said by some to have deliberately developed what later came to be known as the longhorn breed. Shanghai Pierce, one of the shrewdest among the old-time Texas cattlemen, has left a large estate southwest of Houston. The King Ranch, biggest of all present-day Texas ranches, is in the southern point of Texas, bordering on the Gulf Coast. The 1950 census shows 90,450 head of cattle in Harris County, of which Houston is the county seat. This is almost fifteen thousand more than there are in any other Texas county.

But until the development of irrigation and petroleum industries, cattle-raising had a practical monopoly on West Texas. While cattle were important all over the state during the early days, they were never as decisive as cotton in the East Texas economy. West Texas, on the other hand, was originally fit for nothing but sheep, goats, and the hardy breed of bovine that wandered wild over the hills and the brush country. Hence, the land above the Balcones fault line was first settled largely by cattlemen, and its present features still reveal much that was put there by the kind of life required for coping with Texas longhorns.

◆◆◆

2. The Cowboy

By 1840, wild longhorns were so numerous in Texas that farmers shot them mercilessly. Dr. J. E. Lay, who lived along the Gulf Coast about that time, says: "Wild cattle and horses were so troublesome in leading astray our gentle stock that the neighbors would occasionally set a day and all go with dogs and guns to kill them. I remember on one hunt about a hundred were killed." The dead cattle were not taken as food back to the settlements, but were left for the wolves to devour. On other occasions, however, the wild beeves were either eaten or sold for their meat.

Although Texas was definitely independent, Mexico still hoped to regain her. Theft from an enemy never having been considered criminal, some reckless souls did not limit their exploits to wild cattle, but extended them to the raiding of Mexican ranches. The more choice loot they would drive north, sometimes also to New Orleans, to be sold, butchered, and eaten. Because their stock in trade was cows, they were called cowboys. Thus from the first, Texas cowboys were not peaceful herdsmen but rambunctious rapscallions for whom the thrill of guerrilla warfare was preferable to the humdrum tilling of the fields. Even when cowboys came to work for legitimate cattle-owners, earning a legitimate wage, much of the word's original meaning stuck.

The nature of the work makes cowboy life in many respects the opposite of farm life. To raise and sell a thousand bales of cotton, a man requires a modest plot of land by Texas standards, with scores of plodding, submissive, unintelligent, unambitious workers. Some unusual spirits love cotton-picking and make it a fine art, but the lint gets into the sack whether clumsily or skillfully harvested.

To raise and sell a thousand head of steers, a man has to have mile after mile of grazing ground with only a few workers. But the workers have to be of very different mettle from those used in the cotton field. A bad field hand gets less done than a good one; a bad cow hand can wreck all the gains made by the good ones. When a picker goes after a sack of cotton, he does not need to be a champion, and he knows he will get what he is going for; when a cowboy goes after a wild bull, he has to be at his best. Even if he has refined his talents to their highest possible degree, he is never certain of success. He might get the bull and the bull might get him. The dangers he faces often call for heroic feats. The hardships of cattle-handling give him a chance to develop and display admirable fortitude, endurance, and self-denial. Isolation on vast ranges makes him a lonesome, individualistic, philosophic figure.

Gradually, the early Texas cowboys brought the longhorns to a state of semi-redomestication. Because there were no fences, these half-wild brutes were known only by their brands. A dozen or more different owners might have longhorns grazing on the same ground. A man who wanted to keep his stock had to spend his time riding over this range, armed with ropes, guns, and a branding iron. Periodically, usually in the spring, groups of them would get together and gather their cattle into big bunches, or roundups, for branding and trading. Any unbranded animal over a year old belonged to whoever could find and brand it first. These unclaimed cattle soon came to be called "mavericks" because Samuel A. Maverick of San Antonio allowed his cattle to roam unbranded for twenty-eight years.

A big roundup where branding has been in progress is always noisy. Mother cows bawl because their calves, in being roped and dragged to the branding fire, have got cut off from them. The calves cry back in smaller voices. Now and then a bull gives vent to a high-pitched, vaunting bellow, but its echoes are soon lost among the plaints of thwarted mothers. In the whirling dust and the hundreds of other lost calves hunting through the bovine throng, cows must depend more on their ears and noses than on their eyes to ferret out their young ones. Each knows her calf's voice and smell, and the calf can often recognize its mother's call, but if they are very far apart, both are drowned in the pandemonium of strange odors and bleats. Sometimes a dozen or so at once, sometimes hundreds in unison, the calls and replies wax and wane, with the seeming endlessness, though not the regularity, of ocean waves against a shore. After sundown, with the darkening of the world, the mothers must rely less and less on sight and more and more on their subtler senses.

At camp, where the fire drives away both the cold and the approaching dusk, where the cooks are fixing bread for next day's breakfast and the boys are talking over their coffee cups about the warmth of the weather and the possibility of a fog next morning, the bawls and bleats are always audible. Gradually, as the stars come out, the calves locate their mothers, or, in the language of the range, "get mothered up." Little by little, the noise of their hunting gives way to the peace of sleep. The conversations or fiddle tunes or songs or crap-shooting or poker games of the boys die down and they unroll their beds across the grass. A couple of hours before dawn, when the cook gets up to revive the fire and put fresh coffee on to boil, a few cows may still be bawling if the herd is large. By daylight, unless some mothers have had unusually bad luck, the cattle will be as quiet as the stars themselves. At such moments, with a fresh horse saddled, a man seems to gain strange power from the great spaces.

Besides being occasions for ascertaining and shaping up each man's property on the hoof, the early Texas roundups afforded rare chances for the exchange of news and ideas. In the warmth of the campfire, while the bawling of the herd wore deep into the night and the breeze breathed peace to the beasts as they mothered up, the range men traded views about the grass, about the need for rain, about the good times they had had and would have again when the sale of steers should reap them fresh fortunes. As they talked, the vacillating red light of the blaze mingled with the steady, silver-tinted moon or starlight. The sparks of their cigarettes brightened and dimmed with the drawing and exhaling of their breaths.

The problem of marketing Texas livestock was a hard one in the early days. Texas beef had value, but the supply exceeded the means of transportation. Buyers inside the state were hard to find, but prices were high everywhere else. New

Orleans was a famous market, but how could you get your cattle there? By a long drive through mosquito-infested swamps?
Not many were willing to brave such a drive. By boat? The
Morgan Steamship Lines had a monopoly on Gulf commerce
between Galveston and the mouth of the Mississippi. They
charged such exorbitant rates that from 1850 to 1856 their
shipments of Texas cattle averaged only a little over four thousand a year.

After the goldrush to the Pacific seaboard in 1849, new
ranches began opening up in California. A few Texas herds
were driven there. It was a long and perilous journey through
savage lands. The plains Indians exacted heavy tolls. There
were deathly stretches of desert with no water for days to mitigate the fiery sun. The new ranches of the far west wanted
breeding stock: cows and bulls. Cows did not travel as well as
steers. Nor was there any way of knowing whether or not the
new ranges would be already stocked by the time a herd got
there.

The best market of all, the steady steer market that you
could count on to keep up, was in the highly concentrated
beef-consuming communities of the northern and northeastern states. There were rich grazing grounds for fattening steers
in Illinois and other middle western states. The demand for
meat was greatest in the east, but there the lean, gaunt longhorn had to compete against the pampered breeds of small
farmers. Easterners did not always appreciate the qualities of
Texas beef. Besides, there were good political reasons for not
sending steers "to feed our abolition neighbors," as the *Dallas
Herald* put it.

Even so, a few herds found their way into the north and
east during the 1840's and 1850's. Anent one of them the *New
York Times* observed: "These would about balance, if suspended by the neck, as the horns were nearly large enough to
'equipoise' the rest of the animal." Concerning another:
"These were barely able to cast a shadow, and . . . would not

weigh anything were it not for their horns, which were useful also in preventing them from crawling through the fences." In Missouri, Texas longhorns were described as "about the nearest to wild animals of any now driven to market. We have seen some buffaloes that were more civilized." Their meat was "not fit for people to eat: they will do to bait traps to catch wolves in."

But the chief source of resistance against longhorns in the north and east was a mysterious disease known as "Texas fever." Although Texas cattle did not seem to suffer from it, it always attacked the domestic stock of farmers through whose lands Texas herds had passed. The first real epidemic of this fever occurred in Missouri in 1855. A second and more disastrous one took place in 1858. The result was a series of protests on the part of Missouri farmers. Meetings were held. Vigilance committees were created to prevent Texas long-horns from entering the state. Laws were passed restricting the admission of "noxious animals." Also in 1858, Texas fever broke out in Kansas. Again there were protest conventions, vigilance parties, laws.

Thus, while Texas cattle were multiplying by the thousands, the few herds that sought external markets were thwarted on all sides. Prohibitive shipping rates kept them off the Gulf. Mosquitoes and swamps barred their land route to New Orleans. Irate farmers forbade their progress northward. Deserts and Indians discouraged their westward outlet.

The Civil War made matters worse. The blockade of the south by the Union forces choked out what little commerce there had been on the Gulf. Traffic with the north was forbidden by federal as well as state decree. Besides, it would have been treason against the south to sell to her northern enemies. No man in the country sensed the situation more keenly than did a farsighted Illinois stock-dealer named Joseph G. McCoy. As he put it, Texas "could not drive north if she would; she would not if she could."

Meanwhile, in Texas, cattle were multiplying more rapidly than ever because, with most of the able-bodied men away at war, only women, children, and old folks were left to brand and castrate the young calves. The best they could do was work the gentler cattle around the ranches. There was nobody to ride the distant ranges, where maverick bulls and cows reached the age of five, six, or seven years without ever feeling a rope. Being numerous, and having no outlet, they were cheap. Cotton could be smuggled over the Rio Grande and out through Mexican ports because it made no noise. Live cattle, with their bawling, would advertise their presence far across the guarded waters. Therefore, while cotton sold for a dollar a pound, grown beeves were offered in vain for a dollar a head. "Then dawned a time in Texas," said McCoy, "when a man's poverty was estimated by the number of cattle he possessed."

When the war ended, roping and branding mavericks became the sole occupation of many a restless veteran. As never before, the best ropers and most energetic branders got the most cattle. For what purpose? To drive north, now that the quarrel about slavery was over. Nobody knows how many herds crossed Red River and the Indian Territory in 1866. The most authoritative estimate is 260,000 head. But the hope for a market was blasted. At the Kansas line the cattle were stopped by armies of farmers whose fear of Texas fever superseded all other considerations: farmers whose families might be denied their sustenance by the presence of Texas cattle; farmers with too much at stake to take a chance on the slow channels of legislation; farmers in whose memories the wounds of war were fresh, who hated slavery and all places where slavery had been harbored, and who therefore believed that only evil could come out of Texas. "Kansas jayhawkers" was the name the Texas drovers gave them. Tales of carnage at their hands spread abroad over the prairie. Texans accused northern cattle-raisers of encouraging the jayhawkers in order to remove the competition of Texas beef. A northern newspaper cried: "We should keep out the Texas cattle on the same principle that we would the smallpox and the cholera. They are pestilential." Between January and June 1867 new and more specific laws prohibiting or restricting the northward movement of longhorns were passed in Missouri, Kansas, Nebraska, Kentucky, Colorado, and Illinois. A few herds got through, but they lost money. Consequently, the northbound drives were reduced to less than 65,000 head for the summer of 1867.

But Texas kept on spawning more and more longhorns. Cattlemen, especially above the fault line, where livestock afforded the only means of support, were in despair until Joseph G. McCoy came to their rescue. During the Civil War, while Texas cattle were so freely reproducing, the north had consumed its meat supply. Moreover, the railroads were pushing their way westward, and new ranches were being created in the midwest. There was a real need for Texas cattle, if they could somehow be brought around the jayhawker frontier.

The Kansas law had a loophole which Joseph McCoy quickly perceived and turned to his advantage. It stated that any individual or company giving a $10,000 bond to guarantee the payment of all damages to native stock might drive Texas cattle into western Kansas at any season of the year. There were a few other restrictions which could be easily met. The route of the Texas herd must not be within five miles of any settler without his written consent. Longhorns could not be fed or driven along a public highway, but must be taken straight to a railroad terminal and shipped somewhere outside of Kansas.

In 1867 a railroad had just been built westward across Kansas. McCoy rode it with his eyes primed for the best possible shipping point. After careful inquiries he chose Abilene, built shipping yards there, and sent a horseman south to tell Texans where they could take their cattle. The big drives of that year were by that time badly dissipated and discouraged. Many of the herds had turned back. A few had tried to go around the western edge of Kansas. Even so, on September 6, 1867, the first shipment of twenty cars left Abilene for Chicago, amidst high festivities and much publicity.

Then McCoy started a campaign for a big movement in 1868. He sent circulars to all Texas towns, newspapers, and ranchmen whose names and addresses he could obtain, "setting forth the contemplated purpose of the Abilene enterprise and inviting the drovers and stockmen of Texas to bring their herds of marketable cattle to that point, assuring all who would do so of a cordial reception, fair dealing, protection from mob violence, perfect equality upon the market and shipping facilities, and a concerted joint effort to get buyers for their stock." Newspapers throughout Texas copied the circular. Many of them gave it favorable comments in their editorials. McCoy also sent "two gentlemen of tact and address" into Texas to inform Texan drovers of Abilene.

The results were not disappointing. In the spring of 1868 the epic era of trail-driving began. With occasional interruptions from jayhawkers, bad weather, and financial panics, it lasted twenty years. In the words of the *Dallas Herald*, Texas became "the cattle hive of North America." In 1871, when the jayhawkers moved into Abilene and made it unfavorable, the herds veered westward for new cow towns, among which the most noted was Dodge City.

Nobody knows how many Texas cattle went north between 1867 and 1887. McCoy gave several wild estimates which were accepted by the United States Census. For example, he says that 600,000 head reached Kansas in 1871, whereas the shipping records from the cow towns then operating show a total of only 250,620. Many, of course, were driven on to midwestern ranges and were therefore not included in the shipping figures. For the entire twenty years of trail-driving, the best available figures reveal a rough average of 237,-

ooo annually. The usual herd consisted of about two thousand steers ranging in age from five to seven years. Thus, well over a hundred herds were taken north each summer. They traveled about twenty-five miles, or two days, apart, their speed being twelve or thirteen miles a day. Each herd had its trail boss, its cook, its chuck wagon, its horse-wrangler, its *remuda* of fifty or more horses, and ten or twelve cowboys.

After months of lonely, dangerous living, cleaned only by chance rains and swims across deep streams, kept continent by strenuous chases and repeated denials of nourishment and sleep, the Texas cowboy would be ready for a change when at last his herd reached the end of the trail and he got his pay. The first place of business he visited was the barber shop, where he stopped only long enough to get his beard dressed or shaved and his head relieved of any surplus hair that might have grown in camp. Next he went to a drygoods store, where he got rigged out in "glad rags," often including a new pair of high-heel boots with elaborately decorated tops and a new Stetson hat. Then he was ready for a big time.

The cow towns never failed to afford him plenty of entertainment—at a price, of course. High spirits awaited him on saloon shelves, in bottles of all shapes and sizes, representing every color of the rainbow. Women with curves designed to inflame his wildest cravings, perfect as carved statues, yet yielding to his lightest touch, tantalized him and praised his drunken ravings as a sign of bravery. Paid bawds with smooth skins and depraved passions drove him half crazy with brief tastes of their beauty. Professional gamblers lay in wait for his wages. He was trained to face stampedes, angry Indians, and cattle thieves, but he had neither armor nor experience with which to meet these moral scavengers. They baited his curiosity, flattered his extravagance, and left him broke, ready to ride again. The spectacle did not improve his reputation with those pious Kansas farmers who were pouring westward, taming the wild country.

But to the children of such farmers he symbolized a delightful freedom from domestic and religious bonds. He possessed all that had been denied them. Their life was humdrum and comparatively safe from spiritual or physical dangers; his was exciting, varied, packed with suspense, thrills, and hairbreadth escapes. He had to make quick decisions and keep alert through every waking hour. The small farmers could live only by counting every penny and denying themselves all expensive pleasures; the cowboy threw money around as if it were confetti.

Farm boys, not only in Kansas but in Texas and elsewhere as well, yearned to emulate the cowboy. Farm girls longed to marry him. Hence, he became a favorite figure for dime novelists, whose stock in trade was the vicarious satisfaction of such occulted, thwarted wishes. Hence today, cleansed of his sins but not his color, daring, skill, resourcefulness, and generosity, he enjoys a leading role in literature, movies, comic strips, and television.

Thus, fortified by two-hundred-million-year-old fossil deposits and blessed with a subtropical climate, Texas made the longhorn and the longhorn made the cowboy. Except for a few small herds kept as relics, the longhorn has passed on, but the cowboy remains. His spirit pervades Texas customs and ideals. The rodeo, with its contests in roping, bulldogging, and riding, is the principal yearly celebration of most Texas towns. The cowboy's broad-brim hat and high-heel boots, originally designed to mitigate the sun and fit the stirrup, are now worn by businessmen, factory workers, preachers, and politicians as emblems of loyalty to the giant state.

Texas has long been regarded as the source of cowboy standards and the home of the nation's best artists with rope and spur. The Texas and Southwestern Cattle Raiser's Association, largest and oldest organization of its kind in the United States, has spread over the entire southwest since its launching at Graham, Texas, in 1877. The cowboy tradition, vocabulary, and way of life are current on western ranches from Illinois to Oregon, from Kansas to California.

With more than eight and a half million cattle in the state and an annual calf crop of over three and a half million, Texas has kept the lead for years in beef-production. Most of her stock, especially to the north of the brush country, is now from British breeds, brought in since the early 1870's. The importation of these noble creatures was long hampered by the same Texas fever that caused such animosity in northern states. In 1889 this fever was found to be conveyed by a tick which passed from animal to animal by attaching itself periodically to grass blades. A method of immunization against the fever was developed by Dr. Mark Francis of A. and M. in 1899, and a dip to kill the tick was soon devised. In 1906 the United States government instigated a thoroughgoing campaign which has now resulted in the complete eradication of the tick.

◇◇◇

3. New Horizons on the Range

ACROSS THE PANHANDLE PLAINS, where the landscape's spaciousness and grandeur are still further magnified, stretches the Palo Duro Canyon. Burnished with the beauty of formations whose age embraces and antedates the day of dinosaurs, with colors ranging from deep purple to bright pinkish, yellow, and blue, its banks rise more than three thousand feet above the tiny stream that cuts into its floor. Being extremely steep, and extending a hundred and twenty miles from east to west, these banks furnish a natural pasture, where cattle can be kept safe from bad weather at no cost to the rancher. In 1876 a puritanical Illinoisan named Charles Goodnight drove 1,800 head of English cattle into this canyon. Goodnight's ways and stock were distinct from those traditionally associated with Texas. His cowboys were never allowed to gamble or drink on duty. His cattle were usually tinged with foreign strains, though he experimented in crossing some of them with buffalo.

As the longhorns were thinned out, the foreign breeds spread southward into the other parts of Texas. The first important British importations were Durhams and Devons, but Herefords and Angus have now become the most popular breeds north of the brush country. These heavy beasts, developed in the equable climate and moist meadows of England, cannot well endure the subtropical heat and drouthy prairies of South Texas. For this reason the Brahman, from the stern environment of southern Asia, has been brought in. Since the purebred Brahman is not a good beef-producer, South Texas ranchers customarily cross Brahmans with Durhams or Herefords, thus combining Asian hardihood with British corpulence. From a mixture of three-eights Brahman and five-eights Durham, Robert J. Kleberg of the King Ranch has developed the first distinctly American breed of high-grade cattle: the Santa Gertrudis.

Just as the longhorn was a product of primeval Texas, the Santa Gertrudis is a product of modern Texas. Of a deep wine-red color and highly uniform composition, the latter possesses many virtues which both its parent stocks lack. The Brahman is tall and rangy. Santa Gertrudis cattle have thicker frames and more beef to the bone. Each year 85 per cent of the cows in an average Santa Gertrudis herd will have calves, whereas among British breeds only 70 per cent can be expected to give birth. Santa Gertrudis calves at weaning time outweigh Hereford and Durham calves by an average of one hundred pounds. On pure grass, four-year-old Santa Gertrudis steers will average fourteen hundred pounds for the market.

Moreover, the Santa Gertrudis have a high intelligence

and can find food where the British breeds would starve. The
cows are excellent milk-producers and, as one writer puts it,
"natural-born baby-sitters." When a large drove of cows with
calves is turned loose in a pasture, a few of the mothers will
guard the young in shifts, herding them together, while the
majority are grazing or going for water. Longhorn cows used
to do the same thing when water was some distance away.

Santa Gertrudis genes are so dominant that a pure-bred
Santa Gertrudis bull, mated to a cow of any other breed, will
beget Santa Gertrudis characteristics. If for four generations
he is remated to his crossbred progeny, the final offspring is
eligible for classification as a genuine Santa Gertrudis. Selling
for as high as $40,000 a head, Santa Gertrudis bulls have been
exported to Mexico, Guatemala, Panama, Cuba, Costa Rica,
Colombia, Brazil, Venezuela, Peru, and the Philippines, as
well as to many ranches in the northern United States. Thus
for breeding stock as well as for beef, Texas may soon become
the cattle hive of the whole world.

With the coming of fences, gentler strains, and more modern equipment, the methods of handling cattle have been
modified. Like any other change, these first met with considerable resistance from individuals who were profiting from the
old order and lacked the ability to readjust. Owners of livestock who depended on the open range rather than on acres
they had paid for were naturally opposed to fences. Farm communities were often cut off from their markets and sources of
supply by the newly built fences. Consequent grievances led
to an epidemic of fence-cutting which began in 1883 and
lasted, with occasional interruptions from the state government, until the end of the decade.

Since then, many minor changes have been derived from
the machine age. Jeeps have partly replaced horses for herding
in open country, and helicopters help drive wild cattle out of
the brush. Much of the brush is being removed by huge machines. Instead of being chased down and roped, elusive steers

are now caught in small pastures surrounding water wells. In many instances, new agricultural insights have brought about a merging of range with farm. Goats, sheep, hogs, chickens, and vegetable crops are mingled with cattle-raising to the advantage of both.

Even so, the range man's basic way of life remains the same as it was at its inception over a century ago. The King Estate in South Texas, the Waggoner Ranch near the Red River, and many others have their own open ranges: pastures extending for miles in every direction, where roundups are made as in the early days and the cowboy's arts are all brought into play. There is no likelihood that the horse and the roundup will ever be entirely displaced by machines and pens. No mechanism, however cunningly devised, can match the keen senses and quick movements of a good cow pony. No set of pens, however complex, can duplicate the roundup as an opportunity for viewing and handling cattle in their natural habitat.

As on large cotton farms, much of the feudal tradition remains intact on the large ranches. But the cowboy is more like the knight errant than like the Old World peasantry, and his circumstances, plus the general trend toward democracy, have given the old standards a new tone. He is a companion of his boss, a proud and loyal peer, but his dignity rests on personal achievement rather than on an illustrious ancestry.

Because of such ancient sentiments, and because ranch workmen are kept at a safe distance from the economic hazards of city life, there have never been any notable labor troubles on the range, although wages have always been extremely low. The only cowboy strike on record occurred between March 24 and April 3, 1883, when 325 cowboys from several Panhandle ranches struck for higher wages and the right to run their own small herds on the large fenced ranges. As a result, wages were increased from $1.18 to $1.68 a day. The strikers were reimbursed for time lost during the work stoppage, and their right to run their stock on the boss's range was recognized. Led by a man who himself owned a few cows, the strike was on behalf not only of wage-earners, but also of small enterprisers whose free range was being crowded out by large companies buying and fencing the land.

Although the man on the horse demands and gets more respect than the man with the hoe, both the cattle baron and the cotton baron preserve considerable isolation and independence on their far-flung Texas estates. They want to feel that all economic improvements stem from their own voluntary generosity, rather than from coercion on the part of employees or control on the part of government. To some extent they have had their way, and their viewpoint has been carried over into the newer Texas industries. They have kept unionization of labor at a minimum, and their voices in government have not often gone ignored.

Not only the size of their holdings, but also their economic interests tend to make these barons anti-social. Their market is never at home, but always in distant industrial districts. Cattle cannot graze on sidewalks and paved streets. The big rancher does not depend for his income on a prosperous, populous neighborhood. To him, even more than to the big farmer, small farmers are a nuisance, civic promoters are pests that must be tolerated and kept as ineffective as possible, and progressive towns are an abomination. They cramp his style and hamper his ambitions. One of his keenest dreads is the land tax. By outnumbering him at the polls, towns can levy high rates on his vital acres to support their schools and other community assets. Such assets do him little good. If he has children, he will want either to train them for his trade or to send them to some remote private school. Why should he be burdened beyond all others to educate those swarms of village urchins who only get in his way? To escape such burdens, he will essay to control the politics of his vicinity. His efforts are often clumsy and result in bitter conflicts. In the local arena he may lose his lonely fight, but in state politics, where the distances are greater and the issues less widely understood, he frequently wins. Whether or not he gets his way, much animosity is aroused, and in many a small Texas town ill will smolders behind the scenes even on rodeo days.

Whereas the cotton baron ruled during the days of the republic and early statehood, the cattle baron enjoyed a precarious ascendency in state government from the Civil War to the beginning of the twentieth century, when the big industrialist began to take over. Texas's first truly large fortunes got their start in the trail-driving bonanza. Many of the men whose money has built Texas's great institutions were originally range men, with the range man's habits and philosophy. The railroads got their first big boost from ranchers shipping cattle north. Since the grazing of cattle demanded that ranchers own large tracts of land, they cashed in on the oil discovery to an extent beyond the hopes of any other enterprise. This accidental, unexpected windfall has more than made up for their land-tax losses, and thus tends to mitigate their anti-social inclinations. There is a catty saying abroad in Texas that "cattlemen always do well where there is oil under the grass."

4. *San Antonio, Where Warm Winds Converge*

A SAN ANTONIO LASS once asked her father: "Papa, who laid out this town?"

"Lord knows; I don't," replied the father, who had been born and reared in San Antonio. "It was here when I came."

"Well," said the daughter, "whoever he was, he must have been drunk."

Actually, San Antonio was never laid out. It grew like a vine or a stream, seeking blindly the land's most favorable contours and anchoring spots. This original planlessness is stamped indelibly in the narrowness and winding of its streets and the scattered aspect of its sky line. The big buildings are not grouped in a single place, but spread over hundreds of rolling acres. The streets are cramped and crooked because they first came into existence in the days of carts and wagons, which could travel straight or turn a curve with equal safety. Being the oldest of the state's great cities, San Antonio preserves more than any other the atmosphere created by those warm winds of human influence which have been blowing for over a hundred years across the state from the south, the east, and the west.

San Antonio was named in 1691, when it was a mere Indian village, by the Spanish explorer Domingo Ramón, because he happened to arrive there on the saint's day of San Antonio de Padua. Since it has been a relatively large and well-known center of commerce and industry for over two centuries, its metropolitan culture is the richest in Texas. It has a greater variety of racial tints, economic interests, religious missions, political crackpots, and artistic ambitions than any other city in the state.

The Gulf Coast cities have a wide variety of different nationalities, but they are relatively recent arrivals. San Antonio's racial groups have had more time to get themselves woven into the fabric of the community. There are exclusive Spanish-speaking families descended from a group of Canary Islanders who came, at the Spanish king's command, to start the city some two and one-third centuries ago. There are Mexican peons who have been pouring in ever since because they can think of no better place to go. They are less lonely here, where there have long been many of their kind. There are middle-class Germans whose ancestors left those ill-starred early settlements of New Braunfels and Fredericksburg to live and trade in this more populous town. There are Negroes hailing from the decadent plantations to the east, Irishmen originally brought in to work the railroads, soldiers stationed nearby because of the city's militarily strategic location, aviators trained in the dry air above, where clouds are scarce and winds are mild.

This diversity of backgrounds, interests, and viewpoints has made San Antonio the scene of many bitter battles, whose scars remain apparent in both its physical and its spiritual life. In the old days those battles were bloody, with knives and swords flashing, pistols smoking, and tortured flesh decaying. Today they are limited to politics, but they are often just as ruthless as ever, motivated as they are by ancient loyalties and deeply ingrained hatreds among both leaders and followers.

At the same time, San Antonio's racial and cultural cosmopolitanism has given it a glitter, an atmosphere of rapid activity, a versatility, and a consequent resilience that no other Texas metropolis can match. A multitude of permanent circumstances perpetuates these qualities. Lying as it does across the Balcones fault line at a point where the change of terrain is particularly abrupt, the city has natural geographical allure for individuals of diverse temperaments and propensities. These are expressed in window displays and electric signs which reveal widely divergent tastes and an originality stimulated by a swift exchange of ideas and a fast pace of competition. Such impressions are emphasized by San Antonio's mellow age and consequently confident informality, by her slightly sloping terrain, by her curving streets, by her wide sidewalks, by her bustling, haphazardly mingled pedestrian traffic.

The heart of the city is Houston Street, running roughly east and west, flanked by a sea of business area which stretches in irregular waves, street after street, on both sides. People of every conceivable description swarm along Houston Street's relatively gentle bends: peons from the depths of Mexico, dressed in straw hats and rags; army officers, privates, and

pilots in sparkling uniforms; millionaires; human derelicts begging for dimes and nickels to soothe their living pain with a
bit of food, or a cup of coffee, or a little drink of liquor, or a
cigarette of the forbidden but often irresistible Mexican dope,
marihuana, or a drugstore sedative, or a sip of remedial tea.

At the eastern extremity of Houston Street stands the
Medical Arts Building, a monument to the triumphs of modern science. Its triangular base divides Houston Street into a
Y. Followed westward from the Medical Arts, Houston Street
runs into an area more characterized by Indian, Hispanic, and
religious traditions. On the right stands the Santa Rosa Hospital, built and administered by the Roman Catholic Church.
On the left is the municipal market, where Mexican farmers
and merchants bring their produce to spread before the public
in ancient Aztec fashion. The market thrives from three or
four in the morning until deep into the night, selling sharply
odorous peppers and fast-ripening fruits in the hot wind.

Nearby shops display religious trophies and charms. Can-
dles burn in the crowded show windows before effigies of
Christ, sundry saints, and divers apparitions of the Virgin
Mary. Tiny arms and legs of pewter can be bought for a pittance and pinned to the robes of church statues for the curing
of ailments in the arms and legs of worshippers. Loadstones
with steel filings clinging to them are sold because, if kept in a
household, they are supposed to hold the family together.
Remedial brush-country herbs, considered efficacious through
centuries past, are offered on sale to the faithful; the *toloache*
for forgetfulness, the *chaparro prieto* for loose teeth, the
peyote for dreams.

Behind the market place is a wide public park known to
the Spanish-speaking inhabitants as *La Plaza del Zacate*—that
is, The Plaza of Grass. It is one of those social safety valves,
so common and so necessary in large cities, where preachers
and reformers of all brands gather the idle masses to tell them
about the world's myriad evils. Mexican singers roam the mar-

ket place and the Plaza of Grass, with their guitars and their glittering *charro* suits, selling their performances for nickels, dimes, and quarters. Texas Mexican versifiers sell their ballads on gaily colored broadsides. Such a one is Bartolo Ortiz, a broad-faced, smooth-tongued peon who draws his crowds by sawing out "Over the Waves" on a violin made from a battered oil can and by pounding out other familiar tunes on a zylophone made of frying pans. Written in phonetic Spanish, his compositions deal with everything from the cotton field to international politics, and they cost only a nickel per copy.

Thus San Antonio's Houston Street, stretching from the sky-high Medical Arts to the mellow-smelling Mexican quarter, connects the youngest with the most ancient elements in American society. Like that of other cities in this oil-supported state, San Antonio's sky is free from smoke. The Gulf breeze, which cools the afternoons of East Texas and the coast, reaches San Antonio late in the evening and often lasts beyond midmorning. Sometimes it carries a few glistening, sun-kissed clouds into the west at a low speed. From the tops of skyscrapers, the American and the Texas flags wave side by side. The solid red segment of the lone-star banner is often of a lighter hue than the wine-colored stripes of Old Glory, but the white of both emblems matches the crystalline purity of the rainless clouds.

Running southeastward under Houston Street, the San Antonio River winds through the center of the city. Naked Mexican girls, as unashamed of their nude bodies as was Eve in Paradise before the fall, used to bathe in it, swimming nimbly as fish under its ancient bridges in the midst of the Spanish-Mexican town, displaying their curved figures to the craving eyes of young men with all the brazen frankness of mythical nymphs. That was a hundred years ago, when San Antonio was only a century and a quarter old and modern civilization had not yet come to throw up barriers around its warm half-Indian blood.

Now the face of things, at least, has changed. The river passes under forty-two highway bridges. It is a haven of calmness rimmed with concrete. Its shores are floored with carpet grass and wide sidewalks, protected from the metropolitan turmoil by ten-foot retaining walls, shaded by willows, cottonwoods, magnolias, and pecan trees, bordered with palms, banana plants, elephant ears, cannas, and oleanders. Young couples come here to enjoy the dense, cool shadows on the green, to take advantage of the partial seclusion from the roaring machines above the retaining wall. Sometimes they lie side by side on the grass, reading newspapers, novels, and comic strips. Sometimes they sit on heavy brown log benches, holding hands and whispering supposed secrets. Sometimes they tumble among the elephant ears, fondling each other for hours. The hubbub of passing cars goes on above the wall. The chirping of birds continues from dusk to dawn.

Mexican boys, too young for shoes or wooing, come to the river to fish, using grocery-box splinters for poles, package twine for lines, bent pins for hooks, and crusts of bread from garbage cans for bait. At a bend in the river there is an open-air stage known as the Arneson River Theater. Across the water from it, the bank is terraced into a grandstand of earth with seats of grass which can accomodate an audience of approximately one thousand. On clear nights, local groups perform here for large crowds, presenting plays, operettas, orators, and artists. Farther up the stream there are Mexican restaurants which serve enchiladas, tacos, and other special dishes of mixed Indian and Spanish origin, at outdoor tables along the shore. There is also a raft: a floating floor supported by empty air-tight oil barrels, where you can eat at portable tables while riding the water's buoyancy.

Much thinking and hard work have made possible these pleasures of the San Antonio River. To prevent its overflowing and inundating the restaurants, benches, trees, stage, grandstand, and bridges, a short-cut ditch has been dug to carry the

White-faced Herefords being rounded up by helicopter. Waggoner Estate Ranch near Vernon.

San Antonio.

surplus water from the meandering main bed. This ditch is also walled with concrete and can hold the river's maximum expansions. Dams have been built to keep the current from becoming too strong.

The master mind behind these and many other achievements in San Antonio was that of Maury Maverick. Maury had bulldog features, lazy eyes, and explosive opinions. A direct descendant of that early gentleman whose name was given to maverick cattle, Maury served as congressman for one term and as mayor of San Antonio for two, then settled down to practice law and died of a heart attack in 1954, leaving his son, Maury junior, to carry on. It was during Maury senior's administration as mayor (1939–41) and under his direction that the river was changed from a flood hazard to a place of safe amusement. The project cost $442,900, part of which was raised by a local bond issue and part of which came from the Works Progress Administration. Twenty-one city blocks of riverbank are clothed in masonry and concrete. Thirty-one stairways, each with a unique design, lead from the street level down to the seventeen thousand feet of river walks. The stream is illuminated at night by colored electric lights set beneath the water amidst the cannas, the flag lilies, and the hyacinths.

Another important child of Maury Maverick's brain is modern La Villita, on the southern edge of the beautified river as it meanders below Houston Street. La Villita's values can be appreciated only after a review of San Antonio's early history. Originally, San Antonio was not one town, but three. First, there was the mission settlement, made up mostly of Franciscan priests and pacified Indians. Four of its missions still stand, providing places of worship for the pious and historical relics for the curious. Second, there was the presidio, inhabited by soldiers whose job was to protect the missions. Third, there was *la villita*, the little village, originally a native Indian town, but soon invaded by artisans, merchants, camp-followers, and adventurers who came offering their services at a price to the priests, soldiers, and recent converts.

When the three towns merged to form the modern city, *la villita* became one of its worst slums. It remained a den of poverty, sin, and decay until Maury Maverick was elected mayor. Under him, the place was bought by the city government. With the help of N.Y.A. and Carnegie money, he cleaned out the slum and restored the old buildings to their original glory. Under the name of La Villita, the place has now become a cultural center run by the city but entirely self-supporting. Its houses and halls are rented out for conventions and meetings. In it, Latin American youths are taught the arts of woodworking, metalworking, pottery, leathercraft, shell-craft, weaving, doll-making, glass-blowing, portrait-painting, and costume-designing. The schools are supported by the sale of their products to tourists. There is also a class in Spanish and Mexican folk dancing. In the midst of these simple pursuits stands the Bolívar Library. With a repository for United States government publications and a growing collection of Latin American books and pamphlets, it is now used extensively for research. Thus at La Villita the poor of San Antonio's oldest ethnic group can find an outlet for their abilities. Fine talents, instead of being crushed by mass production, are trained here and rewarded from the abundant wealth of modern industry. Peaceful, quiet, imbued with the beauty that accumulating years alone can bring, and deeply appreciated by all who pass through its cool, shady streets, La Villita is a piece of the past which has found a place in the present-day world, to the mutual enrichment of both.

Because of its convenient location and its heavy Hispanic element, San Antonio is a leading center for Latin American trade. Approximately one half of Mexico's trade with the United States is cleared through the San Antonio Customs district. Also, San Antonio sits squarely in the midst of Southwest Texas, with the Gulf Coast to the east, the Rio Grande

Valley to the south, the brush country with its livestock to the southwest and west, and the bleak but mineral-pregnant uplands to the west and northwest. With an average altitude of seven hundred feet and a relatively dry but moderate climate, it provides favorable conditions for manufacturing, with low heating costs and little loss from rust and exposure of machinery.

In addition to its income from foreign trade, meat-packing, agriculture, oil, tourism, and manufacturing, San Antonio carries on a lucrative business with the personnel of the great military and aviation bases in its vicinity. In its northeastern edge lies Fort Sam Houston, comprising more than 3,300 acres of land and occupying more than 1,900 buildings. These include the 320 buildings of the Brooke Army Medical Center, largest military medical center in the world, and the San Antonio General Depot, which is the south's largest army supply center, with its own railroad system and 2,500,000 square feet of covered storage space. Camp Bullis, a training area and chemical school, lies eighteen miles northwest of Fort Sam Houston. All around San Antonio are military air fields: Randolph to the east northeast, Brooks to the south southeast, Kelly and Lackland to the southwest.

San Antonians are fortunate in having a supply of shrines and special establishments for their instruction and amusement such as can be found in no other Texas city. Any time they wish, they can visit the Alamo, where those early heroes died for Texas liberty, or the missions, or La Villita, or the beautified river, or Brackenridge Park, where one of the nation's major zoological gardens has been created in the bed of an abandoned rock quarry, or the palace where the Spanish governor held sway when Texas was a part of Spain.

On Houston Street, about halfway between the Santa Rosa Hospital and the Medical Arts Building, stands the Buckhorn. In the olden days the Buckhorn was mainly a saloon, a lone place of refreshment for brush-country range-riders. When Prohibition closed its bar, it survived as a curio store. Now its bar is open again, but it sells only beer, wine, and soft drinks, and it is devoted mostly to relics and mounted animal heads of every description imaginable. The Buckhorn could belong to no state except Texas and to no Texas city except San Antonio. In its inclusiveness, its compactness, its diversity, its disorder, its half-accidental evolution, and its haphazard growth, it expresses the quintessence of its native town.

Just as San Antonio has drawn people from every corner of the world, the Buckhorn has accumulated hides, horns, and relics from every known quarter. Cattle, buffalo, goats, wild hogs, deer, horses, rhinoceroses, giraffes, monkeys, and hundreds of other species are represented, mostly by their mounted heads. Rattlesnake rattles—over thirty-two thousand—have been woven into tapestries portraying wild life and cowboy scenes. Mexican talent is heavily represented in the baskets, handkerchiefs, luncheon sets, scarves, walking-canes, watch fobs, belts, leather bags, and mounted fleas on sale.

Like San Antonio, the Buckhorn is crowded, for the world has many curious things, and if they are to be enjoyed all at once, they must be crammed into a concentrated space. There is not enough room on the walls for all the mounted heads. Hence, poles have been raised throughout the saloon, and heads bristle all around them. The sheer quantity and heterogeneity of the specimens prevent any semblance of logical order. From a saloon, the Buckhorn has evolved into a museum, but no museum in any other part of the earth was ever arranged with such serene disregarded for the nature and origin of its creatures. Never in their lives did these mounted beasts keep such strange company. Over the bartender's cash register hangs the head of an African ox, the largest in the world. On each side hang Mexican javalinas. Jungle-born monkeys rub noses with Texas jack rabbits. A man-sized gorilla towers above a coiled rattlesnake. An arctic walrus, with long white ivory tusks, hangs between an American antelope and a giraffe from the tropics. A zebra gazes from between the horns of an elk. A moose extends its antlers like spreading umbrellas over rows of southwestern deer. Yet through the whole saloon there runs a sense of fitness, a balance in the arrangement: an artistic if not a biological organization.

The Buckhorn was founded by a San Antonio-born merchant of German descent named Albert Friedrich, whose business was liquor, whose hobby was horned heads, and whose wife liked to arrange rattlesnake rattles in unique artistic designs. Texas ranchers have always been pestered by rattlesnakes, especially in the brush country. To get rid of these dangerous reptiles, they customarily paid a few cents for every rattlesnake rattle that a cowboy brought in to the ranches. The rattle served merely as proof that a snake had been killed, but the ranchers soon began to accumulate barrels of rattles and were bewildered as to how to get rid of them until Friedrich took them into the saloon for a small price and turned them over to his enterprising wife. Deer horns and heads were also bought widely.

By gradual degrees the hobby became the saloon's principal attraction. Hunters who yearned to bring down wondrous wild monsters went to the Buckhorn to mingle their drunkenness with gazing at the great elk heads and weaving mighty dreams around them. Later, when they told their wives and children about the marvelous place, and when the state was invaded by prudent northern farmers and camp meetings, whole families became interested, and the roughness of the male element had to be smoothed. The thrust of Prohibition fixed the Buckhorn's fate. It gravitated inevitably to its present state: half museum, half curio shop, with a bar and a few tables bearing judicious drinks for old times' sake. The drinks being milder now, the horns don't look so big, and the Buck-

horn adds its bit to the culture of the area. Children from all
the country around come to see and learn about its wonderful
contents.

Except for its junior college, which, under the presidency
of J. O. Loftin, has built an impressive modern plant from
public funds, higher education in San Antonio is entirely
church-endowed, with two Protestant and four Roman Catholic colleges. Notable among them is Trinity University, a
Presbyterian school which had a long and transient history,
wandering from Tehuacana in East Texas to Waxahachie near
Dallas, before it merged in 1941 with the University of San
Antonio. It gives undergraduate work and carries on a large
adult-education program. Because of the heavy Latin and
Irish elements in the population, the Roman Church is particularly prominent in San Antonio. Many of the city's outstanding leaders in politics and economic problems as well as
in education have been Catholic clergymen.

V

STERN WINDS FROM THE NORTH

◇◇◇

1. *Panhandle, High Plains, and Red River*

EXTENDING NORTHWARD beyond the headwaters of the Red River is an oblong stretch of elevated plains. If Texas were a pan, this oblong would be its handle. Hence it has come to be called the Panhandle.

It is a land of violence and high velocities. Gales whirl over its lofty waves of bare gravel and treeless prairie. A blazing sun bakes its earth into great cakes of crust. Cold spells freeze it over with glassy coats. Avalanches of snow hurry across it, propelled here and there not by gravity, for the slopes are not steep nor long enough, but by wind.

Wheat is the leading agricultural product of the Panhandle, and every time the land is broken, whirlwinds carry part of it into the sky. Cattle are also raised on a large scale here, and their hoofs help load dust on the whirlwinds. Trees did not grow on the Panhandle's high plains until men came to plant them, and now they can be found only in the towns and farmyards. Wild life has not yet learned of this recent importation; hence the trees are empty of birds and silent except when torn by wind.

Human habitations in the Panhandle have to be sturdy and equipped with an artificial climate to offset the inclement out-of-doors. Ventilation is from electric air-conditioners and fans boxed into the windows, with damp filters to keep out dust and increase indoor humidity. Tame shrubbery and flowers, being vulnerable to the gales, are shielded behind solid yard fences which often have the sturdiness of walls.

This land of ghastly bareness has a lavish economy derived from a complex series of superimposed and vastly different enterprises. First came cattle, to eat the grass and release long-dormant sands. Next came wheat, and the plows set whirl-winds going. Then came oil and gas, and as the world's largest natural gas reservoir underlies the upper Panhandle, this new resource has remarkably changed the complexion of the land and its cities. Since 1940 about fifty-six important plants de-voted to gas products alone have been built and expanded there. The Panhandle produces 80 per cent of the nation's carbon black: soot derived from the flames of burning gas. It has also grown famous as the world's principal source of helium, the inert, odorless, tasteless, non-inflammable gas which originally served principally to lift airships and balloons and which now finds a place in deep-sea divers' suits, medi-cines, neon-type signs, and research laboratories. The original copies of the United States Constitution, the Bill of Rights, and the Declaration of Independence are now preserved against decay in air-tight cases filled with helium from the Texas Panhandle. Since this rare gas has exceptional value for military purposes, the United States government holds a monopoly on its large-scale production.

Amarillo (72,246), chief city of the Panhandle, conserves and nurtures all the successive endeavors that have invaded the upper plains. Her petroleum and gas interests, her status as the world's helium capital, and her many manufacturing

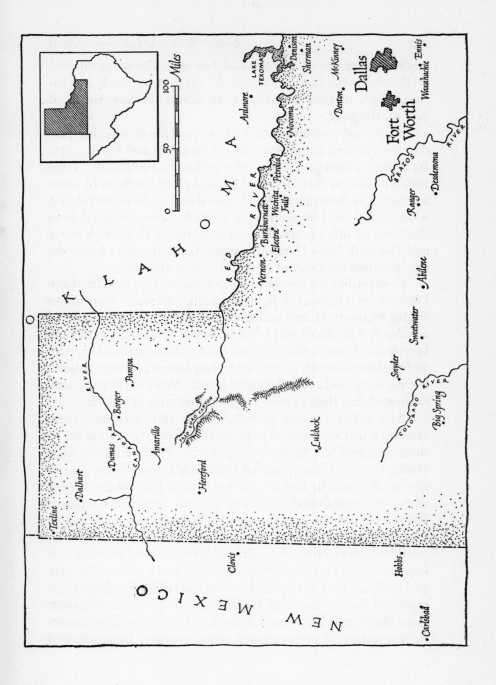

establishments have not weaned her away from wheat and
cattle. She is the home of the world's largest livestock auction
ring, which in 1951 sold over sixty million dollars' worth of
beef on the hoof.

Stretching southwestward from Amarillo is a highly productive irrigated region specializing in grains and truck crops.
Its center is Hereford, "the town without a toothache." Den-
tists now concur that Hereford is a bad place for them to make
a living. The minerals in the Hereford soil are so plentiful that
foods raised in it contain more tooth-building material than
the foods of other lands. The same is true of Hereford's water
and the milk from Hereford's cows. Consequently, tooth decay is almost nonexistent in the Hereford vicinity.

Comprising the southern part of the high plains, the Lubbock area is a blanket of light chocolate and sandy loam six to
twelve inches thick and underlain by heavy clay with a layer of
caliche at a depth of three feet or more. The clay and caliche
keep water from sinking beyond the reach of small roots. The
surface loams absorb water slowly, but have a high water-hold-
ing capacity and are inherently fertile. Water will soak into
them and stay there, giving crops a maximum of benefit.

The entire blanket of caliche and clay-supported loam
rests on a soft mattress of water-bearing sand, two hundred to
three hundred feet thick in many places. All around the high
plains, the winds have torn off the blanket and whipped away
the sand beneath. But across the Texas Panhandle, except
where the east-bound Palo Duro Creek and the Canadian
River have cut canyons through them, both the sand and its
protecting clays remain intact.

The water in the sand mattress is replenished by rains falling into lakes and streams whose beds reach below the clay
and caliche. It is extracted by about fifty-five hundred wells
scattered mostly south of the Palo Duro Canyon. Irrigation
from these wells has made Lubbock (71,747) a leading center
for commerce in cotton, truck crops, poultry, livestock, and

dairy products. Recently, however, the water level in the wells has fallen, and many of the erstwhile opulent agriculturists have perforce returned to dry farming. Here, as elsewhere in Texas, the hazards of an agricultural slump are eased by oil, there being some twelve thousand producing oil wells in Lubbock's retail-trade area.

Lubbock is also one of the nation's neatest cities. All paved streets in the residential districts are cleaned weekly and those in the business sectors are cleaned daily. Seven hundred miles of gutters are swept each week. The result is that for eleven consecutive years the National Clean-up Bureau has awarded Lubbock the title of Texas's cleanest city. Morally, also, Lubbock is immaculate. No liquor is allowed in Lubbock County, for Lubbock's people are of the same God-fearing stock that has filled North Central Texas.

The Red River Valley also enjoys a combination of good land and oil. Oil wells have spread almost to the riverbanks. Unlike the Rio Grande, the Red River has no mountains to hamper its flow and make it bank up its silt in a few favored spots. Its valley is fertile all the way down its length. The result is that a long string of cities, ten to thirty miles apart, has grown up along its basin's southern edge, the largest being Vernon, Wichita Falls, and Texarkana.

Notable among the Red River Valley's smaller towns is Nocona (3,022), leather-goods center of the southwest. Joe Justin, pioneer maker of cowboy boots, came to Nocona in 1887, when the Missouri, Kansas & Texas Railroad brought a track across the river and into the village. Here he established a boot factory. He devised a system whereby cowboys all over the west could measure their feet, send the figures to him, and have boots made to order. As his reputation grew, he taught his craft to his seven children. After his death his sons resolved to move the factory elsewhere, but his daughter Enid was determined to remain in Nocona. Under her direction the Nocona Boot Company has spread the name of Justin farther

still. She has had the honor of fitting the governors of Hawaii,
Alaska, Guam, Puerto Rico, the Virgin Islands, and all the
United States with Texas cowboy boots. In 1952 she furnished
boots for all models in the Paris style show known as "Texas
Week on the Riviera."

At present Nocona has three other leather-goods concerns.
The Justin Company, started in 1919 by Joe Justin's sons,
makes billfolds, ladies' purses, key cases, and various other
small products cut from leather scraps. The Nocona Leather
Goods Company, started in 1926 by a group of Nocona's citizens, specializes in sports equipment. The F & E Leather
Goods Shop makes watch fobs. But Enid Justin holds undisputed supremacy in the making of cowboy boots.

As in the Panhandle, the wind is often strong in the Red
River Valley. It rolls up dust in tight little scrolls that squirm
over the streets of the towns like thousands of living snakes or
worms. It makes the fields billow like oceans and the trees
bow gracefully though noisily along the sidewalks. Leaves
dance over the lawns among waving blossoms, like animated
figures in a movie cartoon. But the winds of human migration
and the natural attractions of mutual interest have brought
to the Red River a remarkable convergence of our best human
traits: of devoutness without intolerance, of competition without malice, of diligent work without oppression, of spontaneous cordiality. In the Red River Valley there are no
wetback swarms to encourage sloth and bigotry among farm-
owners. Nor is there any large Negro labor class to wean people away from the frugality and equality of pioneer days.

Just as South Texas society has been largely molded by the
Mexican element; just as East Texas and the Gulf Coast were
first developed under the deep-south cotton-plantation system;
just as West Texas owes its character to the exigencies of cattle-raising, so was North Texas settlement originally conditioned by the development of Texas railroads. The climax of
the Mexican drama came between 1821 and 1836 and gave

birth to the culture patterns on which much of South Texas life has since been built. King Cotton held the ascendancy from 1836 until diversified farming began to claim attention after the Civil War. Cattle-raising was paramount during the 1870's and 1880's, its epoch overlapping and affecting in several ways the great period of railroad-building. The iron horse has added its bit to the complex of assets and habits in all parts of Texas, but the high plains and the upper Red River basin were mostly empty wastes before the railroads came. Hence, railroads are the basic pace-setting element in North Texas society.

◇◇◇

2. The Iron Horse

ON JULY 16, 1872, John Neely Bryan sat in a chair that had been reserved for him on a platform that he had helped design under a grove of oaks whose trimming he had helped direct. He had seen many big days during his sixty-two years of action-packed life: days of indelible achievement, of unforgettable change. But this would no doubt be the biggest of them all.

In 1841—thirty-one years before this biggest of big days—Bryan had chosen this spot as the most favorable site in all the land for a great city. Before his arrival in Texas, he had been a Tennessee lawyer, but his physician had advised him to go west for his health, and this region of gently rolling prairie in Northeast Texas, where two streams converge to form the Trinity River, was the best place he could find. He was wise in his selections, and searched with long and patient care before settling on this site. All alone except for his Indian pony, called Neshoba Tenva, or Walking Wolf, he built a pole hut ten by twelve feet in size on the east bank of the river. Wearing clothes of buckskin, and breaking the ground with a plow made from a forked *bois d'arc* log, he lived as a hermit for more than six months. Then in 1842 other settlers began coming, and on February 26, 1843, he married one of their daughters. He named the place Dallas, publicized it widely, and gave a town lot to every newly wedded couple in the settlement.

During its first thirty-one years of existence Bryan's dream city had grown to a village of two or three thousand. This was not a rapid rate of growth: only about a hundred new citizens a year. Bryan was not satisfied. But he knew what the place needed: railroads. And now this biggest of his days was to be made memorable by the coming of the first regularly scheduled steam-locomotive train into Dallas.

Old-timers did not all agree with Bryan in welcoming the train. From the moment Texas broke away from Mexico, she had vacillated between a desire for railroad transportation and a fear of the monopolistic possibilities entailed in forming a company big enough to lay rails. On December 6, 1836, just eight and one-half months after the San Jacinto victory, the Texas government issued a charter for the formation of the "Texas Railroad, Navigation, and Banking Company." Although passed by a majority in Congress and signed by President Sam Houston, the charter was at once assailed as an "odious monument of legislative folly" and a "betrayal of the people, jeopardizing their rights, their property, and their liberty, putting them in bondage to a moneyed aristocracy," a "hydra-headed monster" which would "control our currency and curse our prosperity." Some of the protests were due to the fact that the company was to have banking privileges as soon as a fifth of its capital stock (five million dollars) had been subscribed. Because of the opposition, the company collapsed, achieving nothing other than a number of personal antagonisms which were to plague Texas politics for years to come. Three subsequent charters were issued by the republic, but none of the companies thus formed ever reached the point of laying rails.

The days of early statehood brought only a little more success. Fifty-eight charters were issued between 1845 and 1861. The state government gave 5,324,039 acres of land to railroad companies and lent them $1,816,500. Yet Texas had only ten short roads, totaling but 468 miles of track, at the outbreak of the Civil War. These operated only in East Texas and along the Gulf Coast. During the war many of them were demolished. The rails were taken up and stacked to form barricades against northern attacks.

After the war, transportation in Texas remained miserably primitive. On his visit to the state in 1871 Horace Greeley observed: "Her rivers, creeks, and bayous, rarely bridged, are subject to great and sudden floods, whereby teamsters are often imprisoned for days between two creeks which in dry seasons are waterless, and halted by rivers for weeks. But for railroads, Texas is doomed by nature to stagnation, impotence, and barbarism. . . . As yet she has barely begun to be penetrated by railroads."

Meanwhile in England and New England the steam engine was growing in power and grandeur. New inventions were progressively improving it. Mechanical and social mistakes were being revealed and eliminated. Conservative farmers of the Atlantic seaboard failed at first to see any advantage in the "steam carriage." Its rails cut up their farms and endangered their livestock. Sparks from its filterless smokestack set their fields ablaze. Soot blackened the clothes on their wives' lines. But they found that the frail trains yielded to almost any obstacle. They could easily be derailed by a stick of wood across the tracks. Often they balked or stalled for want of fuel or because some clumsily fitted part had gone wrong. Passengers were forced to walk for miles, sometimes pushing the train. Railroad-promoters made diplomatic blunders which dampened public enthusiasm and partly spoiled the romance of the great venture.

The bulk of these trial-and-error episodes had been accomplished and their resultant wisdom put into practice before the majority of Texans got a glimpse of a real railroad. The great venture therefore struck them with more impact than had attended its more gradual introduction to northerners and easterners. Its romance was more telling when it burst in all its full-fledged glory upon this fresh audience. Some travelers from the east had seen the marvel in action, and the wonder of it increased with repeated narration to admiring listeners.

Hence, on that memorable July 16, 1872, when John Neely Bryan and his fellow pioneers of Dallas gave a barbecue of buffalo meat to honor the iron horse, over five thousand souls, drawn by unsullied awe, gathered to see it. They came in ox-drawn carts, mule-drawn wagons, and horse-drawn buggies from as far away as the Red River on the north and the headwaters of the Brazos and Colorado on the west and southwest. They brought lunches to supplement the barbecued buffalo, children to see and remember the great sight, banners and ribbons to adorn the picnic grounds under the oak grove. To ward off the sun, women wore bonnets of all colors and men wore broad hats of felt and straw. Overflowing beyond the borders of the grove, they threw up canvas shades propped on crudely cut poles. According to the historian John Henry Brown, who was principal orator for the occasion, all the drinks were soft. Not a drunk could be found on the grounds, for the farmers of North Texas are hard-working, peaceful folk who feel no need to dull their joys with strong intoxicants. Water and lemonade prevailed.

The weather was perfect for such a celebration. There had been a light shower of rain the day before, just enough to freshen the grass and brighten the oak foliage. Tiny white clouds were flying fast across the sky. A breeze from the southeast, cooled by the Gulf Stream and cleaned by three hundred miles of nature's greenery, sweetened the event's momentous thrill.

At eleven thirty that morning, under the measured throb of drums and the bracing tunes of a brass band, the crowd grew dense around the speakers' platform, where Bryan and Brown sat among railroad officials. Suddenly the music stopped. Fathers hushed their sons. Mothers muffled their babes. All lifted their faces, shaded by hats and bonnets, to listen and learn. Above the twitter of birds and the whisper of the breeze in the oak leaves John Henry Brown told them all those things they loved to hear: things such as he wrote later in his history of Texas, to be repeated by other historians and taught in all the schools. John Henry Brown, erect and hale at fifty-two, with eyes dancing under shaggy brows, cheeks shaved smooth, and a clean beard flowing from his lips and chin, spoke in a voice clearly intended to be echoed through the oak grove and remembered through the centuries.

"He commenced," says the reporter for the *Dallas Herald,* "by referring to several important epochs in the history of the world, which had materially changed the aspect of human affairs. Among them was the revolution, which established the independence of Texas and its annexation to the United States. Its consequences were the Mexican War and the further annexation of New Mexico, California, and Arizona, with the rapid spread of civilization from the Atlantic to the Pacific. The great mineral discoveries and developments had affected the world at large. It was difficult to appreciate the great results of Texan independence. He defended the Texan people from the charge of indolence and supineness. They had exhibited energy and activity and large-mindedness. No state in the Union, under such adverse circumstances, had accomplished so much, had made such valuable progress in the same length of time. She had made liberal provisions for the building of railroads, and had given them all the encouragement

within her power. Today, this joyous crowd, made up mostly
of the hardy cultivators of the soil, the pride and strength of
this or any other country, had assembled to honor the comple-
tion to this point of one of the greatest railroad enterprises
in the state. They hailed the arrival of the iron horse with
joyous welcome. But no feeling of selfishness was mingled
with it. They would not detain it at their threshold. They bid
it onward, with lightning speed, until it met its snorting brother
from the colder regions of the north. . . ."

The recipient of these tributes was the Houston & Texas
Central Railroad, popularly known as the Central. Besides being one of the greatest, it was the first railway enterprise to be
chartered by Texas after her annexation to the United States.
For four years after its creation on March 11, 1848, it remained
dormant. Aroused to action in 1852 by the impatient farmers
of a little settlement called Chappell Hill,[1] sixty-two miles
northwest of Houston, it was reorganized. By 1860 it had laid
eighty miles of railroad, running in a broad arc first northwestward from Houston, then almost due northward toward
Dallas. At the end of the Civil War its tracks were badly damaged, but in 1867 it resumed construction, beginning at a rate
of twenty and soon rising to about forty miles per year, creating towns as it went, naming some of them, such as Bremond
and Groesbeeck, after its own pioneer officials. In 1870 it had
thirty locomotives and its net earnings amounted to almost a
million dollars. The citizens of Dallas paid $5,000 in cash,
$8,250 in bonds, a right of way in their business section, and
115 acres of land to persuade the Central to lay its tracks
through their city.

Thus coaxed, the iron horse came, to be praised in eloquent phrases by John Henry Brown. After the speeches and
the feast on buffalo meat, the people flowed over the prairie
from the oak grove to the town to see the train. By this time it
had developed far beyond the stage of the toy contraption that
a stick of wood or an angry bull could knock off the track. It

[1] The spelling of this name has since been changed to "Chapel Hill."

had become a monster whose cars could hold ten tons of cargo each. No muscle of flesh and blood could match its steel sinews, and its iron lungs breathed fire and smoke rather than air. Like the dragons of ancient myth, it terrified the bravest spirits and staggered the wildest imagination. Super-human though it was, its powerful puffs so resembled the human breath, its plowpoint-shaped cowcatcher nosed its way with such seemingly conscious care through the spellbound crowd, its headlight, fed by kerosene oil, peered ahead with such reminiscence of the Cyclops' eye, that it was partially personified by all beholders. The heat of its long cylindrical boiler and the heave of its sighs were so measured by its de-gree of effort that even the most prosaic merchants could not avoid feeling an impulse of sympathy for its Herculean strug-gles, especially when it pulled a line of cars loaded with prof-itably priced merchandise. Its detractors having long before acknowledged their fight lost, few complained when the clouds were hidden, the sun veiled, and the prairies shadowed by the long, curved funnel of black smoke tumbling from its stack.

The Central Railroad's progress beyond Dallas was more rapid than ever. All the towns to the north wanted the road to pass through them, and offered generous gifts to woo it. The lucky ones were McKinney, which gave a bonus of $20,000, and Sherman, which gave $50,000. Early in 1873 the road reached the Red River. After a struggle over junction points and a sudden flood which washed away its original Red River terminal, it made connections at Denison with the Missouri, Kansas & Texas Railroad, popularly known as the Katy. This was the first rail contact between Texas and other states, and the Katy spared no pains in making the fact known. Its lines were plastered with giant posters showing cowboys astride longhorn steers and designating the Katy as the "gateway to Texas."

Meanwhile, within the giant state, as the Central Com-pany built northward it sent out branches westward. One of

these had already reached Austin when the main line got to
Dallas. Another reached Waco in the fall of 1872. But
San Antonio, Texas's largest inland city at the time, had to
wait five more years before she got her first look at the iron
horse. It finally reached her in 1877, on the Galveston, Harrisburg & San Antonio Railroad, an enterprise initiated and
run by an ambitious Bostonian named Thomas Wentworth
Peirce.

Before the Civil War there had been a road running
eighty-one miles west from the little town of Harrisburg,
which is now a suburb of Houston. It was called the Buffalo
Bayou, Brazos & Colorado Railroad. Promoted by a hero of
the Texas revolution named Sidney Sherman, and begun in
1852, it had the distinction of being the first railroad ever actually built in the state. Like the Central, it suffered much
destruction during the war and was still badly dilapidated in
January 1870, when Peirce bought its properties, changed its
name, and began its extension to San Antonio.

Peirce worked convicts and paid wages in gutta-percha
tokens which passed as currency in Texas restaurants and
grocery stores, so good was his credit. But it was not without
financial help that he reached San Antonio in 1877, to be
feted with festivities no less elegant than those of Dallas five
years before. Samuel A. Maverick—the same man from whom
maverick cattle got their name—donated a plot of ground in
San Antonio for a depot and shops. The city gave Peirce $300,-
000 in bonds, and the state granted him 1,432,960 acres of
land. In his effort to create a community capable of supporting
his railroad, Peirce organized an immigration bureau and
awarded a special rate of fare to anyone promising to settle
the country.

Meanwhile, the entire eastern half of Texas was being
streaked with rails. Despite the panic of 1873, the decade of
the seventies saw the total trackage in Texas increase from
711 to 3,244 miles. Its effect on the state's inland cities was

tremendous. The population of Dallas was more than trebled, rising to 10,358 in 1880. In 1876 the Texas & Pacific, only railroad in Texas operating under a federal charter, pushed westward as far as the village of Fort Worth, thirty-two miles from Dallas. By 1880 Fort Worth had 6,663 citizens. Waco grew in the same ten years from 3,008 to 7,295. Austin almost trebled its population, leaping from 4,428 to 11,013. Although the rails did not reach San Antonio until late in the decade, it had 20,550 people by 1880, as compared with only 12,256 in 1870.

To say that this growth of cities along the Balcones fault line was due entirely to railroads would be an oversimplification. It was due to a combination of railroad-building and the post-Civil War growth of farming and ranching, each helping the others. But the railroad brought an entirely new note into the symphony of progress. Unlike the farm or ranch, it is a highly social undertaking. A farm depends for its existence on edible plants. A ranch depends on its livestock. A railroad depends on its iron tools plus public whims. To sell their commodities, farmer and rancher need access only to hungry people, and a normal person, whatever his views, interests, or talents, can be counted on to get hungry two or three times a day. But a railroad sells transportation, and the demand for transportation is created not by any universal urge like hunger but by a peculiar desire of certain persons to move from place to place or to get something from somewhere else. This desire recurs with a frequency directly proportional to the number of people living in all areas to be connected and to their need for long-distance communications. A large, widely distributed population with local specialties calling for heavy exchanges is therefore vital to the success of a railroad.

Since farm communities are more populous than range lands, and since an acre of ground can produce more freight tonnage in farm products than in beef, the railroads spent millions in Texas throughout the last decades of the nineteenth and the first decades of the twentieth century on a campaign to "turn the lariat into a plow line." In selling the land granted them by the state, they were always partial to farmers, making extremely easy terms to encourage rapid settlement. They were also stimulated by the government's requirement that all railroad land be either sold within twelve years or returned to the state. After 1882, when land grants were discontinued, the railroads bought large tracts, divided them into small blocks, and sold them to settlers, sometimes at a loss.

Anxious to make sure that their generously distributed land tracts would eventually be paid for, the railroad companies were extremely careful in their selection of prospective settlers. They chose only those pious farmers of strong God-fearing bent who placed a high premium on the punctual payment of debts. Such honest, hard-working folk would be more apt to reimburse the railroad companies, both in regular installments on the land and in profitable business, than secular-minded speculators. Thus the new farmers brought by the railroads intensified and solidified the strong religious mentality of those older North Texans who could rejoice without liquor at such gatherings as the Dallas picnic where John Henry Brown first greeted the Houston & Texas Central: those plain-spoken, plain-living agrarians whose pioneer prudence now pervades the state, but can be found in its purest form along the Red River and on the high plains around Lubbock.

But the industrialization of Texas and other western areas, which would increase the home consumption of agricultural products and thus reduce the need for long hauls across the country, was not to the interest of the railroads. Therefore, they did not encourage it. The old habit that many Texans had of exporting their own farm produce and living on imported foods was exactly what the carriers wanted. The *Galveston News* sensed this tendency early in the career of the

Houston & Texas Central. Said the editor: "A railroad has neither a soul to be saved nor a body to be kicked. It is governed entirely by interest. This is the reason the Central will not accommodate the wheat business. The road can make more money by carrying Missouri and Illinois flour than it can by carrying Texas wheat."

Since the general welfare of the populace was vitally affected by the conduct of the railroads, they had to be kept under close governmental supervision. They could not operate without charters which circumscribed their activities in considerable detail. Without the co-operation of national and state lawmakers, they could not get their way. Hence, the temptation to bribe politicians has always been strong among railroad magnates both in Texas and in other states. Dishonest legislators and congressmen have often capitalized on this weakness by introducing bogus laws which, if passed, would seriously hamstring the railroads. Only by issuing free passes and otherwise soliciting the goodwill of these politicians could the carriers offset such legislation.

Railroads also brought large-scale corporate enterprise into Texas for the first time. One of the first really formidable monopolists to extend a tentacle into Texas was a burly ex-merchant named Collis P. Huntington, whose money enabled Thomas W. Peirce to continue his Galveston, Harrisburg & San Antonio Railroad on into the hills until it joined an eastbound road from California, thus for the first time traversing the entire state from east to west and establishing a railroad connection between the Gulf of Mexico and the Pacific Ocean.

To the businessmen of San Antonio in those days, Peirce was as big a fish as any ever seen in America's great commercial sea, but compared with a whale like Huntington, he was a minnow. Together with three other money barons, Huntington had built the first railroad across the center of the United States to the Pacific, largely on federal-government funds. One highly lucrative stunt of these industrial tyrants was to glut their corporation with government subsidies, then form a construction company in which they owned most of the stock and pay it an absurdly fabulous sum to build the road. Thus they sold their own services to themselves, paying themselves generously.

Being alone in the field of transcontinental transportation, they monopolized California traffic, swallowing up even the wharves and local boat lines. They raised their rates to such a height that their Pacific Coast customers were crushed under the burden. Huntington used the money to bribe United States congressmen and buy state legislatures. Californians nicknamed him King Collis and published scathing pamphlets on his methods. One contemporary described him as "a hard and cheery old man, with no more soul than a shark." Another found him "ruthless as a crocodile." Some of his correspondence, revealing his manipulations in Washington, came to light in a court trial and appalled the whole nation.

But by the time Huntington's influence touched Texas, his brutality had been somewhat curbed. The granger movement of the early seventies had demonstrated to him and his fellows that they could not exploit the western farmer with impunity. In 1877, while T. W. Peirce was paying his Texas hands with gutta-percha tokens, railroad workers of the other states were teaching their employers through riot-provoking strikes that they had to have a living wage.

Hence, King Collis had mellowed slightly by 1878, when Peirce was on the verge of stopping his rails at San Antonio. Peirce had almost given up the idea of building beyond San Antonio. His funds were nearly gone. Besides, West Texas was too arid and wild to promise a railroad any local profit. The six hundred miles between San Antonio and the five-year-old village at the westernmost tip of Texas called El Paso had nothing to offer except limestone hills, longhorn cattle, coyotes, and cowboys. The hills were costly to circumvent or tunnel or climb with rails. The cattle were bony and could provide scant returns for the space their horns would take up in a railway car. The coyotes killed all attractive animals and filled the nights with a ringing, blood-chilling howl which would numb the bones of easterners and nullify the effect of a fortune spent in railroad-advertising. The cowboys were worse than the coyotes, because they could sometimes be seen and heard by day.

So it seemed to Peirce until King Collis came along. Huntington expected no more from West Texas than Peirce did, but he wanted a transcontinental route that would couple the deep south with the wild west, swinging through New Orleans, skirting the Gulf Coast, and running clear to California. He had even organized a company for the purpose, calling it the Southern Pacific, and had begun building eastward from California through Arizona and New Mexico. In return for financial support, Peirce agreed to extend the Galveston, Harrisburg & San Antonio road westward and meet the east-bound rails somewhere near the mouth of the Pecos River.

Work began about the same time at El Paso and San Antonio: June and July 1881. Peirce's west-bound line crossed the Pecos near its mouth the following summer. The banks of this river are steep and bordered with high chalky cliffs. This made progress so slow that the two lines did not meet until January 12, 1883, when Peirce drove a silver spike into the tie beneath the last two rails. The ceremony amidst those lofty hills must have been most impressive.

"In the majestic presence of these great canyons," said Peirce, ". . . which speak more eloquently than words the insignificance of man, and on the other hand man's significance in his great triumphs over the forces of nature, of which we have abundant evidence all around us, I proceed to drive this spike which connects by rail the waters of the Pacific and those of the Gulf of Mexico."

He asked Divine favor for all his associates who "with

brain and muscle have periled their lives in this Herculean work." He was grateful to God for preserving his life until he could see this dream fulfilled. It would "assist to bind the different sections of our country more closely together, and to make our continent the highway of the nations of the earth."

But for years thereafter the land beyond the Pecos gained little more than the noise and smoke of the locomotives. While the rails were being laid, little tent towns sprang up to serve the workers. Then they disappeared almost as quickly as they had been born, leaving no trace of their passing except a few garbage heaps which were soon cooked by the sun and eaten by the coyotes. Peirce employed Irishmen for his westward extension, while the Southern Pacific, working eastward from El Paso, hired Chinese. Between these there was much rivalry. The fiery Irishmen despised the Chinese and, well fortified with liquor, expressed their feelings in fights. Their employers were hard put to it to preserve the peace.

Fortunately, the railroads found an ally in a fifty-two-year-old rapscallion from San Antonio named Roy Bean, who followed Peirce's gangs westward, throwing up temporary saloons to sell them liquor. Since the nearest authorized magistrate was at Fort Stockton, over two hundred miles northwest of where the railroad crossed the Pecos, the cantankerous Irishmen could not be conveniently punished for their offenses. To get around this difficulty, Roy Bean was made Justice of the Peace and relied upon to keep order among the workers. He himself was just wicked enough to contend with the situation admirably. Armed with a lawbook, a pair of pearl-handled pistols, a sawed-off shotgun, a meager education, and an amazing fund of audacity, he kept order beyond the Pecos.

He had help, to be sure. There is in Texas a famous organization known as the Texas Rangers. Unlike a local police force, the Rangers have the whole state for their beat. Although they have no uniform and are not subject to military regulations, they can be sent anywhere in the state to take care of situations that get beyond the control of the local peace officers. At the request of the railroad companies, a detachment of Rangers was sent to the Pecos with orders to enforce Roy Bean's decisions.

Roy knew very little about law. His lawbook was more of a symbol than a tool. It gave him dignity, but he never let it boss him around. For instance, an Irish hothead once killed a Chinese and was brought in by the Rangers. Roy thumbed carefully through his book, then announced that he could find in it no law against killing a Chinaman.

Since no locomotive of the day could go the whole road from San Antonio to El Paso without fresh water, stations had to be set up along the way. One of these was Langtry, twenty miles west of the Pecos and five miles north of the Rio Grande, named, according to railroad officials, for a Southern Pacific construction engineer. At first, Langtry had little more than a tank where the train could get water, but in 1882 Roy Bean moved there and built a shack where the passengers could get other liquids. On the spur of the moment he could transform the saloon into a courthouse and dispense justice.

In addition to his legalistic originality, Roy had a yen for theatrics and a love for beautiful women. When he arrived at the Langtry station there lived in Europe a famous actress named Lillie Langtry. Roy saw in this coincidence a chance to capture public attention and at the same time possibly slake his thirst for female charms. He wrote Lillie a letter, introducing himself as the law west of the Pecos, announcing that out of profound admiration he had named his town after her, and inviting her to come and see it sometime. She had been born on the isle of Jersey, sixteen miles off the coast of Normandy, and to do her further honor Roy christened his saloon "The Jersey Lilly" [*sic*]. Since he needed some way to let the world know what his place was called, he announced a court session, found two Irishmen guilty of drunkenness, and sentenced them to hard labor until they had painted him three large signs

reading: "Judge Roy Bean, Notary Public," "Justice of the
Peace, Law West of the Pecos," and "The Jersey Lilly." These
he placed above his saloon door.

The actress was not deaf to Roy's flattery. She answered
his letter, regretting that she could not visit Texas at the time,
but promising that if later she should have occasion to ride
the Sunset Express across America, she would certainly stop
by and see "her town." The occasion came late. Roy waited
and waited. At last he died a natural death and Lillie stopped
by Langtry ten months afterward. For twenty years Roy Bean
was law west of the Pecos. Today his Jersey Lilly is a shrine
reminding all travelers of the isolation and independence that
characterize the great West Texas spaces.

In its early days the railroad's contributions to West Texas
were sometimes unintentional. The bridge over the Pecos was
three hundred feet high, and the floors of other canyons sank
to frightening depths. Freight trains often weighed so heavily
on the bridges that their cars tumbled into the gorges. More
than once Roy Bean stocked his saloon with their spilled contents. Once Roy complained that a train had killed his "prize
Kentucky jack" and suggested that the Southern Pacific con-
sole him with $1,500. According to a neighbor of Roy's, his
jack was worth no more than fifty cents, being old and blind,
but the railroad came across with $500.

Peirce's Galveston, Harrisburg & San Antonio was not the
only line that fell into the hands of Collis P. Huntington in
1878. That was also the year when the great steamship monopolist Charles P. Morgan died. In addition to his control
over Gulf shipping, Morgan owned a number of railroads running from Louisiana into East Texas. After his death, these
and his steamship interests were sold to Huntington. Between
1880 and 1883 Huntington bought up several roads running
through East Texas. Between 1884 and 1889 he slowly got
control of the Houston & Texas Central.

One painful thorn in his side was the San Antonio &

Aransas Pass Railroad, which ran southeastward from San
Antonio to Corpus Christi. This road had been built by a
New Yorker named Uriah Lott on faith and a borrowed five-
dollar bill. Starting at San Antonio, Lott graded the first mile
largely with his own hands. He borrowed enough old rails for
a mile of track and found a locomotive that had been condemned and sent to the shops six years before to be dismembered for scrap iron. Hitching it to two discarded freight cars,
he rolled it into San Antonio, loaded with foodstuffs from
local farmers. Slowly his business picked up until his faith
drew the attention of two range men named Mifflin Kenedy
and Richard King. Kenedy not only contributed cash, but also
contracted to build part of the road, agreeing to take stock in
Lott's company as payment. Bee County gave the road $55,-
830.15. The citizens of Corpus Christi donated $102,950. But
Lott was more of a promoter than a financier. With all this
help, he could not make his railroad pay, and on June 16,
1892, Huntington bought him out.

Huntington continued picking up one small company after
another until he controlled most of the lines in South and
Central Texas. He died in 1900, but his Southern Pacific al-
liance kept appropriating and constructing until in 1934 all
its subsidiaries were consolidated into one mammoth corporation. Today it is the second-largest system in Texas. With a
total main line trackage in the state of nearly thirty-six hundred miles, it serves all areas except the Panhandle and has
stations in every city of over thirty thousand people except
Amarillo, Lubbock, San Angelo, Wichita Falls, Tyler, and
Laredo.

But Huntington never succeeded in monopolizing Texas
transportation as he had monopolized that of California.
Even as he started building his Southern Pacific road across
West Texas back in 1881, one greater than he had come. Jay
Gould, a frail, black-bearded little consumptive who suffered
from stomach trouble, described as "the wizard of Wall

Street," "the greatest manipulative mind of the period," "the
Napoleon of finance," and "the most phenomenal personality
in the national race for money," had begun laying rails into
Texas from the northeast. His International and Great Northern reached San Antonio on February 16, 1881, and struck
westward, paralleling T. W. Peirce's track for twenty-five
miles, then veering southward for Laredo. He bought out the
Texas & Pacific and in the same year extended it from Fort
Worth along the base of the Panhandle to El Paso, giving
West Texas its second railroad. With a dominant interest in
the Missouri Pacific, the Cotton Belt, the Katy, and the Galveston, Houston & Henderson, he controlled about one third
of the rails in the state.

On November 26, 1881, Jay Gould and Collis Huntington
signed an agreement that spelled doom to the hope for any
genuine railroad competition for the time being. Because their
west-bound lines converged near El Paso, they agreed to share
the Southern Pacific track from there to California, splitting
the proceeds equitably. They were not to undersell each other
or encroach on each other's territory. For five years thereafter,
except for the many short lines in East Texas which they were
buying as fast as they could, these two tycoons had the state
to themselves. Then in 1886 another big enterprise came in.
This was the Atchison, Topeka & Santa Fe Railway, popularly known as the Santa Fe.

The first Texas line to be absorbed by the Santa Fe was
born of yellow fever just after the Civil War. In those days
Galveston was the largest, most prosperous city in the state.
She had the biggest banks and the richest depositors. Retail
stores in all other cities got their goods from her wholesale
houses. Since water was still the principal avenue of transportation, Texas farmers customarily looked to her as a market
for their cotton and their chief source of hardware, drygoods,
groceries, and whisky. Some forty miles up the bayou was

Houston, a would-be rival to which the island metropolis hardly gave a second thought.

Then in 1867 an epidemic of yellow fever hit Galveston. More than a thousand people died. Assuming that yellow-fever germs could be carried in freight cargo, and being acutely alert to any excuse for hampering the rival city's trade, Houstonians concluded that Galveston merchandise was pestilential and must not be allowed to pass through their city. Since the state constitution permitted local quarantines, Houston used the yellow-fever epidemic as a pretext for clamping an embargo on all goods coming from Galveston.

Galveston might have survived both the disease and the quarantine with her traditional aloofness had it not been for the railroad situation. From Houston, rails had begun radiating in all directions; Galveston's only track ran through Houston. Hence, Houston's embargo blocked Galveston's only inland outlet. The farmers who had habitually sent to Galveston for supplies now sent to Houston. Since they had to buy their goods in Houston, many of them decided that they might as well take their cotton there. The inland cities, no longer able to draw on Galveston's wholesale concerns, sent to Houston for their hardware, drygoods, groceries, and whisky. Houstonian merchants obliged them for a good price. Consequently, Houston flourished while whisky aged, groceries rotted, clothing gathered dust, and hardware rusted in Galveston's warehouses.

The embargo proved so lucrative to Houston that her leading citizens became extremely fearful of yellow fever: so fearful that they repeated the quarantine year after year about the time of the cotton season. There was always a good reason, fully substantiated by expert medical opinion. One could not be too careful about a contagious disease. If a person in Galveston looked suspiciously discolored or spent a day in bed, Houston would surely hear of it and forbid all movement of

Galvestonian merchandise lest it endanger the health and prosperity of her citizens.

For five years this maddening state of affairs persisted, with Houston growing and Galveston languishing. At last Galveston thought of a way out. She must build a railroad into the mainland which would not pass through Houston. Accordingly, in the year 1873 her men of means assembled and formed the Gulf, Colorado & Santa Fe Railway Company. With a capital stock of $750,000, they began their road on May 1, 1875. It reached the village of Richmond, thirty-three miles southwest of Houston, early in 1879 and went bankrupt.

Galveston's redemption would have been lost if a plump-faced, hook-nosed Galvestonian named George Sealy, already president of the company, had not bought up the balance of its stock for $200,000. With Sealy as sole owner, the road resumed construction. First it shot northwestward to a point thirty-five miles south of Waco. Here it created a town and named it Temple after its chief construction engineer. From Temple it sent out two prongs which wound in diagonal directions like the horns of a Texas steer. One went west into the chalky highlands. The other meandered northward to Fort Worth. Smaller branches contacted Houston, Dallas, and the east Texas timberlands.

At that time one of the most successful companies operating north of Texas was the Atchison, Topeka & Santa Fe, organized by a strong-minded abolitionist named Cyrus Holliday. Beginning at Atchison, Kansas, it had first built southwestward to Topeka, then extended west across Kansas with many branches shooting south. By the beginning of the 1880's it had reached the ancient trading center of Santa Fe, New Mexico, and gained the popular name which it still bears: the Santa Fe. Good management and square dealing had made it prosperous. Throughout the early eighties, it earned an average of over seven million dollars a year, which was a good return for an independent railroad in those days.

*Grain elevator along the Santa Fe track just north of Happy,
thirty-five miles south of Amarillo in the Panhandle.*

Corpus Christi.

But the Santa Fe was as yet an inland road. It needed an outlet to tidewater. For this reason it bought Sealy's line from Galveston in 1886 with the understanding that he should extend its north branch to meet a south-bound line of the Santa Fe at a point in the Indian Territory to be named Purcell, three hundred miles from Fort Worth. The connection was made within three hundred days.

Since its entrance into the state, the Santa Fe has become Texas's largest, most progressive system. By 1890 it had a line halfway across the Panhandle. By 1901 it had crossed the northern Panhandle, and by 1911 it had completed a road from Central Texas to Lubbock at the Panhandle's base. Its total main-line trackage in the state in 1953 was 3,618.3 miles.

The Santa Fe was not the earliest road to begin operations in the Panhandle. That vast area of elevated plains, still an "unpeopled immensity" in the early seventies, was first entered by an independent line from Fort Worth which was headed for Denver, Colorado. The early days of Fort Worth, like those of Galveston, were plagued by the presence of an ambitious and dishearteningly successful neighbor. Fort Worth needed railroads which would draw on lands independent of Dallas. Accordingly, the Fort Worth & Denver City was chartered on June 6, 1873, but the panic of that year caused it to postpone construction until 1881.

At that time Grenville M. Dodge, who had been a general on the Union side in the Civil War, found himself out of a job with a hundred miles of unlaid rails on his hands. Jay Gould had engaged him to extend the Texas & Pacific through El Paso to California. General Dodge had built the line a few miles beyond El Paso when Gould's agreement with Huntington suddenly halted the project. Dodge thereupon contracted with the Fort Worth & Denver City to lay his unused track between Fort Worth and a town near the Red River called Wichita Falls. He reached Wichita Falls on September 1, 1882, and his road transformed it into a prosperous shipping point for Texas cattle. For four years the road remained unchanged, then in 1886 it resumed construction. It reached Texline, in the northwest corner of the Panhandle, on January 26, 1888.

Adjoining its course in the center of the Panhandle lay the Frying Pan Ranch, comprising 250,000 acres, owned and run by a tall, black-mustached barbed-wire salesman from Chicago named Henry B. Sanborn. The railroad touched Sanborn's domain about twelve miles north of Palo Duro Canyon, where a broad alkali lake exposed its banks of yellow clay. To serve the construction gangs, a village of buffalo-hide tents and huts called Ragtown was thrown up in a low place near the sloping banks. Twelve hundred settlers, attracted by the railroad's presence and the land's promise, soon gathered there, designated themselves the county seat, and built a $30,000 courthouse.

Sanborn did not approve. The place was in a draw cupped out by dreadful winds. Rains might gather there and wash the houses away. His own land, a mile to the east, would be much better. The town must be moved. The settlers refused to budge, but Sanborn was not discouraged. He laid out a new site in the proper location and built thereupon a $50,000 hotel. Then he bought the smaller hotel in the original town, put it on wheels, rolled it over to the new site, and called it the annex. From that time on, every week or so he would drive over to the old town, buy a store or similar place of business, mount it on wheels, and move it to the new location. Having nowhere else to do their trading, the settlers were forced to follow. At last only the courthouse remained on the old site. It could not be moved because a Texas law requires a courthouse to remain five years on the spot of its erection. For five years, therefore, it stood alone on the high plains. For five years the county officials walked to it and back each day.

Deploring the motley designation of Ragtown, Sanborn changed his city's name to Oneida, but his cowboys called it

Amarillo, the Spanish word for "yellow," because of the lake's yellow bluffs. To show that he respected the will of the people, Sanborn adopted the popular name and painted his hotel yellow. Soon he went even further and put yellow paint on all his other places of business. From this union of ranch and farm, brought together by the railroad, was born the famous Panhandle metropolis.

With the Fort Worth & Denver City traversing the Panhandle, and with the roads of Gould and Huntington stretching across West Texas, the 1880's saw the whole state laced for the first time with railroads. This second great decade of railroad-building increased Texas's total trackage from 3,224 miles to 8,710 and attracted three giant capitalistic enterprisers (Huntington, Gould, and the Santa Fe) into the state.

Of these the most powerful, the most banal, and the most unscrupulous was the sullen-eyed, thick-bearded little dyspeptic, Jay Gould. A farsighted, law-abiding capitalist blessed with a normal regard for his fellows and motivated by enlightened self-interest can be a priceless asset; a sign of vigor and a source of pride to a community. But Gould was none of these. His farsightedness was fixed only on the stock market's fluctuations, which he forced up and down for his own enrichment. He obeyed the law only when he could twist it to suit his selfish ends. Like a vulture, he loved tragedy and picked nourishment from the bones of economic slumps. His ambition was never to build; always to draw nectar from withering hopes. He was never a leader, but always a drone, draining vitality from his far-flung possessions.

All through the eighties, Texas presented fine prospects from Gould's point of view except for one difficulty which bothered him more and more toward the end of the decade. There was in this wild western state a politician whom he could not buy: a man of vast proportions and sympathies named James Stephen Hogg.

In more ways than one, Gould and Hogg were exact op-

posites. Gould was small, mild-mannered, and sickly. Hogg
was huge, robust, and blessed with boundless energy. Gould
was cold, soft-spoken, and secretive. Hogg was warm-hearted,
loud, and frank. Gould believed in himself alone. Hogg believed in the basic wisdom of humanity.

On July 15, 1885, Gould's railroad companies met with
their would-be competitors in Galveston and formed the Texas
Traffic Association for the express purpose of keeping up their
rates. Shortly thereafter Hogg became the state's attorney
general and compelled Gould's association to dissolve. Hogg
was also instrumental in enacting laws to make all railroads
with lines in the state move their central offices to Texas
towns. "Railroads," he said, "are public highways." They must
be subject, he maintained, to public control. Their purpose
was to serve the people in the areas they occupied, not to fill
the pockets of Wall Street stockholders.

In 1890 Hogg ran for governor and Gould made a hurried
trip to Texas to prevent his election. Hogg stumped the state,
proclaiming that Gould and others had disgraced Texas with
some fifty-three million dollars in watered stocks and bonds.
Gould's method was more cultivated and subtle, if not more
delicate. He merely visited the principal cities, dropping remarks to the effect that there would be no railroad-building
in Texas during the election year, since "capital has grown
rather timid for certain reasons." He even went so far as to
say that "the attitude of the attorney general of the state is
such as to cause some fright among capitalists." People were
left with the impression that if they elected Hogg, no new
railroads would be built through their cities and the lifeblood
of their prosperity would be taken away.

As soon as they had fittingly entertained the wizard of
Wall Street, Texans cast 197,000 votes for Jim Hogg, electing
him to the governorship with the largest majority they had
ever given a candidate up to that time. As soon as he was in
office, Hogg established the Texas Railroad Commission, the

only one in the country whose law was patterned after that of the Interstate Commerce Commission. Its three commissioners were not allowed to engage in "any commercial, agricultural, mining, or other avocation." Nor could they own any stocks or bonds in any railroad company. For two years after leaving office they could not hold any public position of honor or profit. Thus were they removed from the temptation to take bribes. They had full power to enforce fair rates upon the companies, and they used that power tellingly.

On one occasion a group of citizens besieged Hogg with protests against his treatment of the railroad companies. Hogg was a mountain of a man, towering high over the mob, but the protestors seemed numerous and their leader spoke with moving animosity. When the leader's speech was done, Hogg smiled broadly and blared forth with his favorite slang expression:

"Well, by gatlins, boys, I am most glad to see you. Now all of you who didn't ride here on free passes come into my private office and we'll talk this business over."

None of the protestors accepted this invitation. They had all been given free passes by the railroad companies and sent there to agitate.

Thanks partly to Hogg, partly to the granger movement and labor unions, which softened the big companies before they got to Texas, and partly to the large number of big enterprises hitting the state almost simultaneously, Texans have never suffered under continuous exploitation by railroads. Contrary to Gould's intimations, new roads went on appearing and thriving after Hogg's election. Gould's own system, the Missouri Pacific, has since come to be the third-largest in the state, exceeded only by the Southern Pacific and the Santa Fe. Moreover, several other big systems have come into Texas since Hogg created the commission. Notable among them are the Burlington (which took over the Fort Worth & Denver City), the Rock Island, and the Frisco. Also, in 1895 a handsome young New Yorker named Arthur Stilwell brought his Kansas City Southern to touch tidewater on the Gulf Coast, established a town, and named it Port Arthur for himself.

In supervising the policies of these lines, the Texas commission has insisted that rates within the state be no higher than interstate rates. By lowering the cost of long hauls between Texas and the industrial east, railroads could perpetuate the old condition under which Texas specialized in producing raw materials and depended on the east for manufacturing. Since, as we have noted, this condition involved more business for the railroads, they did not wish to see it pass away. But the equal rates required by the commission have facilitated the industrialization of Texas and made it mandatory that the railroads rely for business on improved service rather than on artificially prolonged regional specializations.

In 1905, Ex-Governor James Stephen Hogg was on his way from his plantation home to Houston, riding an inadequately controlled train. Its sudden movements jolted him so that a vertebra was broken in his neck. He never regained his health.

He had dominated Texas politics for over twenty years. Besides circumscribing the harmful activities of large railroad interests, he initiated laws to prevent big pasture-owners from fencing in their less successful neighbors, to keep town and county governments from imposing extravagant bond issues on their citizens, to insure voters in cities against intimidation and fraud, and to improve the efficiency of public schools and other governmental institutions.

In the twentieth century, the railroads met with another check on their activities. The competition of automobiles began making itself felt in the 1920's, forcing the rails to further improve their services. Truck hauling, which grew significant in the 1930's, caused many short tracks to be abandoned, so that in 1954 Texas had only 15,474.04 miles of railroad as contrasted with her all-time peak of 17,078.29 miles in 1932. Air lines, with eleven companies serving the state, are another

important competitor. As of August 1, 1952, forty-seven air-
ports served certified commercial air lines in Texas. Since
Hogg's time, all three modes of transportation have operated
under close though often hotly opposed governmental surveil-
lance.

Jim Hogg did not live to reap in old age the benefits of
his good work in the state's highest office. He clung to life
only a little over a year after the railroad accident which had
injured him. On March 3, 1906, he drove to Houston for a
few pleasant days at the home of his law partner, Frank C.
Jones. Here he hoped, if he could ever get well, to resume law
practice, surrounded by the love of his family plus the pleni-
tude and personal independence which his high principles and
political profundity had helped secure for Texans. But he
doubtless suspected that both his pleasures and his troubles
would shortly cease, for at his host's fireside he told how he
preferred to have his grave decorated:

"I want no monument of stone or marble, but plant at my
head a pecan tree and at my feet an old-fashioned walnut. And
when those trees shall bear, let the pecans and walnuts be
given out among the plain people of Texas, so that they may
plant them and make Texas a land of trees."

Next morning his daughter Ima went to his room to wake
him and saw that he was not breathing any more. When word
of his death went out, the whole state mourned. Newspapers
that had lambasted him in his campaigns for office now la-
mented his passing and paid him reverent tributes. A nut-
growers' association was organized for the paramount purpose
of choosing the best pecan and walnut trees in Texas to fulfill
his last request. Public schools and private citizens were urged
to plant memorial trees which could be budded from the final
selections. Vast crowds gathered to hear exhaustive lectures
about the art of growing, grafting, and budding the land's native nuts. No more wild pecan trees fell, as they had fallen for
almost a century, under the ax of the invading cotton farmer.

Today many a Texas home and playground is shielded
from wind and sun by wide-spreading pecan and walnut trees,
but Texans maintain that none produce with such abundance
and succulence as those whose seeds or buds came from the
two father trees shading Governor Hogg's grave in the Austin
cemetery.

VI

OUT OF THE DEPTHS

◇◇◇

1. Boom Towns

THE TOWN of Kilgore (9,638) in East Texas is a jumble of oil derricks with homes and business buildings scattered sparsely among them. The row of cafés, pharmacies, and shops which lines its main street is framed in a dense background of derrick towers. Its hardware stores are packed with huge oil pumps and other such oil-well equipment on sale. You don't come and buy this hardware to have it packaged with sticker tape for carrying away under one arm. Trucks with twenty- to thirty-foot trailers have to go along on every shopping trip.

The oil-well spacing regulations that govern younger fields do not apply to Kilgore. If a man owns a lot in the city limits, he may perforate it with wells as close together as the derricks will fit. This is because the discovery of East Texas oil antedates the regulations. Since Kilgore had begun to grow before the oil was discovered, store-owners along its main street lopped off the rears of their establishments to make room for wells.

Dwelling houses are surrounded by derricks, some with pumps at their bases, run by coughing gasoline engines, draw-

ing oil from under front walks and lawns. Back yards are
heaped high with oil-well pipes, some of them ten to twenty
inches in diameter. Thanks to its oil, Kilgore's city government
is debt-free and its fine public buildings have been erected
without bonds. Tax rates are extremely low, and the assess-
ments are based on estimates seldom more than 25 per cent
of actual value. Kilgore's yearly celebration is fitly called a
jub-oil-lee.

From Kilgore south, towns have boomed since the beginning of the twentieth century with many sudden gusts of
wealth from oil and gas. Most lasting has been the prosperity
of those along the Gulf Coast, which provides oceanic outlets
for petroleum products. While Beaumont and Houston mingle timber and agriculture with their seaport facilities, a more
purely maritime economy prevails in the three leading coastal
cities: Port Arthur (57,530), Galveston (66,568), and Corpus
Christi (108,287).

The Beaumont port serves four large railroad systems: the
Missouri Pacific, the Kansas City Southern, the Santa Fe, and
the Southern Pacific. Freight trains, when they come to Beaumont with cargo for ships, are in no danger of being held up
by bad weather. The boxcars can be rolled inside a brand-new
warehouse, where unloading and loading can be done rain or
shine with no danger of damage to the merchandise. Another
important asset of Beaumont is the Lamar State College of
Technology, a fully accredited four-year college that turns out
graduates skilled in the technical trades of the Gulf Coast.

In addition to its immense mineral and agricultural
wealth, the Texas Gulf Coast is blessed with a trade-winds
breeze, which brings cool air across the land from the waters
flowing south in the Gulf Stream. This breeze usually begins
blowing softly about mid-morning and gradually gathers
strength until at dusk it is often almost a gale, causing the
lofty foliage of oak, willow, ash, elm, cottonwood, pecan, and
palm to tumble noisily above the awful roaring of the Gulf.

Toward midnight the wind dies and the waves grow quiet.
This Gulf breeze keeps the coast refreshed despite its subtropical location, so that the mean annual temperature, from
the Sabine to the Rio Grande, is between sixty-nine and
seventy-nine degrees. The average yearly rainfall ranges from
about fifty-four inches around the mouth of the Sabine to
only twenty-seven at that of the Rio Grande.

All three of the leading coastal cities depend largely on
foreign trade for their prosperity. All three draw much from
oil and chemicals. All three have the slum life that seagoing
traffic ordinarily generates. All three have a complexity of foreign groups washed in from the sea: Italians, Germans, English Canadians, Irishmen, Frenchmen, Syrians, Dutchmen. All
three have a vibrance fed by the constant influx of new peoples
and fresh sea air. All three have fine fishing facilities and many
professional fishermen.

Port Arthur is the youngest of the three. It did not exist
even as a village under its present name until near the end of
the nineteenth century. Situated in a low flat swamp near the
mouth of the Sabine, it has a pleasure pier, but no beach. Its
wharves are served by a seven-mile channel. Its streets are so
low that rain water has to be pumped out of them. Fifteen
miles of dikes surround the city in the form of a U to keep
out water from nearby bayous.

In 1900 Port Arthur had less than 1,000 people living
within its city limits and its immediate vicinity. By 1910 it
had grown to 7,000 and by 1920 it had 22,251 persons. Early
in its history two large native Texas oil companies made it the
site of their refineries. They were the Gulf Corporation and
the Texas Company. Since then, the Atlantic Refining Company has built a refinery in Port Arthur and the city has become the home of many chemical industries.

Thus, unlike most Texas cities, Port Arthur owes none of
its growth to agriculture. It was born in the mind of Arthur
Stilwell, who needed a terminal for his Kansas City Southern

Railroad. It was nursed by oil and matured on the chemical industries, which depend for raw materials on petroleum and natural gas. The port's major docks are still controlled by the Kansas City Southern, Gulf Oil, and the Texas Company. Of course, some cotton and grains are handled at the port. There is also some lumbering, and iron and steel foundries have been built in the city. But the principal commodities are petroleum and chemical products.

Port Arthur is so devoted to oil that half its people sleep in the daytime. It is just a cluster of disk-shaped and spherical and cylindrical tanks, caught in a tangle of pipes and derricks, with patches of dwelling houses and shopping centers here and there. Since the wells and refineries must run day and night, everybody works in shifts. At regular intervals of two weeks or so, the houses display signs that read "MAN SLEEPING" through high noon. Thus, the natural rhythm of night and day is blotted out by the demands of the earth's black gold.

Yet Port Arthur has not the clamorous hubbub of older industrial centers. Its noises are muffled and steady, for the refineries are not machines with moving parts to bang and rub against one another. Except for a few auxiliary motors, they have no wheels to grind against axles or plunging pistons to throb under explosions in cylinders. They are just groups of containers painted white, black, red, and silver, varying widely in size and shape, all standing still as soldiers at attention. Actually, they are nothing but big collections of kettles, boiling oil rather than water, sorting out the vapors through their complexity of pipes and valves. Intense pressures are built up in them, but they are of the steady rather than the bursting kind. Day and night they roar, exuding little streams of cottony smoke. Their silvery pipes slither here and there, sometimes running like monster snakes along the ground, sometimes humping up, then plunging down again, sometimes rising fifty or sixty feet high, with little red ladders along their sides and little red platforms at their summits. At night they are lit up brilliantly with electric lights garlanding their edges as if they were Christmas-tree forests. They draw their crude oil from underground pipelines which often extend into the fields of neighboring states. Their finished products, being varied and having divers destinations, are carried away in trucks, trains, and steamships.

At the north end of Port Arthur's Houston Avenue lies the Texas Company's largest refinery, with buildings and tanks covering forty-eight hundred acres. It has within its area a network of railroads totaling twenty-two miles of track. Its tank farm has over fourteen hundred steel tanks, with a total capacity of over twenty-three million barrels. It manufactures its own cans, with capacities ranging from two ounces to five gallons, on its 105-acre Texaco Island near Port Arthur. It also has a marine division with tankers, motor ships, tugs, and barges. These Port Arthur enterprises alone employ some seven thousand persons.

Adjoining the western edge of Port Arthur, the Gulf refinery covers four thousand acres with Highway 87 running through the midst of it. Its big black pipes extend in clusters over the highway, high enough so that through traffic can pass underneath. Its ships come right up into the midst of its congregated storage tanks, in a channel dug for the purpose. Its twelve hundred tanks have a capacity of eight million barrels. It has its own complete fire department, electric power plant, medical staff, ambulance service, and radio broadcasting station.

The human relations of these major companies are wisely directed. They avoid labor troubles by keeping either ahead of or on a par with other plants in their wage scales and working conditions. The Texas Company has a $200,000 modern assembly building for employees, built of concrete, marble, and glass bricks. Its auditorium can seat twelve hundred persons. Gulf's Refinery Park, providing recreation for employees, has a clubhouse with bowling alleys and billiard tables, a library of current periodicals, and an assembly and dance hall. There is also a tennis court, lighted for night play.

After passing through the Gulf refinery, Highway 87 heads for the open sea and skirts some sixty miles of pleasure beach, with the Gulf's white-specked blue stretching endlessly to the left and an equally endless sea of prairie to the right. The green of the prairie is just a little lighter than the Gulf's blue and almost as monotonously smooth, without a house or a tree to break the straight horizon for miles and miles. When breaks do occur, they are usually caused by oil derricks or pumps. The entire coast is free to anyone who will park his car or set up camp on the wide expanse of damp sand along the shallow shore.

The sun commands this beach most of the time. The clouds, though legion, are newly formed. Together with the foam caps, they glitter in the sun. When they pass over, they throw shadows, but they seldom shield off more heat than would a shelter of thinly spread cotton lint. Like the Gulf waves, they move steadily toward the northwest. Progressing inland, they must eventually lose their substance, just as the waves, sliding shoreward, visibly decrease in size.

Swimmers assemble for miles along these wind-whipped shores. Manual laborers and office secretaries spend their spare time here. Ship-builders on vacation help their children make sand houses in the shade of outstretched tarpaulins. Tender teen-age belles with sculpturesque bodies swelter blissfully in the water's edge. The bright sun bores through their two-piece bathing suits to blister and tan their skins.

Oil derricks are built out over the water. Bolted to black wooden piers, they maintain an awful stillness while the breakers beat about their buttresses and bite deep into the earth around their sustaining pillars. The crews work in shifts on the derricks, just as they do in the refineries. All night they use electric lights to supplement the soft-shining moon and stars, which are often veiled by clouds. All day they endure the torrid sun, but there are joys to spice the roughest of their jobs. Breathing the high, salt-laden air of the space around their derrick tops, they can gaze down at thousands of near-nude vacationers and feast their eyes on graceful female forms. But the derricks are not continuous. Unlike those of East Texas, the Gulf Coast oil wells stand in groups, usually scattered over little mounds where underground salt domes place the petroleum within their reach.

Scattered along the shore are little beach villages built entirely for happiness and relaxation. Their houses are flimsy lumber boxes with wide, rambling screen porches designed to catch a maximum of fresh air. Resembling giant spiders, they stand on tall, gangly, stilt-like legs which keep them safe from high tides. A majority of them are owned by families who also have homes in the cities. Since they express the less restrained moods of their builders and owners, no two of them are alike except that they enjoy the same seaside environment. The wind is always in them. So are the roar of the Gulf waves, the smell of sea and fish, and the beauty of the unshielded sky. Most of the inhabitants in these beach villages are temporary. They come for a few sweet hours on Sunday afternoons, or a whole week end, or a dozen or more days at a time in the summer, to recuperate from their industrial worries, to swim in the breakers, to woo their women in the moonlight, to play canasta or bridge or chess over gate-leg tables, to fish, or just to sit on the porches and breathe the refreshing wind while the mosquitoes whine in vain outside the screens. Butane gas in big red tanks beside the houses furnishes flame for cooking and for warmth when the winds become too brisk.

As these families bring what they need with them, there are not many stores in the beachside villages. You cannot get drugs or drygoods there, except a few patent medicines, suntan lotions, and swimming trunks sold along with groceries and fish bait at the snack joints on the highway. The storekeepers stay through the winter, deserted by their public, sur-

viving the cold months with what little they can pick up from
through travelers, selling gasoline, sandwiches, and beer.
Meanwhile, the oil keeps flowing and the ships keep passing
by. The roar of motors is seldom remote along the coast, even
when the cities are far away.

Galveston communicates with the thin neck of land above
its island by means of two large ferry boats. The rides are free,
financed by the Texas Highway Department. The ferries are
named after R. S. Sterling, a forthright governor of East Texas
oil-boom days, and Cone Johnson, who played a leading role
in getting Woodrow Wilson nominated for the presidential
race. They ply the bay on twenty-minute cruises among bell-
ringing buoys and leaping porpoises. Steamships lie all around,
waiting to be loaded or serviced.

While Port Arthur is one of the state's youngest cities,
Galveston is one of its oldest. Her age is apparent in her ancient, stately homes, her huge trees, and her long rows of
oleander plants, whose seed was brought to the island in 1841.
Three major factors have prevented Galveston's keeping pace
with Houston in the race toward metropolitan greatness. The
first is the hurricane hazard. Gulf hurricanes damage the island
city badly. When a really destructive one hits, Houston becomes a haven of refuge. The storms reach Houston too, but
usually lose much of their force before they get that far inland.
The Gulf used to inundate Galveston in bad hurricanes, but
today a seventy-foot sea wall protects it.

The second important factor deterring Galveston's growth
is its island location. The island is thirty-two miles long but
only about two miles wide. The city's development is cramped
and its shape distorted by the surrounding waters. New homes
cannot be built without extending the costly sea wall. Railroads and highways cannot reach the city without long, expensive bridge structures.

The third obstacle to Galveston's development has been

a human one. Yet for a long time—until 1947—it seemed as impregnable as the geographical obstacles. The story of its hold on Galveston and its final removal shows how a seemingly profitable monopolistic business policy can harm the monopolist himself. Houston owes its growth largely to Galvestonian shortsightedness.

The story begins back about the middle of the nineteenth century, when Galveston, with a little over four thousand people, was the state's greatest city, being twice as large as Houston and almost ten times as large as Dallas. In those golden years just a century ago there came to the island city two good men, churchmen and merchants, upright citizens, believers in freedom, disciples of thrift. One was John Sealy, of railroad fame. The other was William Lewis Moody. Twenty years later came Harris Kempner to make three. Financially, the descendants of Sealy, Moody, and Kempner became the three leading families of Galveston. They were consistently and sternly moral. For generations the Moodys never used tobacco in any form. Like all good merchant tribes, Galveston's three big families kept alive the tradition of thrift. But their thrift was of the narrow, shortsighted kind. Being the most illustrious households on the island, they soon got control of its most precious asset: the port. As chairman of the Galveston Deep Water Committee, W. L. Moody got government funds to deepen the harbor before the turn of the twentieth century. Kempner's sons soon became part owners in the port's warehouses. George Sealy, Jr., was for many years president of the wharves. In the interest of thrift, they kept the wharf rates prohibitively high. Nothing could be done about it because there was no place else for ships to go.

At last Charles Morgan, himself in possession of a thrifty heritage on the steamship side, could stand no more. In 1873 he went to the Galveston Wharf Company and begged them to reduce their rates. When they refused, he set his wires to work for the transformation of Buffalo Bayou to a deep-water channel, and the ships began passing Galveston by, going to Houston instead.

For years the island city struggled to get the wharves under municipal control, to modernize the obsolete equipment and set the rates on a competitive level. At last, in 1947, with the help of an able wharf-manager named E. H. Thornton and the co-operation of W. L. Moody, Jr., the deadlock was broken. The wharves were turned over to the city. Rates were revised. Promotion and modernization were begun, and the port now carries on an active business. Its exports of cotton and grain led the nation in 1952, and it is now the world's largest shipping point for sulphur. More than 70 per cent of the sulphur consumed in the United States is extracted from the Texas Gulf Coast, and Galveston has the most modern equipment in the country for handling it. The Galveston loading tower can pour six hundred tons of sulphur into a ship per hour. Approximately thirty thousand tons can be stored in the port's two concrete bins. Some twenty sulphur vessels are loaded every month at Galveston, for, unlike farm produce, sulphur comes in the year around. Galveston also handles most of the tin ore for the Texas City plant, and hundreds of other commodities.

In the port, as in the city of Galveston, there is an atmosphere of mellow age. The harbor has been navigable and navigated longer than any other in the state. The pavements are old and broken. Their cracks and scars blend strangely with the heaps of yellow sulphur and the twelve million dollars' worth of new equipment: gantry cranes, warehouses, grain elevators, sky-scraping sulphur funnels fed by conveyor belts. The sulphur comes out of the depths in different shades, depending on the oil content of the underground formations. Some of it is a yellow as bright as that of candle flames. Some of it is more dusty, more subdued. All along the railroads it is piled in dunes, its smell mingling with the odors of great age to help give the port of Galveston a character all its own.

To the right of the freeway as you leave Galveston lies a heap of oil tanks, tall black funnels, intricate coils of pipe, smokestacks pouring out yellow vapors, and spigots exuding flame, steam, and sulphury odors. This is Texas City (16,620). When you approach it from the south, you see no sign of human habitation: no houses, no stores; only those nets of pipe and giant containers. After you pass through blocks and blocks of refineries and chemical plants, the human receptacles begin, with the humbler homes next to the industrial section.

Like Port Arthur, Texas City is a child of modern industry. Its early growth was due to the erection at its port of a Pan American refinery in 1933. This was followed by Carbide and Carbon Chemicals in 1938 and Monsanto Chemicals in 1943. Meanwhile, the nation's first tin-smelter, operated under a Dutch company's auspices to process Bolivian ores for the United States government, was begun at Texas City in 1941. Today, Texas City's Longhorn Tin Smelter produces twenty times as much tin as all the other smelters in the western hemisphere combined. Texas City is also a port of Seatrain Lines, a new concern that rolls whole freight cars into its ships and carries them, ready to ride the rails, to other terminals. This saves the transference of cargo from train to ship and from ship to train again.

One unfortunate circumstance, often neglected but nevertheless important to the future of the upper Gulf Coast, is the presence of insect pests. There is no sense in letting such an otherwise healthful area be marred by the whine and sting of mosquitoes, for instance. During World War II the region was temporarily free from this menace because the United States Army systematically eliminated it. But with peace the mosquitoes have returned. I have heard northerners say that they would love to come to Texas if it were not for the insects. Their elimination seems most readily accomplishable through some foundation or governmental agency. Private enterprise alone, with its screen-wire windows and its Flit guns, is not apt to make much lasting progress against these little spreaders of disease and pain.

Another region which owes its recent prosperity to metals and chemicals is that of Freeport (6,012), down the coast from Galveston. This region is fortunate in having large underground reservoirs of fresh water which are constantly being replenished by the heavy rainfall on the level ground southwest of Houston. A layer of porous clay absorbs this water and conducts it southeastward under more recently deposited sands so that it builds up considerable pressure beneath Freeport and vicinity. This plentiful water supply, in conjunction with the chemical content of deep formations and the Gulf's brine, has revitalized the whole area.

Sulphur-mining was begun at Freeport as early as 1918, but the real rejuvenation of this decadent old-south region came with Dow Chemical Company in 1940. In addition to the Gulf brine from which Dow extracts magnesium, its plants use about three million gallons of fresh water per day, all of it coming from wells drilled in the Freeport vicinity. Producers of many other chemical end-products, including plastics and gasoline, have since migrated to the area, so that all the little towns west of Freeport: Lake Jackson (2,897), Brazoria (776), East Columbia (200), West Columbia (2,100), Sweeny (1,393), and Bay City (9,427) now have a new lease on life.

But the city best equipped to profit from these combinations is Victoria (16,126), on the Guadalupe River, about seventy miles west of Bay City. First settled by Mexicans in 1824, Victoria has enjoyed successive influxes of affluent groups to form a highly cosmopolitan population: Germans, Irishmen, Italians, and Anglo-American planters. Being in the neighborhood of the Shanghai Pierce estate, it early developed a substantial livestock industry. When oil was struck on the nearby McFaddin ranch on December 1, 1931, Victoria already had an unusually large number of wealthy families.

Therefore, it did not suffer from the sudden fluctuations of a boom. Chemical industries have entered it with the same lack of convulsions. Its families have an average bank deposit of over eleven hundred dollars—the highest in the state—and it has begun preparations for a deep-water outlet to the Gulf.

From Victoria south, the rainfall slacks off so markedly that rice, which must be underwater throughout at least three months of its early growth, gives way to cotton, which does better on less moisture. Oak trees give way to scrubby mesquites, though live oak mottes are scattered in patches all down the coast. On the beach their branches are permanently bent northwestward by the wind from over the water.

Of the three coast cities, Corpus Christi is by far the most versatile, the most progressive, and the most promising. It also shares some of the advantages enjoyed by the large inland cities of the coastal plain. Like Victoria, it had a substantial fund of individual and family wealth from ranching and agriculture before its oil bonanza came in 1934. Like Galveston, it has a beautiful and extensive pleasure beach and rich historical traditions. Like Port Arthur, it has become a booming seaport for petroleum and petrochemistry. Like Houston, it is extremely well located. Being in the midst of a prolific cotton-growing region, it is as convenient to the lower Rio Grande Valley as Houston is to the black waxy strips below Dallas and Waco.

To these assets must be added the $125,000,000 Naval Air Training Center built in 1941, with its central station about ten miles from the heart of Corpus Christi. This is the world's largest naval air training base. It covers over twenty thousand acres of land. Known collectively as the "university of the air," it has six auxiliary stations in the vicinity.

Thanks partly to the naval base, partly to the Gulf breeze, Corpus Christi's environs are free from mosquitoes. The base has eliminated all still fresh water, which serves as breeding grounds for the larvæ. The Gulf breeze prevents invasions from inland swarms. This breeze is particularly strong in Corpus Christi, where it pours with refreshing force through all the little rambling bayside houses. It begins around eleven in the morning and rises to boisterous heights by dusk. It is cool, but not cold enough for blankets even at its peak, which it reaches around midnight. By morning it has usually died down.

Both the waves and the buildings of Corpus Christi's North Beach are smaller than those of Galveston and the upper coast. Galveston's beach faces the open Gulf, where the breakers are often too large and rough for actual swimming; Corpus Christi Bay, protected as it is on all sides, has smaller billows in which you can swim or float, yet at the same time enjoy the rhythmic rocking of the sea. Galveston's houses are aged and dignified. They are often two or more stories high, rising at a respectful distance from the shore. Corpus Christi has scores of little one-story cabins. Unlike those of the upper coast, which must rise on high legs to avoid the open Gulf, these bayside cottages stand low and intimately close to the water's edge, so that guests can step from them whenever they wish for an after-supper swim, or a bedtime swim, or a moonlight swim, or a midnight swim, or a daybreak swim, or a sunrise swim. Most exciting are the late-evening or night swims, when the palms and oleanders, of which Corpus Christi has a combined supply from the south and north, are bending and bowing in the gales, and the waves throw foam almost against the front porches. Most invigorating are the early-morning swims, when the trade-winds breeze is gone, the oleanders and palms are still, the waves are shrunk to little quiet moving lumps, and the impending sunshine makes the water's coolness welcome.

In many ways Corpus Christi's physical situation is particularly fortunate. Mustang Island, spanning the mouth of its bay about five miles out, forms a perfect land barrier, shielding it from the Gulf's more violent winds and waves.

Situated as it is in a concave curve of the bay shore, the city can spread indefinitely, its additions radiating like the folds of a fan to embrace ever larger lots and blocks. Its industrial area, lying along the docks at its northern and northwestern extremity, affords maximum convenience and minimum annoyance, for the Gulf breeze carries its noise, smoke, and dust away from the business sector and the beach playground. The swank residential sections, strung southeastward down the coastal curve, catch the breeze while it is clean. The ultramodern contours of its new air-conditioned buildings further emphasize the city's atmosphere of cleanliness. Beauty is cultivated both in the city's architecture and in its fine-arts movements: a symphony orchestra, a civic music association, a little theater with its own building, an art foundation, a fine-arts colony, and a writers' club.

Corpus Christi's many advantages have made it the fastest-growing city on the coast. Its population has approximately doubled during each decade since 1900. While its oldest elements date back to its establishment in 1839, over 90 per cent of it is less than half a century old. Almost three fifths of its manufacturing establishments were begun within the last ten years. This youthfulness and constant rejuvenescence bring to Corpus Christi a freedom from entrenched interests which other cities of its size seldom enjoy.

Because of its rapid growth, Corpus Christi faces both cultural and material problems. Its public schools, though in a process of rapid expansion, are bursting at the seams. Its public library, with only about fifty thousand books, is far too small. Its water supply must be enlarged. This last problem will presently be solved by the Wesley Seale Dam, to be built across the Nueces River just above where its mouth freshens the brine of Corpus Christi Bay.

Meanwhile, in West Texas the four young oil cities of Kermit (6,912), Odessa (29,495), Midland (21,713), and Big Spring (17,286) are growing fast from apparently bottomless petroleum pools. Secondarily, they rely on large-scale cattle-ranching. The principal boom towns in the Panhandle are Pampa (16,583), some fifty-two miles east northeast of Amarillo, and Borger (18,059), fifty-one miles north northeast of Amarillo. Pampa is the older of the two, with stable landowners in exquisite brick mansions. Borger is younger, more febrile, and more given to extremes. Born of oil and gas in 1926, it was a shambles of iniquity until the Second World War gave its industries a new market. Today, good city management has given it every convenience that a modern citizen can want: paved streets, copious electric lights, and first-class hotels, schools, and churches.

2. Houston, Queen of the Boom Towns

OF ALL THE MAJOR TEXAS CITIES, Houston is the most happily situated. Far enough inland to be relatively safe from hurricane hazards, she nevertheless enjoys seaport facilities through her fifty-mile ship channel. She has rice farms to the east, timberlands and diversified agriculture to the north, rich blackland cotton, rice, wheat, and truck farms to the northwest and west, the infinitely varied and productive Gulf Coast to the south, and cattle and oil all around. The land within two hundred miles of Houston produces more than any other region of the same size in the world. The climate provides a pleasant variety, combining Gulf breezes with frequent rains and semi-tropical sunshine. Winters are mild, and natural gas is almost as ubiquitous as air. Heating costs are therefore almost nil. Materials are so plentiful that houses can be built or bought for a song. Because the handling of Texas industries, based as they are on liquid fuels and volatile chemicals, requires more brain than brawn, the average intelligence quotient is high and incomes are accordingly substantial. Home-ownership is unusually widespread. Almost 50 per cent of Houston's residences are owned by their occupants, as compared with Boston's 24 per cent, Chicago's 31 per cent, and San Francisco's 35 per cent.

Unlike the towns in Northeast Texas's rolling timberlands, Houston is a city of straight lines, right angles, level surfaces, perpendicular columns. The walls of big buildings seldom slant or curve, but meet to make sharp corners and points. The streets are amply wide, most of them shooting straight over the flat ground, and free from streetcars. The trees, where left to stand in private yards or on the 3,300 acres of public park area, are erect and clean underneath. The city is spread over 163 square miles, with moss-hung groves interspersing the business centers. The tree trunks grow straight up. The moss hangs straight down. The land runs straight across, forming deep, cool, heavily shaded retreats where life is sweetly peaceful.

Houston's Main Street extends in a beeline for a little over five miles out of the southwest to bridge Buffalo Bayou in the northeast. At the southwestern extremity of this straight stretch stand two great showpieces scraping the sky: the Shamrock Hotel and the Prudential Building.

Covering fifteen acres of foundation area, with rooms originally decorated in sixty-seven shades of green, the Shamrock is a veritable palace, built for the pleasure of guests rather than kings, with eleven hundred air-cooled rooms and an adjacent garage accommodating one thousand cars. Originally conceived by the reckless, dreaming oil-well wildcatter Glen McCarthy, it has three public and nine private dining-rooms, a children's playground, and the world's largest outdoor hotel swimming pool.

Ice can be hardened in the public dining-rooms so that skating champions can entertain the eating crowds in the middle of summer. The children's playground has a slide, a see-saw, and swings for the free use of guest families. The pool, built in accordance with Olympic requirements, has nine lanes for swimming competitions and a towering spiral set of diving-boards. Such features have given the impression that only millionaires come to the Shamrock. As a matter of fact, its rates are fairly low, and many families of average means stay there.

When the Shamrock was built in 1949, it stood alone on the prairie. Now it is in the midst of the city's fast-growing grandeur. Across Main Street, several blocks to the east, the Prudential Building rises 318 feet into the sky. Like the Shamrock, it is a palace, but for employees rather than guests. It is the regional home office of the Prudential Life Insurance Company, serving seven southwestern states. For the health of its office workers it provides a health center; for their comfort and entertainment, large lounges and auditoriums; for their pleasure, a swimming pool. It is another monument to the wisdom of farsighted American business, which can envision a permanent profit from liberal dealings with both employees and clientele.

In front of the Prudential Building, over an oblong granite-rimmed fountain, is a statue of a family group: man, woman, and child, in classic nudity. The man half reclines, half sits, facing the east. The woman, facing west, is draped gracefully across his legs, her thighs rolling in long, smooth curves over his Herculean muscles, her ankle in submissive captivity under his hand, her breasts obtruding generously. The child sits upright between them, supported by their arms as they clasp its back in a mutual half-embrace. The statue was designed by Wheeler Williams of New York.

Bordering on the grounds of the Prudential and the Shamrock are three wide areas devoted to the hygienic, diversionary, and intellectual edification of citizens. They are the Texas Medical Center and Hermann Park to the right of Main Street as you go north, and Rice Institute to the left.

With more than a dozen separate health institutions on its 163-acre tract, the Texas Medical Center is a place where specialists and facilities for many different fields in medicine are situated in one neighborhood. The University of Texas, Baylor University, and many other religious and educational institutes have special branches in this center, whose buildings represent a total investment of some fifty-six million dollars.

Conspicuous among them is the University of Texas's M. D. Anderson Hospital and Tumor Institute, hailed by *Time* magazine on December 13, 1954, as the nation's finest, best-planned place of healing. Named after the rich Houston cotton-broker Monroe D. Anderson, who left his fortune for "good works" when he died in 1939, designed by Cancer Surgeon Randolph Lee Clark, Jr., and faced with pink Georgia marble, it combines the marvels of modern science with the comforts of a normal home. Its orderly arrangement of services cuts confusion to a minimum. Patients enter the building from the west only. Through the south door come doctors and nurses. The southeast entrance is for administrative personnel, the east for research workers, the north for students. All radioactive materials are handled within a vertical "stack" extending from the basement to the fifth floor. Operating-rooms are in pairs surrounding a central group of instrument and scrub rooms, and operations are relayed by television to students in special viewing-rooms. The air- and sound-conditioned private rooms and wards, none of the latter having more than four beds, are decorated in restful grays and greens with occasional relief from lighter colors. Wall pictures have backs shaded to harmonize with the hue of the wall, so that if they displease a patient they can be turned around. Each private room opens on a sun porch, and at the head of each bed is a radio outlet with a plug for earphones or an under-the-pillow speaker, so that each patient may choose entertainment according to his individual tastes without annoying anybody else.

Adjoining the Texas Medical Center on the north is Hermann Park, flat-bottomed and roomy, shaded by great spray-needled pines and huge oaks heavy with the usual beards of moss. It is the place where Houston goes for nearby outdoor recreation. Even its monkey house is air-cooled, for Houston is the world's most air-conditioned city.

To the left of Main Street as you leave the Shamrock going north is Rice Institute, where with the protection of spreading trees, the seclusion of laboratories, and the beauty of wide, quiet halls, scientists and students explore the deep unknown. Much space on the campus is devoted to natural beauty: profusely irrigated lawns; long, straight, close-clipped hedges penning in statues of great and ancient persons; trees of every conceivable variety. The driveways leading to the buildings are like tunnels whose walls and roofs are of growing foliage.

With roots as deep as those of its oldest oaks, Rice Institute refuses to be moved by the winds of economic interest, political whimsy, and public opinion which have made so many great schools miserable. With a student body limited to sixteen hundred, a ten-to-one student-teacher ratio, and complete freedom of research, it will not yield to the pressing demand for technically trained human robots. It prepares engineers, but they do not get away without thorough learning in the humanities. While other institutions turn out engineers with only four years of training, Rice keeps them for five, making sure that they get a broad general education as well as the specialized knowledge of their chosen fields. Students are admitted principally on a basis of high-school records. Since no tuition is charged, rich and poor alike may attend, their success depending purely on their ability and diligence.

The five miles between these retreats and the bayou are rapidly being filled with skyscrapers, not only along Main

Street but also along the streets which parallel it on both sides. So far, the highest concentration of big business buildings is in the last mile, next to the bridge. But the banging of steam hammers, the clamor of dredges, the clatter of rivet guns, and the moan of concrete-mixers can constantly be heard above the normal street noises all along these thoroughfares. Since the Second World War an average of over $100,000,000 per year has been spent on peacetime construction within Houston's city limits. Ground has been broken for a bank with aluminum walls; it will cover a whole block and will have twenty-four floors. This is only one from dozens of examples.

Although not spectacularly tall, Houston's buildings serve their purpose well. They were built more for business than for show. The tallest so far is the Gulf Building, which rises thirty-seven stories above the pavement. Facing each other across Main Street are Houston's two leading retail stores: Foley's and Sakowitz. Foley's, a general department store, has carried modernization to the windowless stage, obtaining all its light and ventilation by artificial means. Chutes and conveyor belts save the expense of room-to-room deliveries. Sakowitz is a clothing store serving everyone from "the common man to the common millionaire." It gives daily luncheons at a dollar a plate for working girls; while eating, they can view the latest dresses modeled by the store's selected beauties. Every Tuesday afternoon at the tea hour, Sakowitz holds a more elaborate fashion show. It also stages large shows, often in the interest of charity. One example was a Havana show, whose proceeds went to the Cuban-American Research Foundation for inquiry into the causes of tropical diseases. Sakowitz's twelve models were flown to Cuba for the purpose.

Passing under Main Street almost at right angles, Buffalo Bayou meanders east southeastward, first to become a barge channel, then to widen into the famous Houston Ship Channel.

Protected on all sides by land, yet on a level with the Gulf itself, this channel has made Houston the nation's number-two seaport, second only to New York in total tonnage moved. The public wharves, which lie along the channel's turning basin, can berth seventeen large vessels; the four privately operated terminals farther down the channel can accommodate nineteen, so that thirty-six ships can be docked in Port Houston at one time. The port's total foreign service alone touches two hundred and fifty other ports in eighty-five other countries.

With all the state's new industrial developments and agricultural diversification, cotton is still the largest-volume commodity that leaves the Houston wharves. It is loaded at the rate of about one million bales per year, half of it bound for some thirty foreign nations. Next to cotton in quantity comes wheat, then oil-well supplies, then milo maize, then gasoline, then carbon black, then lube oil, then sulphate of ammonia, then rice, then machinery. Commodities of less volume are too numerous to name. Note that, except for cotton, milo, and rice, these leading exports are industrial products refined and processed in Texas. At their destinations they are further molded and combined with other substances for human use, but they are by no means raw materials when they leave Houston. The principal imports also range from raw to finished goods. In the order of their quantity, they are coffee, crude oil, oil-well supplies, bags and bagging, newsprint, tubular products, canned pineapple, sugar, structural steel, and asbestos. Yet with crude oil ranking second in its list of imports and oil products ranking fifth and seventh among its exports, Houston is the world's largest petroleum port, as well as its largest cotton-exportation point. Principally, the city is an oil-refining center. The crude comes in; the gasoline and lube go out. Its large cotton business is due partly to the presence of numerous cotton presses which can prepare the bales for shipment at a minimum expense of space, time, and money.

Below the public wharves, lying along the channel's edges, is a seemingly endless array of factories producing foods, tools, and every conceivable means for increasing human power. They represent investments in excess of one billion dollars. A partial grasp of their vast scope and influence can be gained by naming a few of the companies interested: Consolidated Chemicals, Lone Star Cement, Arrow Mills, Southwestern Sugar and Molasses, Sinclair Oil, Champion Paper, Diamond Alkali, General Tire and Rubber, Hercules Powder, Sheffield Steel. Shell Oil has a large refinery near the channel, with its yellow emblem stamped on long rows of shell-white storage tanks. There are a hundred and fifty major plants in all, thirty-eight of them producing chemicals. These webs of columns, pipes, and ladders cover hundreds of acres and keep the humid air heavy with exotic fumes, odors, and smokes. Their oil and chemical containers, some of them disk-shaped, some of them long and cylindrical with rounded ends, lying like enormous sausages across the ground, some of them spherical, like little planets standing on thin metal legs, bubble up all around. Among them, show windows measurable in city lots rather than in feet display oil-well machinery as if it were fine apparel. Others display boats in the same way. Behind the windows, thousands of experts are hired. Sheffield Steel alone employs thirty-five hundred specialists. They turn out hundreds of different alloys for different purposes, testing each for its intended use by such bizarre methods as observing the color of the sparks it throws from contact with a whirling emery wheel.

Strung among these gigantic productive establishments are the private terminals. Behind and between them weave railways. Connecting the port with the city's six trunk lines, the Port Terminal Railway now runs new Diesel locomotives exclusively. While the bulk of Houston's tremendous tonnage is handled by boat and rail, much of it also leaves and comes by truck, especially for local consumption. The port serves thirty-four regular motor express lines and seventy other specialized carriers.

The hulls and spires of vessels going to and coming from the Gulf can be seen far beyond where the land hides the channel, so that they appear to be moving over dry ground, among cotton fields, cattle ranches, oil wells, refineries, and electricity lines. Their movement is as slow and steady as that of the black and white smoke pouring from the factories and refineries. Their quiet, gliding, uninterrupted drift contrasts strikingly with the fitful flit of birds in the air and the swift flow of auto traffic on the highways around them. Almost 4,000 ships and more than 10,500 barges plowed this Houston channel in 1952, carrying some forty-seven million tons of cargo worth about two billion dollars. More boats pass through these wharves, leaving their money in Houston, than through the Panama Canal. Twelve cents of every Houston dollar are said to be generated by the port.

Running roughly parallel with the bayou from the channel to the center of town, bearing much of the truck traffic for the city's business, is a wide, divided thoroughfare called Navigation Boulevard. Rife with noise, grease, and odorous vapors, the environs of Navigation Boulevard and the bayou constitute the major part of Houston's back yard, where the big wholesalers, warehouses, and manufacturers meet the boats, trucks, and railroad trains. It is always full of motion, directed and undirected, but motion just the same, loud, coarse, and heavy. Percheron horses pulling wagons loaded with watermelons clop among the trucks and buses. Cranes heap gravel in high piles. Many of the streets and alleys are paved with ancient red brick too rough for smooth and easy travel. But along them progress all the vigorous ugly jobs that must be done. All down the parking lots and block-long loading platforms, part of the vehicles line up while others pour through: railroad cars

Galveston: Part of the beach-front on the Gulf of Mexico.

Houston: Main Street, looking northeast.

by the dozens, trucks by the hundreds, automobiles by the hundreds of dozens.

Dealers in junk, used cars, lumber, and secondhand furniture come here in swarms to set up shop. Construction men sweat sparkling beads of perspiration that cool them as the breeze whips over their muscles. Buxom girls with robust legs and round hips frankly molding tight blue jeans work at service stations, ready to fill your tank, wipe your windshield, and sweep your floor board clean. Some of them willingly furnish comfort and entertainment for the sailors and other itinerants attracted by the port. Car hops in suggestive costumes serve fancy foods in an endless variety of combinations. Dust whirls around them, mingled with gusts of smoke from struggling trucks and big industrialists' cigars.

There is a brutish beauty in this conglomerate of rude power and newly gained sophistication, of whispering trees and monstrous machinery, of industrial co-operation and individual pleasure-seeking, of cool breeze and pitiless sun, of force and flexibility. Never before since the world began has there been such a mixture.

Running about a mile south of the channel, a fifty-mile divided highway with viaducts at all intersections penetrates Houston's business sector like a giant fork. This is the Gulf Freeway, connecting Galveston with Houston, built at a cost of $28,643,521. Its right-of-way was paid for by the City of Houston, Harris County, and Galveston County, and the construction costs were split evenly between the federal and state governments. As it nears Houston's business district, it divides itself, its four lanes becoming one-way feeder streets which intersect Main Street like fork prongs.

To the left of the Freeway as it enters Houston stretches the University of Houston's fabulous campus, principal living monument to the city's philanthropy, particularly that of the oil millionaire Hugh Roy Cullen. Contrasting sharply with the deeply rooted, heavily secluded recesses of Rice Institute, the University of Houston is shining new and growing fast in size, with wide fresh lawns and glaring masonry bare in the bright sun.

Having started as a technical junior college with a heavy enrollment of working people, the University of Houston has developed an organization admirably suited to its dual role as public-service institution and intellectual center. Its freshman and sophomore courses are in a separate division known as the Junior College. The junior and senior years are administered under the Senior College, and the graduate courses are kept together in the Graduate Division. Students whose abilities and resources point to their stopping school at the end of their sophomore year can do so without losing anything, since they can take away a technical degree from the Junior College.

At present the University of Houston's thirteen thousand students have fourteen permanent, air-conditioned buildings on a campus grown to 275 acres. Recent acquisitions further include a 160-acre experimental farm, large supplies of laboratory equipment from oil and chemical companies, extensive welding and machine shops where students learn by undertaking actual jobs, and a television station which offers regular college courses for credit over the air. The central building on the campus is the Ezekiel W. Cullen Building, dedicated by Cullen to his grandfather, whose words appear on a large slab near the entrance: "Nothing is so essential in a free government as the general diffusion of knowledge and intelligence of every kind."

West of Main Street, on the opposite side of town from the ship channel and the Freeway, lie the high-class residential districts. Of these, River Oaks is the richest, with palatial mansions in yards measured by the acre. More modest additions stretch to the west and north, cut off from the center of town by the belt of slums which fast-growing cities inevitably generate around their business sections. The Houston slums are filled almost exclusively with near-destitute Negro and Mexican families.

The large concentration of different enterprises and commerce has brought the best expressions of present-day culture to the Houstonian's doorstep: a public library system with almost four hundred thousand volumes, a fine-arts museum with permanent exhibits valued at more than three million dollars, two legitimate theatres, and a symphony orchestra of eighty-five musicians. Directed by the world-famous Leopold Stokowski and underwritten by the Houston Symphony Society in co-operation with the public parks, the Houston Symphony plays twenty-one free outdoor concerts each year in addition to its subscription concerts.

There are some drawbacks to life in Houston. Her high proportion of home-ownership, together with individualistic traditions, has caused considerable resistance to city planning. Public school grounds are crowded. Surrounding home-owners refuse to budge an inch. The railroads, shooting out in all directions, were laid before the bulk of the city was built. The streets, laid across them later, have some three thousand grade crossings.

Houston is implicitly, almost desperately, dependent on foreign trade. Every time the traffic slacks up a little, her businessmen get jittery and her publications issue frantic remedial recommendations. The city needs more end-product manufactures to consume the commodities of her processing plants and make them ready to retail locally. Too much of her industry is one-sided: it takes raw materials only part of the way toward human usefulness and ships them off to be finished in other lands. This weakness opens new opportunities for enterprise, however, and end-product establishments are growing fast. Even when such establishments become adequate, Houston and the other Texas boom towns will continue owing their principal growth and hence their basic traits to the nature of ancient formations underneath the Texas earth.

3. The Depths

To THE SUPERFICIAL OBSERVER, Texas is a gently rolling watershed, tilted slightly toward the southeast. But her underground structure is fantastically rugged. Situated at the meeting-place of the western highlands and the Gulf of Mexico, she is a funnel into which five important configurations or geological fabrics of North America converge.

The first of these configurations is the Gulf Coast, clothed in recently deposited layers of soft sand and clay, but internally puckered with dozens of salt domes. These domes were formed from prehistoric seas which, being cut off from the world's larger bodies of water, increased in saltiness with repeated evaporation. Eventually the brine thickened into beds of salt. Seemingly unfriendly, yet essential to the final triumph of living things, these salt beds sparkled for centuries under the primeval sun, growing thicker and bleaker as era followed era. Dust and ash from volcanic eruptions eventually covered them. Where there was water, the dust sank to the lake floor and formed coverings. These coverings became hundreds, then thousands, then tens of thousands of feet thick. The dinosaurs, notwithstanding their previous record for persistence, were unable to survive the changes. Their bodies, together with those of all other land and sea life belonging to their era, were buried deep beneath the reach of any drill shaft yet made.

But the salt was lighter than the silt that settled above it. When a thin place weakened the covering crusts, the weight of surrounding accumulations pressed down on the salt bed, causing it to break through the weak spot and ooze upward. Thus, an underground lump of salt was formed, too far from the top of the earth ever to see the sun again, but rising toward it nevertheless, squeezing the silt above into cakes of rock and lifting the surface into a mound. Around this mound, more silt accumulated. Its weight again pressed down on the salt at the root of the underground bulge, causing the lump to rise until its added bulk, plus that of the crusts above, again became equal to that of the surrounding earth. Again the surface of the earth was lifted into a little hill. Again the silt settled around the hill's base, upsetting the equilibrium, which could be restored only by a new rise of the salt bulge. Thus a massive column of salt, sometimes a mile or more in diameter, gradually forced its way toward the top of the earth, shattering the hardened layers of stone above it into splinters with cracks and gaps that radiated irregularly in all directions.

Yet the remaining fragments, especially at the summit of the salt dome, had been pressed into such firmness that they preserved their form even after penetrating chemicals had eaten out large cavities within them. These chemicals could not change the salt. They merely followed the contours of the compacted earth, which had been bent upward by the rising plug.

From rains and rivers, water seeped down to the surrounding salt bed. Being heavier than the oil from the deeply buried dinosaur and fish bodies, it forced this oil up the bent cavities into the cap rock above the salt dome. Fresh rains, sinking around the salt and generating steam from the earth's internal heat, increased the pressure. Natural gases exerted additional force, until the cap rock became taut: ready, like skin over a boil, to burst at the slightest needle prick.

In addition to these salt domes, the Appalachian Mountains reach deep into the heart of Texas: so deep that uneducated tourists do not know they are there. From Texarkana they shoot southwestward to the neighborhood of San Antonio, then turn west toward El Paso. Beyond the Pecos River they have been named the Glass Mountains. Few realize that these West Texas promontories form a continuous chain with the Ouachita Mountains of Oklahoma, the Ozarks of Arkansas, the beautiful Blue Ridge of Virginia, and other ranges in the Appalachian system. The reason is that part of the chain runs under the ground. Its East Texas links are buried beneath four thousand feet of earth. But their presence is proved by the oil well's drill. They form a huge pocket into which petroleum, seeping through the less solid silts and clays above, has drifted since the age of giant reptiles. Moreover, the unseen peaks function in a manner similar to that of the Gulf Coast salt domes, furnishing upward grades on which water pressure and expanding gases can force the oil into the reach of modern human craft.

The third geological fabric invades Texas from the north, filling most of the Panhandle. It is a high shelf of extremely rich soils known as the Great Plains. These lofty prairies have not the monotonous flatness of the Gulf Coast. They undulate so gently that the eye can span miles from wave to wave of wind-swept earth. As old-timers put it: "You can sit on your horse and see ten days in every direction." This is because the high plains were built in the open air by rivers and winds, rather than under the smoothing waves of a receding gulf. Running water and uninhibited gales rather than brine are still the principal carving and eroding forces of these high plains. Situated as they are about halfway between the two-hundred-million-year-old Appalachians and the sixty-million-year-old Rockies, they were not broken or wrinkled by the underground impulses that created these two great mountain systems. Just as the dinosaur era was cradled in time between those two upthrusting movements, the Great Plains are cradled in space between them. Those plains were therefore merely raised and quilted with tempest-driven sands until they attained an average elevation of thirty-five hundred feet above sea level. Shielded from the sea to east and west by mountains, divorced from humidity by altitude and distance, these Panhandle plains have never known much moisture. Since the rainfall is scant and the streams are small, there is neither the volume of water nor the swiftness of current required for fast fluid erosion. Mountain rivers grow sluggish when they reach these level highlands. Their waters grow warm, soak into the thirsty soil, and rise into the sun-scorched air. Their load of western dust is left to lift their beds and make them change their courses, spreading new earth far and wide.

The winds are violent, but while they take tons of earth away daily, they also bring dust from farther west and leave it piled about the low bluffs and gulleys. Thus, being relatively level, the high plains have kept much of their potential agricultural wealth. The drill bit and seismograph have now revealed that at enormous depths below these plains are mountain ranges whose age surpasses that of the Appalachians by untold millennia.

The fourth major geological configuration enters Texas from the southeast corner of New Mexico. Largely underground, it extends southward beyond the Pecos River Valley, eastward as far as the present city of San Angelo, and northward for unknown distances beneath the wind-borne heaps of the high plains. Although its occasional exposures, called "red beds," are ugly and rugged, it is rich in hidden wealth because for thirty million years before the Appalachian uplift and the dinosaur era, when the hills of Llanoria still ruffled the eastern horizon, these red beds formed the basin of a vast inland lake known as the Permian Sea. Dust from distant cliffs and refuse from extremely varied pre-reptilian marine life settled to the Permian Sea floor until in places it became twelve thousand feet thick.

The fifth geological fabric is that of the Rocky Mountains. Just as the Appalachians came into existence about the time when reptiles began to dominate the living world, the creation of the Rockies coincides approximately with the beginning of mammalian domination. The Rockies are too young, therefore, to yield much wealth within themselves, although eroded materials from their summits have done much for other areas, notably the top layers of the high plains and the Gulf Coast.

These five strips of differently composed earth—the Gulf Coast, the inundated Appalachians, the Great Plains, the Permian Basin, and the Rocky Mountains—all meet to embrace one another and tie themselves into an extremely complex gnarl of knots under Texas soil. For this reason Texas enjoys a richer compound of natural blessings than her neighbor states. Louisiana has the Gulf Coast and the inundated Appalachians, but no high plains or Rocky Mountains. Arkansas has some Appalachian chains, but most of them are above the ground and do not form oil pools. Oklahoma has fabulous oil reserves captured by underground mountains, and she shares the great plains with Texas, but she has no Gulf Coast, and the Rockies run far west of her. New Mexico has the Rockies, the Permian Basin, and the Great Plains, but she lacks the Gulf Coast salt domes and the vast oil pools that have gathered above the buried Appalachians.

◇◇◇

4. Early Oil

So EXUBERANT are the petroleum veins converging under Texas that oils and gases rose to the surface long before well-drilling, even for water, was invented. Extreme underground heat plus deeply buried peaks beneath Nacogdoches, in East Texas, had forced petroleum to emerge from the earth before the migration of Europeans to America. Indians bathed in the mysterious Nacogdoches springs and used the oil as an ointment to eradicate insect pests and skin diseases. At Sabine Pass, where the Sabine River flows into the Gulf, salt domes and hot gaseous pressures caused oil to leave the soil and form a thick scum over the water. By 1543 this scum had grown so firm that the Spanish survivors of the De Soto expedition, on their way back to Mexico, used it as calkage for their ships. Subsequent chronicles describe Spaniards greasing their cart wheels and anointing their bodies with East Texas oil.

Anglo-Texan colonists took up the tradition of the land. The strange eruptions became favorite health resorts among them. Frederick Law Olmsted, who traveled through Texas in the middle of the nineteenth century, paid a visit to one of these resorts. He describes it in his *Journey through Texas*, first published in 1857:

"Near the western limit of Jefferson County is the odd natural phenomenon of a 'fountain of lemonade.' The supply is abundant, and a barrack has been built for summer visitors, who frequent the spring for the relief of every variety of disease. . . . There are two springs, of cold, clear, acid, slightly astringent water, boiling with the outburst of an inflammable gas, having a slight odor of sulphuretted hydrogen. The overflow forms a pond of an acre in extent, which gives to the locality its name of 'Sour Lake.' Upon the banks and bottom is a deposit of sulphur. The approach to the rude bathing houses is over a boggy margin, sending up a strong bituminous odor, upon pools in which rises a dense brown, transparent liquid, described as having the properties of the Persian and Italian naphthas."

Yet the full potentialities of this fabled naphtha as fuel and lubrication for machines were far from apparent even to experts. The first piddling, pedantic step toward geological investigation began in 1858, when the Texas legislature authorized a survey of the state to be made by a state geologist, an assistant state geologist, and a chemist. Some specimen bits of rock were collected and placed in special rooms at the state capital, but the Civil War seriously interrupted the study. The geological rooms were used for making percussion caps.

The sample stones were thrown in heaps on the floor by frantic war workers who knew nothing of their significance. Their arrangement according to geological age was destroyed and the cabinet that housed them was badly damaged.

Their messages to science might have been entirely lost but for a plant-collecting New Yorker named Samuel Botsford Buckley, who became state geologist at the close of the war. He set the rooms in order and initiated other field trips, but personal contentions led to a second suspension of the work. About the only contribution Buckley made to the approaching oil age was his discovery—from reading a newspaper!—that kerosene was good for getting rid of roaches, ticks, and similar annoyances. He reported to the government that "its liberal application in the crevices of bedsteads or in the cracks of a room will expel the vermin."

While Buckley was sprinkling imported kerosene around his pebble collection at the state capital, an altogether different sort of exploration was taking place deep in the East Texas woods. Around the year 1867 a couple of hunters named Emory Starr and Peyton Edwards found themselves without water about fifteen miles southeast of Nacogdoches. In a creek where the earth was damp, they dug some holes into which water might seep during the night. Next morning the holes had the expected water in them, but upon its surface floated a thick layer of oil. Starr and Edwards knew that at Nacogdoches there were saddles and harnesses which could be softened if rubbed with this untasty scum, so they skimmed it off and took it to town. This encouraged the boring of shallow wells, seventy to one hundred feet in depth, from which oil was pumped or baled. The Nacogdoches drillers built a refinery, a pipeline, and a 2,000-barrel storage tank.

Then toward the end of the eighties a rancher named George Dullnig began selling oil from two wells of 275 and 300 feet near San Antonio. Other oil wells were drilled along the southeastern flanks of the Balcones fault line about this

time. Notable among them was one by Major Alexander
Beaton on his Gem Hill estate in the outskirts of Corsicana,
fifty-five miles south by east of Dallas.

Though little public attention was paid to these achievements, the state government re-established its geological survey in 1887 under a Washington and Lee University graduate
named Edwin Theodore Dumble. Dumble and his staff published a series of studies on the surface features of the state,
but their principal interest was in solid minerals: iron, coal,
copper, and building stones. They called attention to the sa-
line heaps under the Gulf Coast, but regarded them only in
terms of salt-production.

Neither Dumble's survey nor the oil seeps of Nacogdoches
and the Balcones area could keep up the people's interest in
the wealth beneath their feet. The focus of Texas life was agriculture and ranching. Projects private or public could gain
popular approval or support only by enhancing the success of
farm and range. Even during the brief term of their employ-
ment (1888–92) Dumble's researchers found it expedient to
call their work the "State Geological *and Agricultural* Survey."

But fortunately for the state's industrial future, farmers
and ranchers needed more water. Their demands stimulated
the art of making deeper holes. Drillers soon began sinking
their shafts over a thousand feet into the ground to tap flowing artesian veins. Then in 1894—two years after the abolishment of Dumble's survey—some water-well experts were drilling for the city government of Corsicana, fifty-five miles south
of Dallas. At 1,027 feet they struck oil. To prevent its con-
taminating the water they were after, they sank a casing
through the stratum and went deeper. Water was found at
2,470 feet, but the oil crept up the outside of the pipe and
forced its way to the earth's surface. Although choked by the
weight of the surrounding soil, it continued to flow until Corsicana's most enterprising citizens became convinced that
money could be made from it. They organized the Corsicana

Oil Development Company and went to work. By 1898 there were 278 producing oil wells in and around Corsicana.

But the real era of oil was created by the puncturing of a salt dome's cap rock near Beaumont at the turn of the twentieth century. The dramatic suddenness of this event combines with the world-wide magnitude of its consequences to give it an atmosphere of fantasy.

◇◇

5. Spindletop

In 1900 Beaumont was a dull, sultry little southern town. Her streets were of God's original dirt, muddy when wet, dusty when dry. Her houses were frail frames of pine, drafty in winter, suffocating in summer. Her days followed one another with uninterrupted, humdrum monotony. Her 9,400 inhabitants were devoted to cotton, rice, lumber, and sitting on the most comfortable public benches. Her leading citizens were conservative and benign. Her darkies were sulky and humble. Rich and poor alike were reconciled to the seeming eternity of their lot. Their only ambition was to live out their years with as little work as possible. Their only visible future was old age.

A few exceptional eccentrics popped up now and then, but they were generally dismissed as nitwits. One of them was a one-armed ex-lumberman of thirty-two summers named Patillo Higgins, who made himself obnoxious over a mound of sand four miles south of town. The level-headed folk of Beaumont could see nothing extraordinary about this knoll. Although approximately one mile wide and two miles long, running northeast and southwest, it was only some thirty feet high, with a summit almost as flat as the surrounding prairie. Local oafs, who had never seen anything higher, called it a hill. Gases and varicolored waters seeped from the earth near its base. Razorback hogs, suffering from ticks, came to wallow in the sulphurous, oily moisture. The strongly odorous slush always brought them prompt relief. A cone-shaped stump on a bluff nearby had caused early Neches River boatmen to name the place Spindletop.

Patillo Higgins had convinced himself that there was oil somewhere beneath Spindletop hill. He insisted that if a well were drilled in the vicinity, it would have the power of a magic wand, transforming Beaumont from a village to a city, converting all her farmers into millionaires. He annoyed and often disgusted the town's businessmen with what they thought were daydreams as vain as fairy tales. He planned a metropolis on the hill and named it Gladys City after a pretty little girl in his Sunday-school class. He even organized a company and offered stock for sale, with a picture of Gladys amidst derricks, oil tanks, and belching smokestacks printed on its letterheads.

But he could never drum up enough interest and cash for a successful well. He did entice three concerns to drill, but a five-hundred-foot layer of quicksand above the hidden salt dome stopped their bits before they reached any sign of oil. Geologists told him he was wasting his time. Oil had never before been found under seacoast sand. Corsicana, whose best wells plugged along at a production rate of some twenty barrels per day, was said to be as good as Texas would ever do.

At last Higgins made contact with a tall, bronze-faced Austrian christened Antonio Francisco Luchlich but subsequently Americanized as Anthony Francis Lucas. Being a trained engineer with considerable experience in salt-mining, Lucas could articulate his theories in convincing terms and command respect even from skeptics. He obtained a letter of introduction from Professor William Battle Phillips, geologist at the University of Texas, to two former operators at Corsicana named James Guffey and John Galey. Guffey and Galey joined forces with Lucas in furnishing money for a test well on the southern edge of Spindletop hill. They contracted Al, Curt, and J. G. Hamill, who had had experience at Corsicana, to drill the hole for two dollars a foot.

Al Hamill was a lean, gangly Texas youth with clear, deep-set eyes and a firm, thin-lipped, receding mouth. He and his brothers fully earned their pay. Day and night they struggled against the slush that rose with mysterious odors through the mouth of the descending pipe. For getting through the quick-sand which had stopped their predecessors, Lucas and the Hamills invented three novel devices.

The first was a system of pipes decreasing in size as the bit descended. Lucas would begin with a large casing, sink it as far as possible, then insert a smaller one through it to greater depths.

The second device was mud. Clear water had previously been used with success in the hard clays of Corsicana, but it lacked the thickness to cope with Gulf Coast sands. So Curt Hamill plowed up a mud pit and drove in some cows to stir up the water, which was subsequently pumped with better results into the drill stem.

The third device was the type of back-pressure valve already being used in pumps. Lucas was the first to think of using it in a well pipe. With its help, Curt Hamill's muddy water could be forced down into the quicksand and held there, making room for the bit while it worked.

The original rig from Corsicana was too flimsy to penetrate the cap rock of the salt dome under the hill. New equipment had to be ordered frequently. On January 10, 1901, a freshly acquired fishtail bit was lowered into the 1,160-foot hole. Before it had descended more than 700 feet toward the partly punctured cap rock, the oils burst from their weakened prison.

The Hamill brothers and their helper, Peck Byrd, barely escaped the first eruption. The new bit, plus the six tons of four-inch casing to which it was attached, plus swivels, blocks,

and tackle, were all hurled through the top of the derrick into
the sky. A high wind in the upper air sundered and twisted the
segments of pipe. When they descended around the derrick,
their momentum drove them like gigantic nails into the
ground.

There followed a momentary pause, broken only by Al
Hamill's words of wonder and regret at the loss of so much
good equipment. His remarks were interrupted by a column
first of mud, then of gas, then of solid oil, soaring hundreds of
feet above the broken derrick top. Soaked in muck, Peck
Byrd hurried to the Lucas home, but he was panting so hard
when he got there that he could do no more than point to the
derrick and shout "Look!" at Mrs. Lucas.

Mrs. Lucas phoned her husband, who was in Beaumont.
Something awful, she told him, had happened. A plume of
blackish liquid was hurtling through the derrick into the heavens. Half in horror, half in hope, Lucas leaped into his hack
and whipped his horse into a run. Standing on the floor
boards, he traveled the four miles from Beaumont to Spindletop at a speed that shook the frail vehicle until it threatened
to fall apart.

When he came in sight of the gusher, he could not hold
back his exultation. As the rumble of the oil column began to
drown out the thud of his horse's hoofs, he jumped from the
buggy, stumbled, and went rolling, sprawling, and somersault-
ing toward the sight. As soon as he could regain his feet he
rushed under the flood of falling oil and stood there like a man
in a shower bath, letting it soak through his clothes and so con-
vince him beyond a doubt of its reality. Then he backed off
and gasped: "A geyser of oil! A geyser of oil!"

A carpenter-farmer named Charley Ingals, whose home
was being drenched in the greenish-black shower, jumped on
his horse and thundered into Beaumont, yelling: "Oil on the
hill! Oil on the hill! And the damn stuff's ruined my farm!"

Half-shaved customers left barber shops and hurried on

foot down the road Charley had come. Merchants left their doors wide open and their stores exposed to thieving hands. In a few hours the news embraced the world by rail and wire. Crowded trains left Houston, San Antonio, Corsicana, Dallas, and all important points to the north, south, east, and west, bound for Spindletop. Hack-drivers got rich charging eighteen to twenty dollars per person for a ride from the excursion trains to the gusher.

Lucas hired forty men by night and fifty by day to keep the spectators far enough away from the well so that the Hamill boys could work. Levees were built to enclose the lake of oil around the well.

Over three thousand barrels of heavy, bluish-green petroleum were leaving the earth every hour. The noise was so deafening that no shouts, however loud, could be heard above it. The Hamill boys could make themselves understood only through signals. To protect themselves from the rainbow-creating showers of greenish mist, they used goggles, nose shields of gauze, and ear plasters.

For six days the fountain of oil spouted some three hundred feet into the air. Then the Hamill brothers rigged a trap to capture the stream and force it into a horizontal pipe, so that the roar subsided, the oil was harnessed for human use, and the applause of the surrounding crowds became audible. The capping of the well and its enclosure by a large sand-filled iron cylinder as a precaution against fire were accomplished just in time, for on March 3 some sparks from a passing locomotive ignited the lake of oil around the derrick. A wall of flame enveloped the vicinity and blackened the sky with smoke. The lake was consumed, but the well remained unharmed.

The land around the hill, formerly offered in vain for six dollars an acre, now brought hundreds of thousands. Those who happened to own it became millionaires overnight. Erstwhile conservatives indulged in dreamlike spending sprees.

Humble darkies were flushed with sudden opulence. Those who had scorned Patillo Higgins, whispering behind his back that he was fit for a padded cell, now revered him for the prophet that he was. One hundred grateful Beaumont citizens gave Lucas a solid gold watch charm larger than a silver dollar, with a gusher of inlaid onyx on one side and a big diamond in the center of a Texas star on the other.

Beaumont boomed. Her days were measured no longer by the monotonous march of hours, but by the pulsating tempo of fresh oil discoveries, with new gushers roaring in sometimes at the rate of twenty per month. Her population rose to thirty thousand in three months, increasing at an average of over two hundred people per day. Her houses were not built to stand this influx. Their frail pine walls waxed thin under the pocket knives of nervous investors from all over the world. Million-dollar oil companies moved into abandoned barns and shacks and built office desks from packing crates. No man had a hotel room to himself, for every nook was crammed with cots. Many were forced to spend their nights resting as best they could on pool tables and sawdust heaps from lumber mills. Tycoons and gamblers paid hotel rates for the privilege of sleeping in barbers' chairs, with their suitcases, often containing thousands in cash, padlocked to their legs.

The rest of the world was no better prepared than Beaumont to enjoy this fabulous bonanza. Shipping facilities were far from adequate. Oil became the most plentiful liquid in Beaumont, and therefore the least valuable. It could be had for three cents a barrel, while water cost five cents a cup. But enterprising industrialists and railroaders soon became aware of the opportunities afforded by this cheap new fuel. Its fluidity not only made it burn with unprecedented smoothness but also saved the strenuous labor of coal-shoveling.

Whereas the nascent market demand had first initiated the discovery at Spindletop, the unexpected magnitude of the supply now stimulated the demand. Within six months after the Lucas well came in, a pipeline had been completed to tide-water at Port Arthur, and two more were being laid. Their cost was from $5,000 to $10,000 per mile. Storage tanks holding from 600,000 to 700,000 barrels each were also built during these first six months of the oil era. Before the year was over, oil had begun replacing coal in Houston, Galveston, San Antonio, and several smaller towns. In 1905 the Santa Fe Railroad Company used 1,592,000 barrels of petroleum. The Southern Pacific was using 2,640,000 barrels a year. On its Galveston, Harrisburg & San Antonio line alone it had 204 oil-burning locomotives.

In addition to initiating the fuel-oil age, Spindletop inspired a new scientific discipline known as salt-dome geology. On March 28, 1901, the Texas legislature passed an act providing for the University of Texas Mineral Survey. Through a study of the muds turned up by the drill bit, previously unknown contours of underground formations were soon discovered. New salt-dome reserves were found all along the coast. Wells around Sour Lake were producing fifty thousand barrels of oil daily by 1903. Batson, forty miles northwest of Beaumont, yielded almost eleven million barrels in 1904. Near the village of Humble, fifteen miles northeast of Houston, farmers had traditionally saved their fruit orchards from freezing by digging little holes near the trees and lighting the jets of gas thus freed from the earth. In 1905 wells at Humble produced over fifteen million barrels of oil. One of the major Texas oil companies was subsequently named after the village. These fields were followed by Goose Creek in 1917, Hull and Barber's Hill in 1918, and scores of minor discoveries.

When the oil had been drained from the cavities and cracks in the stone crown of a salt dome, longer drill shafts pricked the deeper sands around the edges of the cap rock, tapping the source nearer its roots and blessing the locality with a second boom. This happened at Spindletop on November 13, 1925, when a shrewd organizer and student of the earth named Miles Frank Yount brought in a five-thousand-barrel-a-day producer at 2,500 feet, a depth more than twice that of the Lucas gusher.

By this time Beaumont was a thriving metropolis with about fifty thousand people. Her streets were paved. Her principal buildings were of brick, stone, and concrete. She had cultural gatherings and concerts. Men of wisdom came there to lecture. Great musicians came to play. One of them was the world-famous pianist Ignace Jan Paderewski, who had heard of Spindletop's gushers and hoped to see them filling the sky with their blue-green plumes.

But the gushers of the area were by this time tamely pouring their product into enormous pipes, which conveyed it unseen to tanks and refineries. However, Frank Yount had a plug opened under one of his derricks, so that the oil would spurt aloft in all its primitive glory and the illustrious guest would not be disappointed. With Paderewski in the car, Yount and his friends drove out to the field, pointed to the artificial geyser, and remarked that that well must have just come in. The stunt was expensive, but Yount's friends declare that the look on Paderewski's face was worth many times the cost. They regard it as nothing more nor less than the usual show of Texas hospitality.

◇◇◇

6. *The Alchemist's Dream*

MEANWHILE, oil fields were being developed in other regions of Texas. Ancient rock formations under the Red River Valley, raised into arches by uplifting pressures, had forced oil and gas to unusually shallow depths. A farmer of Clay County, drilling for water in 1902, struck oil at 150 feet. Since his livestock could not drink the stuff, he abandoned the well, but his discovery led to the creation of the Petrolia field, which produced more than sixty-six thousand barrels of oil in 1905 and was supplying natural gas for Dallas, Fort Worth, and twenty-one other North Texas cities by 1913.

The great North Central Texas rancher W. T. Waggoner named a shipping point after his daughter Electra and accidentally found oil instead of water in the vicinity. Drillers leased the land, and in 1911 a gusher started the Electra boom, whose peak production of 8,288,000 barrels came in 1914. It was followed by the Burkburnett boom, whose first big gusher came in 1918. Wichita Falls, the cow town first brought into prominence by the Fort Worth & Denver City Railroad, became the center of oil activity in the Red River Valley.

But the greatest of the North Central Texas booms came at the town of Ranger, about one hundred miles due south of Wichita Falls. It was started by a 1,700-barrel producer in 1917. By 1919 the Ranger field had yielded over forty million barrels of oil. In one year Ranger's population leaped from one thousand to thirty thousand. Unlike Beaumont, Ranger did not suffer from a slump in the value of her plentiful commodity. The national government's needs in World War I and the high quality of Ranger oil kept the price above four dollars a barrel. Ranger oil-field workers were paid as high as twenty-five dollars a day plus lodging and board. The Desdemona field, some fifteen miles southeast of Ranger, was developed in 1918 by small operators and reached a peak of over seven million barrels in 1919.

Just as Spindletop and the Gulf Coast held the petroleum limelight during the first decade of the twentieth century and the second decade was dominated by North Central Texas fields, the 1920's saw booms in the Panhandle and West Texas. In the early twenties the Panhandle became the world's largest source of natural gas. Stretching north and south for 115 miles with an average width of twenty miles, its pool yielded more than forty million barrels of oil in 1927. Subsequent production has declined and risen, with a low of sixteen and one-half million barrels in 1932 and a gradual increase to more than thirty-one million in 1947.

West Texas fields burst into prominence almost simultaneously about the middle of the 1920's. Interest in the area was stimulated by a University of Texas bulletin published in 1917, wherein the state's leading geologist, Johan A. Udden, pointed out the identity of the Glass Mountain formations with those of the Appalachian Mountain system and suggested that oil pools might have crept into the great basins north of them. This suggestion led to drilling in the neighborhood of Big Lake and a 200-barrel producer in 1923. The Big Lake area reached its peak production in 1926, with almost eleven million barrels of petroleum. This was the big year for West Texas oil. It saw the opening of fields in Crane and Howard counties, which later merged with others in Glasscock and Upton counties. Ira G. Yates, a rancher west of the upper Pecos, had a birthday on October 29 of this big year. His present was a 70,824-barrel gusher, a close rival of Spindletop. It netted him some fifteen million dollars all told, creating a field which rose to a peak production of almost forty-two million barrels in 1929. It was surpassed only by the Hendricks field, near the southeastern corner of New Mexico, which was also opened in 1926 and which produced over sixty-two million barrels in 1928.

All these West Texas wells drew from pre-reptilian sediments of the Permian Sea. Panhandle and North Central Texas oil came from even older sources. Yet the exploitation of these pools took place in a few years, inciting booms which followed the same rapid pattern. First came the spectacular gusher. News of it brought a sudden immigration of speculators, who hoped to make money from the oil. Then came swindlers, gamblers, and prostitutes, to make money from the speculators. The immigrants caused a housing shortage and feverish building activity, with million-dollar companies housed in five-dollar shacks. The habits, traditions, and moral standards of the permanent inhabitants were shaken and sometimes shattered. Peace officers were solicited to restore law and order. If production slacked off, the human predators passed on and ghost towns remained. If the oil kept coming, adjustments were slowly made. In no case was the place ever the same as it had been before.

A quarter of a century had passed and more than one billion barrels of oil had been drawn from Texas pools before Texans realized that there was a limit to their treasure and it had better not be wasted. Deliberate curbing of oil output began under the Texas Railroad Commission shortly after the Yates discovery.

But the real testing ground for conservation measures was East Texas, where reserves caught by the underground Appalachian ranges began to be tapped in the early 1930's. Previously, in the twenties, pools had been opened farther down the flank of these formations at Thrall, Powell, Mexia, and Luling. Then on October 3, 1930, a seasoned Oklahoma wildcatter named C. M. Joiner and familiarly called "Dad" by the hundreds of small investors with whose money he drilled, struck the southeastern edge of the largest oil pool ever discovered in the world to date.

Dad's well was near Henderson, forty miles north of Nacogdoches. Although it precipitated the usual boom, it came nowhere near revealing the vastness of the reservoir that fed it. It first ran fifty-two barrels in seventeen minutes, but its full daily production came only to 226 barrels. Then on December 19 another gusher, twelve miles north of Dad Joiner's well, caused a boom at Kilgore. Geologists could not believe that the two wells were drawing from the same pool. Heeding their advice, the major oil companies first showed little interest in East Texas and permitted small operators to lease the land between the Henderson and Kilgore fields. They soon saw their mistake, for subsequent drillings revealed that a single solid pool underlay Henderson, Kilgore, and five counties to the north and south, stretching over an area of six hundred square miles.

Despite the Railroad Commission's proration decrees, East Texas soon began giving the world more oil that it could use. Spindletop had done the same, but that was in the days of coal and wood, before the world's industrial genius had adjusted itself to the consumption of petroleum. It took much more to swamp the market in the thirties, when locomotives were almost exclusively oil-burning and automobiles had entirely displaced the horse and buggy. The general economic depression was an important factor, of course, and the petroleum surplus gushing from Gulf Coast salt domes and western fields contributed much to the ominous condition of the world market, but the principal immediate cause of the price slump in the thirties was the sudden inrush of East Texas oil, whose production was under the ownership of numerous small operators and completely without over-all organization.

As in the days of the Lucas gusher, the price of oil fell to ten cents a barrel, then to eight, then to seven, then to five. Still, East Texas operators defied proration, viewing it as a device on the part of major companies to gain a competitive advantage and invade their field. By August 17, 1931, the situation had grown so bad that Governor Ross Sterling issued an order to close down all East Texas wells. He sent the National Guard to enforce his decree.

Sterling was a former major-company executive, and many East Texans suspected him of partiality to the larger enterprises. This fact, plus the price jump that resulted from the shutdown, encouraged the production of "hot," or illegal oil. East Texas still exhibits scars from the ravages of conflict between embittered independent operators, who fought for survival against laws which they considered fatally unjust, and the inadequate representatives of the state government. On September 5, 1931, the field was legally reopened, with a limit of production set for each well. This stimulated the practice, already inherent in unbridled competition, of drilling more wells than were necessary for the most propitious exploitation of the pool. Whereas one well on every ten acres would have been plenty to drain the oil at a rate most suited to the pool's potentiality and the market's capacity, twice this many were often dug by rival owners. This doubled the expense of equipment and labor, but brought no additional benefits. The gravity of such extravagance becomes apparent when one considers that the average depth of East Texas oil sands is 3,700 feet and the cost of one well is $14,000. Yet nobody could be blamed, because since all the wells drew from the same pool, each owner was forced to produce as much oil as he could; otherwise his neighbors would drain it from under him and his investments would be lost.

Through the balance of 1931 and the two subsequent years, bedlam flourished over the East Texas pool. Production rose in 1933 to 204,954,000 barrels: more than ten times the yearly output of any other field. The national market's inability to absorb so much crude oil encouraged the building of numerous small refineries in East Texas. These local concerns, being within the field, in easy reach of the producers, and seeking cheap raw material, further stimulated the running of hot oil. Cheap East Texas gasoline became famous among motorists of modest means. The unpopularity of major companies made it possible for dishonest operators to steal their oil through secretly laid underground pipes. Disgruntled guards and landowners were disposed to protect or at least ignore the thieves.

At the height of the turmoil in 1932 the East Texas Producers' and Royalty Owners' Association was organized. Its purposes were to curb illegal practices, which were bringing calamity to large and small companies alike, and to help the Railroad Commission enforce proration. An emergency act of the Texas legislature in the fall of 1932 authorized fifty special investigators to help uncover the offenders. These investigators worked in shifts, day and night. Franklin D. Roosevelt's petroleum code brought more order to the field in the fall of 1933. The Interstate Oil Compact Commission, created in 1935, improved morale both in East Texas and elsewhere by substituting voluntary state systematization for direct federal control.

Little by little, the East Texas underworld was exterminated. Hot-oil runners and thieves were arrested. Their secret pipes were dug up and destroyed. A three-way equilibrium was gradually reached among small independent concerns, nationwide corporations, and governmental control. By 1938 more than 80 per cent of the field had been brought under the domination of major companies, and by 1941 only three independents were left in East Texas.

Successful oil-production, of course, involves big plans, big risks, big plants, and hence big companies. It is doubtful, however, that the companies have to be as big as they are. A study made at the University of Texas by Melvin H. Webber in 1947 showed that in 1946 over half of Texas's oil was produced by thirteen nationwide corporations, while some thirty-one hundred smaller concerns produced the rest. These thirteen major companies were controlled largely by the Rockefeller, Mellon, and Morgan interests. While their labor policies are often better than those of smaller enterprises, indications were that competition among them was not genuine. It is also probable that the depletion allowance, which permits oil men to deduct 27.5 per cent from their income in rendering their income-tax reports, is too large. However, while vigilance must be exercised without respite to maintain a true balance of competitive powers, there can be little doubt that conditions are better today than they were in the early days of the East Texas boom, when the parties concerned had not yet fully adjusted themselves to the nature of the new resources.

Mutual agreements now prevent the blind rivalry which caused such waste in the early thirties. Oil men now realize that since petroleum products evaporate rapidly, the best place to store them is their original underground reservoir. In its natural state, oil is usually mixed with more volatile substances. When a hole drilled into the pool relieves the underground pressure upon these substances, they evaporate rapidly to form gas. It is the expansion of this gas, often aided by pressure from underground waters, which forces the oil to the earth's surface. Consequently, the oil and the gas gush together from the newly drilled well. Early drillers, ignorant of the gas's contribution, syphoned it off in small pipes and lit the resultant jets to prevent larger conflagrations. Gas flares illuminated all the great fields day and night through the first three decades of the oil era. As the gas was burned off, the underground pressure decreased and one well after another had to be put "on the pump."

Today, however, the gas flare is almost entirely gone. Cylinders, some eight feet high and two feet or so in diameter, distill the gas and either direct it into pipes for human use or inject it back into the earth to mix with the original oil sands again and create fresh pressure. By cutting down the outlets of flowing wells, owners can keep the petroleum in its native environment until the time has come to use it. In some fields, notably in East Texas, salt water from neighboring wells is injected into the oil strata to keep up the pressure.

Texas's annual oil-production rose to over nine hundred million barrels in 1948, and has since maintained an average very near this figure. This is more than 40 per cent of all the oil produced in the United States. Along with the abundant supply of fuel and lubrication has come a mushroom growth of manufacturing. Texas has been transformed from an economic colony, supplying raw materials and farm produce for the east, to an industrial colossus with facilities for supplying every modern human need. She has her own petroleum-refineries, chemical plants, food-packing and preserving industries, cotton and wool mills, wood-product and furniture-making centers, factories for turning out finished airships and all kinds of transportation equipment, paper and printing industries. Her shops supply articles of leather, stone, rubber, clay, metals, and glass.

Of course, these are not all purely local enterprises. Like the oil wells and refineries, the chemical plants, vehicle factories, and food and textile industries are largely under nation-wide corporate ownership, whereas the shops supplying tools for these concerns are often locally owned.

The petroleum industry has become the most vital and pervasive feature of Texas life. More than 98 per cent of the fuel used by Texas railroads in 1947 was oil. Private motor vehicles in Texas used 1,758,004,515 gallons of gasoline in 1948. In 1949 over two thousand Texas motor buses consumed more than 23,000,000 gallons. Fourteen thousand Texas trucks burned over 155,000,000 gallons. Eighty-two per cent of Texas's farm land was cultivated with tractors burning various forms of petroleum fuel. One hundred and seventy-five of Texas's two hundred and one electric-power plants used gas and gasoline generators. Equally staggering amounts of oil and gas products were used by airlines, military installations, and manufactures.

One fortunate feature of Texas oil and gas is their wide distribution over the state. Instead of being bunched up in one spot, where they would benefit only one area, Texas oil and gas fields are spread all the way from the Pecos to the Sabine, from the Panhandle to the environs of Corpus Christi. Of the 254 counties in the state, only 63 are without a direct income from petroleum, and 53 of these have oil-producing neighbors.

But the use of oil and gas for fuel and lubrication is only the beginning. In the Middle Ages, alchemists dreamed of transforming the "baser metals" into gold. Magic words were

uttered, and smoky beings supposedly rose from infernal sulphurous depths. Specialists spoke in rumbling tones and made
their listeners gasp in wonder, but none of them could budge
the stubborn traits of iron, tin, copper, mercury, zinc, or gold.
Nor could ample amounts of these metals be had, for men
were aware of them only in spots where their solid forms had
been stumbled on accidentally.

When Anthony Lucas and his helpers aroused the Spindletop gusher, they did not know that they had evoked a demon
whose power could carry men farther than any former con-
juration along the road toward fulfillment of the alchemist's
dreams. By furnishing more generously than ever before a
wide variety of chemical compounds, Texas petroleum and gas
fields have conspired with human enterprise to catapult the
world into a new era more marvelous than any fairyland ever
imagined, where the supposedly fundamental substances are
no longer fundamental, where heavy things can be made light
and light things heavy at will, where solid bodies can be woven
from thin air and visible objects can be caused to disappear.

Yet strangely, now that we have the power, we no longer
aspire to make gold. For gold has never been more than a mere
symbol of wealth, and we have ceased to confuse the symbol
with the real thing. We prefer to make new substances which
serve our purposes better than gold. Some of these are obtained
from the most commonplace things imaginable, merely by
isolating already existent elements or recombining them in
new ways. The Celanese Corporation takes the air we breathe
and, by bubbling it through butane gas, produces an acid from
which numerous new materials can be made. Notable among
them is acetate, a fiber from a blend of acetic acid and cellu-
lose (cotton linters or wood pulp). It makes comfortable,
easily laundered, wrinkle-resistant clothes. Celanese has two
plants in Texas, one at Bishop, near Corpus Christi, and one
at Pampa in the Panhandle. Dow Chemical Company, with
a large plant at Freeport on the Gulf Coast, derives magne-

sium, a strong but light metal widely used in airplanes, from sea water. Polyethylene, a light, waterproof plastic with excellent electric-insulation properties, is now being produced all along the Gulf and in East Texas. It is made by submitting natural gas to one thousand atmospheres of pressure at a temperature of two hundred degrees centigrade.

By burning natural gas, thirty-seven Texas plants make carbon black, a basic ingredient of inks, paints, and rubber products. Large quantities of aluminum are now produced at Port Lavaca, Rockdale, and Gregory on the Texas Gulf Coast. Antimony now comes from Laredo; cadmium from Corpus Christi, Amarillo, and the Panhandle town of Dumas; copper from El Paso; iron and steel from Houston and the East Texas towns of Longview and Lone Star; manganese from Houston and Brownsville; tin from Texas City; zinc from Houston, Corpus Christi, El Paso, Amarillo, Dumas, and Dallas.

None of these processes disturbs the internal structure of existing atoms; they only modify the relationship of atoms and molecules with one another. The creation of entirely new atoms, achieved but not yet developed, opens broader horizons still. Thus, with ever increasing velocity, we are learning to mold our environment to suit ourselves, whereas in the past we had to make the best of whatever environment we happened to encounter. Real wealth actually consists of nothing more than this ability to control our circumstances: the tools, the knowledge, the consequent satisfactions.

While these strides are being taken on a world-wide scale, Texas has become an important focal center in their accomplishment because of her extremely diversified underground store of key substances, her strategic location, her well-organized research facilities, and the lively intellectual atmosphere generated by her religious and political movements.

VII

OUT OF THE HEIGHTS

◇◇

1. Safe Havens

THE BALCONES FAULT LINE is most distinct through Southeast Texas, where it runs roughly parallel to the bulge in the Gulf Coast crescent. Along this line, between Dallas and San Antonio, lie three comfortable cities: Waco (84,706), Temple (25,467), and Austin (132,459). All of them have absorbed the expansive atmosphere, the grandeur, and the spaciousness of the wide, rolling terrain. All of them bask in complacent self-satisfaction. All of them maintain a stanch moral conservatism. All of them are perennially invaded but never upset by Mexican influence from the south, plantation mores from the east, ranch life from the west, piety from the north, and oil wealth from all directions. Yet each gains a peculiar coloring from outstanding individuals who have been drawn there by real or imaginary attractions or who have happened by sheer chance to inhabit the land.

Waco is a city of long, straight streets and graceful, sturdy architecture. Founded in 1849, it is in many ways a city of ancient memories and deep-rooted beliefs. The Indians from whom it takes its name served for years as a buffer between the wild tribes of the west and the tame tribes of the east. They chose this basin where the Brazos descends the fault because it was traditionally considered safe from storms, earthquakes, and sudden floods of rain. Gulf hurricanes, while they harried the coastal plain, had not touched the Waco basin for many generations. No earthquake had disturbed it since the one that caused the fault, eons before the Wacos or any other human beings came. The Anglo settlers adopted from the natives this idea of the place's security, and Waco soon became a favorite haven for the faithful. Baptist farmers, long famous as lovers of safety for both their bodies and their souls, soon made it their gathering-place.

Today, its staid, solid Baylor University has the world's largest collection of literature related to Robert Browning. Here on the rolling Texas ranges, thousands of miles from Browning's homeland, scholars must come if they would study the British poet exhaustively—all because Baylor happened to hire Professor A. J. Armstrong, who happened to be interested in Browning. The Browning collection is in a special building of beautiful cream-colored brick, a stolid contrast—so say the Wacoites—to the foolish modernistic buildings now being erected in other cities, whose overabundant glass will surely shatter and whose thin walls will surely fall when another storm or earthquake comes along.

Baylor also is fortunate in having Professor Guy Bryan Harrison, who has accumulated the world's second-largest Texana collection; the University of Texas has the largest, of course. Harrison has specialized in dime novels and pocket books that have Texas settings or somehow relate to Texas. With the help of students and colleagues, he is adding to this special collection every day.

Temple, thirty-five miles south of Waco, has become famous as a hospital center because it happened to be well located for employees of the Santa Fe Railroad. This company's workers got together here, founded the Santa Fe Hos-

pital, and hired two exceptionally fine doctors, Arthur Carroll
Scott and Raleigh R. White, to supervise the place. With a
view to creating an institution that would treat patients as
human beings rather than as "cases," they established the
Scott and White Clinic, which has served the ailing from all
over the southwest. Also, besides the usual set of industries
hinging largely on agriculture, Temple has gained much from
the proximity of the army's Fort Hood, about twenty-five
miles to the west.

Although Austin has some two hundred and fifty manufacturing establishments, including the largest chili- and
tamale-canning factory in the United States and the southwest's biggest brick plant, it is principally an intellectual and
political center. Brilliant, crisp, silent, and clean to the point
of severity, it endures a glaring sun without the daily breeze
which refreshes the Gulf Coast and hits the higher hills above
the fault line. It is in rolling land, but its streets are straight.
The only turns they make are up and down. Square corners
and symmetrically measured blocks are laid over unsymmetri-
cal, hard-rocked hills. Some of the buildings are so white that
the sun, glancing from them, is almost painful. But every night
they glow in artificial moonlight from lamps on iron towers
165 feet high. North of the capitol dome, on a hill surrounded
by wide campus buildings, stands the University of Texas
tower, with its rows of oblong windows and its four clock
faces, tolling the hours, chiming the half- and quarter-hours.
It is one of the few places in the city which get as much breeze
as sun.

The skyscrapers of Austin stand along Congress Avenue,
which runs south from the capitol to the Colorado River. The
capitol dome is similar to the one in Washington except that
its outer walls are of locally quarried red granite and its sym-
bolic adornments carry different messages. A woman stands
on the dome's summit. She resembles the Statue of Liberty

except that instead of a torch she holds a lone star aloft, and instead of a scroll she carries a sword.

The towns above the fault, where the winds have sliced the ancient dinosaur land into lofty scraps that look like flat-topped hills, have a bleakness about them that indelibly affects their character. Unlike the Gulf Coast communities, they do not flourish, even when oil is found under them. They boom. They smoke. They build fine schools. They plant domestic trees to take the place of the land's stunted wild shrubs, but they never display the spontaneous exuberance that is apparent along the coast. Their smooth streets and neat brick structures are doomed forever to sit strangely, incongruously, in a devastated and devastating background. The high plateaus in the center of the state are still rather sparsely populated. Devoted largely to livestock and farming where possible, they are watered by dammed rivers with fine hunting and fishing.

On the northwestern edge of the plateau country lie Abilene (45,570) and San Angelo (52,093), two tranquil but prosperous towns with Central Texas livestock on one side and West Texas oil on the other. Like Lubbock and the central fault-line cities, they are devoutly religious, in tune with the finest human instincts and moral traditions. Unlike those of San Antonio, their people are predominantly Protestant fundamentalists. Their habits are steady and abstemious.

Abilene is famous as a family town: a place where families are drawn and held together, "while other communities," as Jack Yeaman puts it in *Texas Parade*, "are shattering and scattering theirs." Abilene has a higher proportion of sons in business with their fathers than any other Texas city. Yeaman describes it as "quiet and deep." This is due partly to geographic and partly to human factors. Until the oil era, Abilene's location held promise only for those who wished to lead a steady, pious life, to keep their sons and daughters safely away from the sins of the big cities—romantics in the best sense of the word. The highly religious population of the North Texas plains soon began to accumulate there in noticeable numbers. When a trend of this kind gets started in a town, other individuals with the same tendencies will go there, where they can share the satisfaction of their dearest desires with persons who understand and appreciate them. People with different proclivities will accordingly become discouraged and go elsewhere. Thus, the process is not only self-perpetuating but also self-amplifying and self-accelerating. Today, Abilene is a place where the majority of families go to church together, worshipping regularly instead of spasmodically. Nor do the children need to go away for a higher education. There are two colleges and a university in Abilene.

San Angelo has long been recognized as the southwest's leading wool center. The Edwards Plateau, extending southward toward the Rio Grande and southeastward toward San Antonio, is the state's largest sheep- and goat-raising area. To this steady source of income San Angelo has added much oil money from the Permian Basin, stretching westward. The Goodfellow Air Force Base, begun in 1941, has added still more impetus to catapult San Angelo from a town of twenty-five thousand inhabitants in 1940 to a city of over fifty thousand in 1950. Another important characteristic of San Angelo is its heavy Czech population. Originally farmers and ranchers, these slowly spreading Europeans have carried their habits of thrift, punctuality, and diligence into the city, to fill leading positions in its politics and give it an enviable economic stability.

2. Dallas and Fort Worth, Where Heights and Depths Converge

THE DELIGHTFUL EXPANSIVENESS of modern Texas life carries more impact than ever as one nears the Dallas–Fort Worth metropolitan area. San Antonio has an ethnic variety and a richness of memories that Dallas lacks. Nor does Dallas have the mammoth oil-refineries and smelly chemical plants of Houston and the Gulf Coast. But this youngest of the state's great cities more than makes up for such deficiencies. High and rolling, though not hilly, Dallas combines the local political harmony of Houston with the fine flying weather of San Antonio and the bracing air of the Panhandle. In comparison, Houston is a comfortable but lung-smothering dungeon of industry. San Antonio hems you in with narrow avenues and petty municipal politics. While the sky's unblemished blue is peculiarly abundant above all these relatively smokeless Texas towns, at Dallas you sometimes feel closer to the heavens than to the rest of Texas.

There is a spacious freedom in Dallas that you cannot find in most places. The Panhandle and the Red River Valley have the same wide horizons and high, rolling landscape, but they do not open to you all the cultural opportunities of Dallas. San Antonio has its own complex blends of culture, not much in touch with the world beyond the brush country. Dallas maintains close contact with the sophisticated east. Houston has its symphonies, its museums, and its literary conventions, but they hang flimsily to its sweating body, like inconsequential baubles, at the mercy of its monstrous whims, tolerated only as a prize fighter tolerates tails at a formal banquet. For Houston, art is a social obligation. For Dallas, it is a part of life.

This difference is not an incidental one, due to a chance gust of culture blown toward Dallas. Nor is it a fundamental one due to a lack of refinement inherent in Houstonians. It is a natural consequence of the equipment for physical subsistence available in the two regions. Houston, with its oil reservoirs, its ship channel, and its pipelines, serves established, corporate customers on a large scale all over the world. These absentee consumers are permanent, impersonal, and aloof from all human considerations such as art, music, and literature. They must have the cotton, fuel, lubrication, and chemicals that Houston can supply. They will pay for these things whether the Houston Symphony plays well or badly. Moreover, Houston is populated largely by people who must go there, whether they like it or not, to guide her precision instruments and drive her giant engines. She has cultural activities only because her more discerning citizens appreciate the fine arts and wish their city to keep abreast of others by indulging in intellectual luxuries.

Dallas, on the other hand, is mainly a banking and mercantile center. It draws its substance from individuals: money-borrowers, middle-class enterprisers, experts in management, retail customers, tourists. Such persons often have highly selective tastes. Their contact with Dallas is dictated not by any lasting need, but by their passing caprices. They must therefore be wooed with beauty, flattered with diplomatic skill, amused with fine drama and literature.

It is for this reason that Dallas has one of the world's most famous fashion shops, the nation's biggest bookstore, the southwest's tallest skyscrapers, the state's best-known and most imaginative exponents of theater, the land's most discerning critics of literature and music. They come to Dallas because they are appreciated here, and they are appreciated because they are needed. This is why the fine arts mean so much more to Dallas than they do to Houston. This is why Dallas becomes apoplectic when Houston or San Antonio or Fort Worth threatens to outshine her, while Houston feels the brunt of no major tragedy when a rival city gains a theatrical advantage. This is why James Street, writing about this highland metropolis for *Holiday* magazine in March 1953, entitled his article "Dazzling Dallas." Dallas has to be dazzling. If she did not dazzle, she could not live.

Dallas is a direct refutation of geographical determinism. The North Texas black lands called for a great metropolis somewhere in the area, but there is no earthly reason why it should be on this eroded shelf of limestone which John Neely Bryan selected as a site for his dream city. Hailing as he did from Tennessee and the environs of the Mississippi, Bryan had river boats in mind when he established Dallas. He thought the place would be a terminal for ships floating up from the Gulf and would at the same time attract land traffic because of a fordable spot just above their imagined docking-point. But the Trinity has always been too shallow and unpredictable for boats of any kind, to say nothing of ships, and bridges and railroads soon spoiled the special value of the ford. Frustrated, Bryan and his fellow settlers found refuge in superlatives. If Dallas could offer prospective citizens no physical inducements, then she would offer them personal and social inducements. She would astound the world with the extent of her inventiveness. Everything she had would be the biggest and the best.

Since Bryan's time, Dallasites have never been satisfied with modest projects. Whatever they do must be done spectacularly, with a transcendent sweep, for this is what impresses their borrowing and buying public. Inevitably, they are dreamers, for they must deal with intangibles. But hard knocks have taught them to anchor their dreams on careful factual study. Every time they make a move, they hire experts to ferret out the possible consequences of each policy. Thus Dallas has become a city where people go around with their heads in the clouds and their feet on the ground at the same time. The reasons for her success are unearthly: man-made; non-topographical. Her amazing growth can be explained only by the fact that a number of peculiarly farsighted and enterprising persons happened to accumulate within her borders. They drew others of the same bent, and their continuous materialization of seemingly extravagant air castles has proved self-stimulating.

In early Texas days, speculating planters, spreading northward from the Brazos, Colorado, and lower Trinity valleys, converged in the Dallas area with the pioneers and northern farmers who came in on railroad money. Here the three groups mingled their divergent views and achieved unusual intellectual breadth. But the two events which made Dallas supreme among the area's towns were: first, its choice as a point for the intersection of the north-bound Houston & Texas Central Railroad with the west-bound Texas & Pacific; second, its selection as the home of the district's federal-reserve bank. These events were due not to any physical advantage offered by the spot, but to the determined efforts of Dallasites, tendering inducements, pulling political wires, advertising their hopes.

A good example of how Dallasites work is the Texas Centennial celebration, held in 1936, just one hundred years after independence was won from Mexico. Either San Antonio or Houston would have been a more logical city in which to hold the celebration. San Antonio had the Alamo, Houston the San Jacinto battleground. Dallas had no such historical monuments. But the centennial was celebrated in Dallas because Dallasites went out and got their city designated as the place for it. Since then the yearly state fair has been held there, on the already prepared grounds which the centennial used. The only physical advantage of this location is its convenience for northern outlanders who might want to see something of

Texas without traveling all the way down into the deep south of Houston or the brush country of San Antonio. Dallas has thus become the state's show-window city, gravely conscious of her public-relations responsibility.

There has always been a tradition of community interest among Dallas businessmen. They know the importance of a vigorous, alert citizenry. They realize that they cannot have lasting success without prosperous stockholders, employees, customers, and competitors. When a new businessman comes to town, they will give him a chance to show his civic spirit. If he fails, they will ostracize him and, first by gentle, then by broader hints, encourage him to reform or leave. If he persists in his error, he will be sidetracked, boycotted, shamed until his dearest wish will be to crawl away somewhere and die unmourned. Large companies with branches in Dallas have learned this. On arrival, they devote generous sums and much time to cultivating the goodwill of those who make the city tick. The employees and representatives of incoming concerns are warned by the management before they enter Dallas that an important part of their duty is to become community leaders. Profits are sought not by lowering wages, raising prices, and choking out competitors, but by seeking to increase the quality of products and service: by maintaining high public esteem. The rapid growth of Dallas is a testimony to the wisdom of this farsighted policy. Her population has doubled since 1930 and is now well above half a million.

The spiritual richness of Dallas is derived partly from the fact that the area was originally settled by religious pioneer agrarians who appreciated the value of brotherly goodwill among neighbors. Farming as they did on a small scale, they acquired their necessities in small weekly lots and had a need for retail merchants. The environs of Houston, on the other hand, were first populated by prosperous planters who had their huge estates to look after and felt no need for close community co-operation. Their slave-cultivated plantations consumed imports in wholesale quantities and obtained them by the wagonload. Since then, both Houston and Dallas have attracted individuals congenial to their respective ways of life and have so perpetuated these original characteristics. Thus have human immigrations converged with geographical environment to give each of the state's leading cities its own peculiar character.

Like San Antonio, Dallas has a river flowing through it. But while San Antonio hugs its river with the loving embrace of long association, Dallas avoids its river, spreading everywhere except into the stream's vicinity, with long viaducts passing at a respectful height above it. This is partly because the early growth of Dallas took place late in the nineteenth century, when men, having begun to get their water from wells, barrels, and pipes, had no more need for rivers except to fish in on vacations and hurry over on bridges wherever business called.

San Antonio, born a century and a half before, became a city at a time when women still carried water in big pitchers from streams and natural springs. Whenever floods came, the ancient San Antonians retreated and let their homes float away or be temporarily inundated. After the destruction they returned to resume their life on the riverbanks, with the fondness and forgiveness that helpless dependence always brings.

But the floods of San Antonio were never so bad as those where the Trinity passes Dallas. The head of the San Antonio River, fed by natural springs, is within the city limits. Its waters, flowing beneath its bridges, are therefore comparatively clean and tame. By contrast, several branches of the Trinity converge near and above Dallas, so that its waters are turgid and often violent. Levees have therefore been built between the Trinity and Dallas's principal business and residential districts.

Unlike those of San Antonio, the skyscrapers of Dallas are jammed together, so that from a distance they look like those of a feudal city on a moat, with a few sharp spires and towers in the center and a wall of lower buildings all around. From a little closer, they appear as one vast heap of brick, concrete, and plaster, varying from dull red to cream and yellow, evenly streaked with signs and windows. This is because the central business section, a capsule of skyscrapers six blocks wide and some twenty blocks long running east northeastward from the north bank of the river, is encased in a sheath of railroads, warehouses, and factories. High in the air above the mass of sky-touching masonry looms a great winged horse made of neon lights, marking the headquarters of the Magnolia Oil Company.

At one time railroads entirely surrounded the Dallas business section, imperiling its traffic and choking its growth. Those living within the oblong scorned to move out of it; nor did newcomers relish the social opprobrium of setting up house "on the other side of the tracks." Now the northeastern end of the oblong has been released by the removal of the old Houston & Texas Central line. The former Central right-of-way has been replaced by the Central Expressway, a six-lane automobile thoroughfare with parallel service roads and viaducts to help avoid intersection hazards. Since no stigma was attached to living "on the other side of the highway," this change helped in more ways than one. Also, automobile transportation has made it possible for city workers to commute from relatively remote suburban areas. The ring of abandoned palatial homes remains along the railroads and the Expressway, now inhabited by human derelicts: harlots, booze-peddlers, drug addicts, men who have lost their fortunes and their souls.

But there is no single slum area or underworld in Dallas. Her sinners are few and far between. Nor is there a unified, coterminous Negro or Mexican district. The racial elements are more intermingled in Dallas than in any other major Texas city. Negroes do live on separate blocks or groups of blocks, and the Mexicans gravitate west of the business section, but people of other races are interspersed among them. This dispersion is visible also in the physical aspect of the residential sectors. Creeks and gulches cut Dallas up into relatively isolated fragments, so that while her business section is compact, girthed by a band of iron rails, the city as a whole is badly scattered.

In the northern edge of the business section looms the Republic National Bank Building, a huge blue-green prism of aluminum, with a sharp rocket-like point and a beacon light piercing the clouds almost six hundred feet above the sidewalk. It is one of the few large structures in which the true nature of new building materials is fully recognized. Before the invention, some seventy years ago, of steel frames for buildings, walls had to serve both as protective coverings and as supports for upper floors and roof. Today, steel has removed this latter duty. Yet most architects, bound by tradition, continue to erect thick walls as if they were still needed for supporting buttresses. Such walls, being extremely heavy, place an added load on the steel frame. They also take up space which could otherwise be put to human use.

The Republic National of Dallas relies frankly on its steel frame for support. Its outer walls are a thin envelope of upright oblong aluminum panels. Each panel has two four-pointed stars radiating toward its corners and sides, reflecting the sunlight in a diffused sheen from several different directions, giving the structure a soft bluish appearance. Although only one eighth of an inch thick, this wall, backed by light insulating and bolstering materials, is fantastically strong. The starry designs on the panels, in addition to mingling the sunlight so as to dazzle the spectator, give the metal a maximum strength per cubic inch. The windows, pivoted so that both surfaces of the heat-absorbing, blue-green-tinted "Solex" glass can be cleaned from the inside, are tested to resist a hundred-mile-an-hour wind combined with heavy rain.

Contrasting in form and hue with this and many similar new creations are the slightly older ones. The pale cream-colored Mercantile National Bank Building, with its lofty metal spire, is most conspicuous among them. With thirty stories and four huge clocks on its tower, it was the city's tallest before the Republic National went up. Now it runs a close second in the race of the spires.

Filling a block across the street from the Mercantile stands the main store of Neiman-Marcus, best described by George Sessions Perry's classic remark: "Neiman-Marcus is not just store. It is a state of mind." This fashion center of world-wide renown is an excellent example of how a few individuals with exceptional skill in some limited field can change the cultural complexion of an entire country. Before the Marcus family made their enterprise famous as a place to buy women's apparel, the fashionable aspirations of the west were all turned eastward. Women of Texas and all points between the central states and California who wanted and could pay for the best bought their dresses in Chicago. Women of Chicago bought theirs in New York. Women of New York bought theirs in London. Women of London bought theirs in Paris. Along with this habit ran the concomitant assumption on the part of literary and artistic snobs that nothing of permanent import could come out of the wild and savage west. All true beauty must originate in Europe, and in all the finer things of life, especially where they touched on feminine attire, Paris must set the pace.

But there lived in Dallas a brother and sister, Herbert and Carrie Marcus. Carrie married a financier named Al Neiman, and the three pooled their fortunes to form the Neiman-Marcus company in 1907. Neiman sold out his interests in 1928. Herbert died in 1950 and Carrie passed away childless in 1953. Herbert's four sons, Stanley, Edward, Herbert junior, and Lawrence, now run the store, with Stanley as president.

The refusal of this company to deal in faulty goods doubt-

less raises the standards of rival stores. Some competitors, of
course, can get some of the same materials. In order to out-
strip them, Neiman-Marcus has learned to "package" the
material differently, that is, to fit it into novel styles and
designs. One method has been to select some color or set of
stylistic traits which fits the region, the trends, and the season.
An ample stock of materials, accordingly dyed and cut, is then
procured. At the psychological moment, the color and accom-
panying characteristics are promoted. "Cactus Colors" were
thus advanced in 1936, the year of the Texas centennial. Then
came "Topaz" in 1938, "Magnolia Colors" and "Madrona
Brown" in 1939, "Chinese Colors" and the "Azalea" series
("Topaque" and "Silver Beaver") in 1940, "American Blue"
in 1941.

This last color shows the impact of World War II, in
which all four Marcus boys served. Stanley was chief of the
clothing section for the War Production Board. Appropriately,
"New Horizons" were launched in 1945. "Metal Grays" and
"Black Rose" followed in 1946. "Pheasant" was reputedly inspired when one of the Marcus boys saw a pheasant's picture
in a magazine at a dentist's office. There was "Thrush"
(taupe) in 1948. There were "Royal Theater" (purple) and
"Turkish Delight" (orange) in 1953.

Elaborate show-window and interior decorations accom-
pany the color promotions. "Say It with Carnations" was one
slogan in 1953. Neiman-Marcus joined the Colorado Carna-
tion Growers' Association in filling the store with 75,000
carnations and matching clothes and accessories with eleven
different varieties and shades ranging from the palest of petal
pink through deep reds, vivid yellows, and starch whites. In
1954 complete collections of summer fashions took a bright
look called "Singing Yellow." Hundreds of canaries hung in
cages throughout the store, flooding it with their songs, and
the whole place was awash with 175,000 daffodils.

New styles are given impetus at an annual fashion show,

in the first week of September, where some thirty-five models display on the average a million dollars' worth of jewels, $250,-000 worth of original dresses, and around $200,000 worth of fur pieces. Some thirty-five hundred tickets are sold at $12.50 apiece, and awards are given to designers, who attend from all over the world.

The result of these selling schemes is that the west's aspiring eyes are no longer fixed on Chicago, New York, London, and Paris. Indeed, people in those regions, as well as in the rest of the world, when desirous of a delightful male or female outfit, often turn to "Dazzling Dallas." Chicago has four hundred Neiman-Marcus customers. New York has fifteen hundred. London has twenty-six. Paris has thirty-two. Neiman-Marcus merchandise has gone to Mexico, the Panama Canal Zone, Cuba, Peru, Ecuador, Turkey, China, Bermuda, Australia, and the Dutch West Indies. Whereas most stores do over 80 per cent of their business within a thirty-mile radius, 50 per cent of Neiman-Marcus's customers are from outside of Dallas.

While the oil booms of Texas have had much to do with the store's growth, while the store has done much to save the state's new rich from making fools of themselves with gaudy adornments, while single sales have run as high as $127,000, the Neiman-Marcus management knows that in the last analysis it draws its sustenance from the common folk. More than half its customers spend less than $500 a year on clothes bought there. Since families in Texas usually attain their most substantial fortunes after their heads have passed the age of forty years, the low-price customers are not slurred as hopeless vagrants, but optimistically identified as "the younger set." They get just as much attention as does the store's more affluent clientele, with a special center, called the "Younger Set World," on the fourth floor.

Neiman-Marcus is also the place where a regional cookbook, *A Taste of Texas*, originated by accident. Back in 1947

Stanley Marcus asked his public-relations director, Marihelen McDuff, to write a letter for a few select friends of the store, asking them what they thought about somebody writing a Texas cookbook and whether, if they favored the idea, they would contribute a recipe. Through an assistant's error, the letter went out to the store's entire mailing list: more than three thousand persons. As a result, hundreds upon hundreds of replies poured into the public-relations office, flooding the place with recipes. Nonplussed at first, McDuff finally un-loaded this mass of good-intentioned correspondence on the home-economics department of the Texas State College for Women at Denton, just thirty-two miles north northwest of Dallas. Teachers and students at this college tested out the thousands of recipes and selected the best three hundred for the cookbook. Published by Random House, A Taste of Texas is now in its seventh printing. By July 12, 1954, it had sold 21,950 copies.

On the opposite side of the Mercantile from Neiman-Marcus is the Cokesbury Book Store. It also extends across an entire block, with openings on both Commerce and Main streets, and fills six floors. With a mailing list of sixty-three thousand, and with twenty-one thousand charge accounts, it sells books by mail to the entire southwest.

Extending across two blocks and facing the Expressway southeast of the business sector is the farmers' market. The other great Texas cities also have farmers' markets, but none like that of Dallas. Houston's market is closed in on all sides, so that the stale odor of decaying vegetables is penned up for all to smell. Few farmers come there, and the place has be-come little more than a wholesale enclosure for stuff shipped in from other states. San Antonio's market is used mostly by Mexicans. Fort Worth's is in a tough part of town and en-closed like that of Houston.

But the farmers' market in Dallas is open on all sides, to the world and to the winds. It consists of two broad sheds running the length and width of the blocks. Customers can drive their cars down the middles of these sheds. Facing outward along the sides are diagonal parking spaces for customers, and before these spaces, strung down the edges of the sheds, are the selling stalls, also open on all sides, where farmers bring their produce for direct sale to consumers. All through the harvest seasons the market is in a ferment. Farming families converge here from all over the southwest. The girls, mothers, and small boys do most of the selling, while the men and older boys are harvesting and hauling in fresh loads of okra, cantaloupes, squash, beets, cucumbers, onions, honey, apples, tomatoes, potatoes, lettuce, dewberries, collards, beans, peas, peppers, eggplants, muskmelons, watermelons. Farm family members take turns at the stalls. At night they sleep on pallets or cots stretched across the concrete under the bright electric lights and the free, odor-laden wind. They do not leave the produce until it is all sold. Prices are low because the land is fructiferous, competition is keen, and perishability is high.

Farther to the east, at the end of the main business streets, lies the Fair Ground where the State Fair of Texas, under the aggressive management of the great Dallas community leader R. L. Thornton, is held yearly. In the center of the Fair Ground stands the Cotton Bowl, biggest stadium in the state. Scattered around the bowl are other centers equally well known: the Fair Park Auditorium, where State Fair Musicals introduces Broadway shows and big-name stars in person to the southwest and originates new musicals that subsequently go to Europe and New York; the Hall of State, a museum devoted to Texas history; a model home built by Harwell Hamilton Harris of the University of Texas and his architecture students; the Dallas Museum of Fine Arts; Margo Jones's theater-in-the-round.

Margo Jones is a Texas girl who believes that every city of one hundred thousand population and above should have at least one professional theater. After thorough training, bolstered by a Rockefeller grant and a trip around the world, she found that modern electric lighting and space limitations made the new theater-in-the-round, where the stage is in the center of the room and the audience sits on raised seats all around, would be her best medium. Since 1947 she has directed just such an establishment in Dallas, with two hundred seats and a weekly budget of $2,225. Her actors work full time and receive a steady weekly check for $75 in and out of season. Over four thousand people see each of the nine plays which she presents every year. She herself reads at least one play each day. While she hopes for more and better contemporary plays, she has been most successful with the classics, particularly Shakespeare, Ibsen, and Chekhov. Hers is the first professional theater-in-the-round.

Her choice of Dallas as a setting for her experiment is in keeping with the city's character. "All roads," she says, "pointed to Dallas. It is practically in the middle of the country. It is in a new, fresh, rich, pioneering part of the nation; it is a city already rich in theater tradition; it had always been a good road town; there were many sincere theater lovers there who were anxious to help; I had gone to school near Dallas and had worked there; it was my home territory. . . ."

Fort Worth (278,778), just thirty-two miles west of Dallas, maintains close cultural ties and keen economic competition with these Dallas enterprises. Spiritually, Fort Worthians gain much from their proximity to Dallas. In a few minutes they can drive there over either of two broad thoroughfares, to shop, or visit friends, or attend banquets, or participate in other social functions.

Unless they wish, however, Fort Worthians need not go to Dallas for the essentials of relaxation and spiritual enrichment. Fort Worth itself has almost 5,500 acres of park and recreational area, with five large artificial lakes. Her public library, with over 216,000 volumes, comes nearer than that of any other major Texas city library to the ideal of one book for every citizen.

Unlike that of Dallas, Fort Worth's business sector has not been encased in railroads, but the Trinity hems it in on the west, north, and east. It rests in a finger of the black-land prairie which is formed by a U turn of the river. Its main business streets extend from the railroad depot on the southeast to the courthouse near an inward dent in the U. While according to the last census of manufactures (1947) Fort Worth was the nation's fastest-growing industrial center, it remains pre-eminently a city of small competitive enterprise. Of its 1,819 business concerns, including governmental and service organizations, 1,456 have less than fifty employees each. Together with Dallas, Fort Worth has derived a major gain from the large aircraft-manufacturing plants which have chosen the region partly because of its clear sky, partly because of Dallas and Fort Worth promoters.

Culturally and economically, Fort Worth supplies much that Dallas lacks. While Dallas might well be called "out where the east ends," Fort Worth has long vaunted the slogan: "out where the west begins." New York business and culture have always viewed Dallas as their western outpost; West Texas ranchers have likewise used Fort Worth as their eastern terminus, where they take their beef to be butchered or shipped and their children to see the sights. Hence, high-heel boots and ten-gallon hats are seen far more often in Fort Worth than in Dallas.

One of Fort Worth's most impressive annual events is the Southwestern Exposition and Fat Stock Show, held in January and February. The grounds stretch along Lancaster Avenue, which skirts the prongs of the U in the Trinity southwest of the business section. Here lie the stadium and the fair-ground buildings. Here lies Pioneer Palace, devoted to eating, drinking, and otherwise making merry. Here stands the Colosseum, with a tall brick tower in front and a life-size bronze statue of Will Rogers on horseback in a carefully nursed patch of prickly cactus, Spanish daggers, and other native plants on the front lawn.

West of the Colosseum lies the Fort Worth Fine Art Center. Brand-new in both materials and design, it is more than a mere museum. It is a place where Texans can come not only to see, but also to learn the meaning of art. Pictures are hung on movable mats so that an expert can display them at will as easily as slides can be flashed on a screen.

Near the art center lies the Fort Worth Children's Museum, also of ultra-modern design. John Ripley Forbes, founder of the National Foundation for Junior Museums, considers it the best and largest in the world. Besides the usual mounted animals and skeletons, it has a number of small live animals which the children can pet and play with, thus learning more about wild life and developing a feeling for conservation. It also has a planetarium, a "theater of the sky," for instruction in astronomy.

Higher education in this north central Texas metropolitan area is served by the two Protestant institutions, Southern Methodist University in Dallas and Texas Christian University in Fort Worth. With a little over sixteen students per teacher, these schools have gained fine reputations for high standards and active research and writing. Southern Methodist University is the home of the *Southwest Review,* a quarterly devoted to high-quality literature and high-caliber thinking. Situated as it is among schools which emphasize technical training, S.M.U. bids fair to become the great cultural university of the Southwest.

Underneath their rapid physical change and progressiveness, Dallas and Fort Worth maintain a deep spiritual devoutness equal to that of Waco and the other safe havens in the state's relatively isolated central and north central highlands. This staid and often fundamentalistic adherence to Christian principles is not due entirely to the character of agrarians imported by the railroads for mercenary reasons. The religious genius of Texas, while it received an important contribution from the railroad-building era, contains equally important strands of influence running back to the earliest days of Texas settlement. Also, while it finds its purest expression in the central, northern, and northwestern regions, it underlies and molds the moral, the political, the intellectual, and even the recreational life of the whole state.

◇◇

3. *Camp Meetings and Current Morals*

JOHN RABB was poor both in spirit and in worldly goods. His entire material wealth consisted of a few fire-tending and farming tools, a stew kettle just big enough for a family dinner, a spinning wheel, some clothes, some quilts, some chickens, some hound pups, some cattle, a sow with nine pigs, a wife with one child, and three horses named Flucus, Nickety Poly, and Tormentor. John Rabb was one of those first Texas settlers around whose graves so much glory has gathered.

His early days on the Colorado River were not glorious at all. Mosquitoes and Indians made him and his family miserable day and night. His wife spun thread galore so that the hum of the wheel would keep her mind off the menace of prowling savages. There was no hope of escaping the mosquitoes, but John heard that the Indians were less troublesome on the Brazos, so he decided to go there. Having no wagon, he loaded his chickens and inanimate belongings in a big bundle on Flucus's back. His wife and babe rode Tormentor.

He rode Nickety Poly, and the rest of the caravan walked.

At least, this was the original arrangement. But they had hardly got started when one of the kine stepped on a pig and crippled it so it could not longer walk with ease. John tied it to the bundle on Flucus's back. Because of its squeals, the horse stampeded and scattered John's property to the four winds, shattering the kettle and bashing out the poor pig's brains.

After days of vexing labor and anxiety, Flucus was recaptured and the remaining possessions reassembled. From then on, Nickety Poly carried the pack. But the grass was tall, and the tender-hearted Rabbs could not stand to think of their poor little hound pups having to hunt their way through it. John tied up the bottoms of a pair of old cowboy leggings or chaps, so that they formed two sacks, one for each of the smaller pups. With the pups in them, he threw them astride Nickety Poly's hips behind the pack and tied them there.

All went well for a while, then the pups got tired of their imprisonment and began yelping to get out. Alarmed by the noise, Nickety Poly bucked them off and galloped away. Again the family's necessities were gone: their bedding, their clothes, their chickens, their spinning wheel, and what was left of their cooking vessels. Until long after midnight they searched for the errant steed. They might have gone on hunting till doomsday had it not been for their blessed little rooster, tied by a leg to the spinning wheel atop the pack. How he and the other fowl kept intact on the pitching horse is a mystery, but they did, and the approach of dawn inspired the cock to make the woods ring with a rousing crow. The sound guided the Rabbs back to their lost goods.

At last they reached the Brazos and built a cabin there. John thanked God for answering his many prayers and bringing his family safe through so many perilous trials. All religions except the Roman Catholic were forbidden under Mexican law, but a Methodist missionary named Henry Stephenson slipped into the Rabb home one peaceful evening and preached a sermon. John Rabb became an ardent Methodist. He gave freely of his land and hard-earned cash for space to worship. After erecting one of the first saw and grist mills in Texas, he made generous gifts of lumber for church buildings. His faith was of the simple, straightforward kind which requires no philosophical elaborations and brooks no equivocating sophistry. He believed that God answered his prayers and warned him against impending dangers through dreams and premonitions.

The frontier permitted little time for study or contemplation, yet frequently presented difficulties which were hard to face without belief in a friendly, all-powerful God. There were scores of others like John Rabb in early Texas, drawn into an ingenuous faith by the contingencies of place and time. Mexico's prohibition of Protestantism, administered as it was with the inefficiency and lack of conviction that characterized her inexperienced government, had several unanticipated effects on Anglo-Texan religious sentiment. It set up a negative selectivity among immigrants from the United States. According to the Mexican colonization law, Austin's prospective colonists must agree to become Roman Catholics. Since most of the sects which made up the Anglo-American community were strongly anti-Catholic, this provision sifted out all serious religious thinkers and admitted only those for whom the prospect of taming a new country was more important than adherence to a particular church denomination. John Hawkins was an example of the latter. Writing from Missouri to his friend Austin, he said: "For my part I . . . know I can be as good a Christian there as I can here. It is only a name anyhow."

Only a name; but the dangers of life in Texas quickly threw these immigrants into conscience-searching remorse. They yearned for the security that they had left behind and the religious worship that had gone with it. Alone in this strange wilderness, torn from the tenets of their childhood

training, having sworn allegiance to a religion that they had
learned long ago to abhor, they soon repented of their pledge
and clung with unwonted tenacity to the scraps of church lore
which they had managed to bring with them. Clarified by
peril, their memories conspired with their imaginations to
crystallize and adorn these cherished bits of piety.

Mexican law required that all previously Protestant families re-enact their marriage ceremonies under Catholic ritual,
but no priest was provided for the purpose. Nor was there a
clergyman to join the young couples who found themselves in
love. They had to content themselves with legal bonds until
the proper church authorities appeared to solemnize their
unions.

Stephen F. Austin bombarded Mexico with requests for
a secular priest, but did not get one until 1831—ten years after
the Anglo-American settlements began coming into Texas.
Consistently and openly, Austin condemned the monastic
friars of Mexico. ". . . Those miserable drones," he declared,
"are the enemies of liberty, of human happiness, and of the
human race. Their convents, instead of being consecrated to
the sacred and immaculate religion they profess, are dens of
corruption, of intrigue, of infamy and vice. There never was
a people so dreadfully priest-ridden and enslaved by super-
stition and fanaticism as the greater part of this nation. The
clergy literally suck the blood of the unfortunate people."
Such comments as these, plus fifteen years of Mexican rule,
instilled in Texans a deep and abiding antipathy for all gentlemen of the cloth.

The priest who finally came to conduct the long-delayed
weddings was not of the type that might raise the colonists'
esteem of clergymen. He was Father Michael Muldoon, described by an eye-witness as a "bigoted old Irishman with an
unlimited capacity for drink." Although he sympathized with
Texas sentiment for independence and befriended Austin during the latter's imprisonment, his habits did not link him in

the colonists' minds with the best principles of Christian morality.

Meanwhile, a new religious point of view, peculiarly fitted to proselyting in the western wilderness, was sweeping across the United States. It rejected not only Roman Catholicism, but also the earlier Calvinistic faiths of Anglo-America. People had grown weary of the Puritan belief in a cosmic aristocracy with a brutal God who from the beginning had chosen only a few for sainthood and doomed the vast majority to eternal flames. The horror and heartlessness of such a doctrine failed to satisfy the blossoming optimism of the westward-pushing frontier. Nor were the scientific philosophers, with their Newtonian physics and their mechanical universe, in harmony with the free-will aspirations of the pioneer democracy. From European romanticism and American transcendentalism came the conviction that man was more than a mere machine and that the common folk merited a better fate than everlasting flames. Cosmic despotism gave way to cosmic equalitarianism.

The new philosophy averred that God's wisdom came not through a network of clerical and governmental dignitaries, but through the inborn intuitions of the natural individual. Christ's spirit infused the willing soul directly, without the intervention of priest or king. God expressed Himself through the untrammeled decisions of free men, and the best of earthly governments were therefore those which interfered least with each individual's freedom of thought, speech, and action. The frontier preachers scorned not only the graven images of the Roman church, but also all complex musical and artistic compositions, dancing, gambling, and other communal diversions. If a man lived simply and honestly, following the dictates of Christ's spirit, which spoke to him from within through the wordless language of pure unspoiled emotion, he might cross the river Jordan free of charge, without registering at any institutional toll bridge.

The best environment for salvation was not an artificially

decorated church house, with its graven images and its thick walls shutting out God's wind and rain and sunshine, but the virgin woods with their singing birds and fragrant blossoms. Texas possessed just such an environment, but until 1836 she remained at least nominally within the Pope's far-flung domain. The tardiness of her release gave the new faith ample time to gain momentum in the east.

Even before Texas independence, the harbingers of this romantic gospel seeped into Texas territory, secretly planting the seed of their new faith. As dissatisfaction spread among the Texans, the Mexican identification of church with state tended to weld political and religious issues into one. Since the authorities continued insisting that loyalty to Mexico involved membership in the Roman Church, Protestantism became an expression not only of homesickness for the blessings of the abandoned United States, but also of resentment against Mexican dominion. The acceptance of Catholicism was looked upon as a step toward submission to Mexican tyranny. To spread Protestant creeds was to oppose Mexico's political control. Protestant worship grew hand in hand with the spirit of revolution. The common man's informal religion was united in the minds of Texans not only with the promise of everlasting happiness after death, but also with personal freedom and well-being here and now on earth.

After San Jacinto, therefore, Protestant missionaries found an unusually fertile field in Texas. The interdenominational camp meeting, where preachers and populace assembled in God's forests under tents to spend several days at a time in undivided worship, had been invented by romantic zealots in Kentucky about the turn of the nineteenth century. By the time it got to Texas, its possibilities had been fully demonstrated and the technique of making it successful had been perfected. To Texans it became not only a vehicle for eternal salvation, but also a symbol of newly won independence and hence of contemporary political, social, and economic betterment. Besides, it appealed to many universal human urges, opened the door to many opportunities, and fulfilled many immediate needs.

The tents and the large assembly suggested an array of battle. Satan was the enemy, and Christ's sacrifice was the sure weapon. Worshippers could enjoy all the rewards of a martial movement—the thrill, the self-approbation, the sense of heroism—without the physical risks and injuries contingent on mundane warfare. The experience of camping out under the trees, uninhibited by roof and floor, appealed to primitive impulses and drew thousands who were seldom seen inside an ordinary church.

To the pioneer farmer, the camp meeting had still other, more practical values. It was his best social outlet, the principal link between him and the rest of the world. It meant a chance to strike bargains and make horse trades with near and distant neighbors. From the preachers and whatever itinerant lawyers might attend the meeting, he could learn what had been going on in the world for the past several months: what new political developments had taken place, how the price of cotton, corn, and hogs might rise or fall, where to find the best and cheapest new farming equipment. For his wife, there was a chance to visit relatives, to exchange the latest gossip, and to compare cloths woven at home with those made by the neighbors or bought in stores. For the sons there was a chance to enjoy the fragrant presence of young girls galore: to choose from a gratifying variety of beauties. For the daughters, there was a chance to be seen by eyes other than those of the family, the slaves, and the livestock. For all, there was a chance to break the monotony of domestic chores.

Camp meetings were generally held in the late spring or early summer, when the fields had been planted and there was not much work to be done around the farms. In Texas, where the summer heat is excessive, they were often more successful in the late fall, about the end of September or the beginning of October, after the cotton was all picked and the corn harvested. A meeting usually lasted a little less than a week, beginning about Tuesday or Wednesday and ascending to a climax on the subsequent Sunday. Weeks beforehand, preparations would be under way. As much of the livestock as possible would be turned out in the pastures, where it would need no daily feeding. Wagons would be greased and put in traveling shape because the meeting-place might be thirty or forty miles away, a whole day's journey behind oxen or mules. Food for the road and the days in camp would be loaded on the wagons: watermelons, cantaloupes, beans, corn meal, sides of beef, and slabs of home-smoked bacon.

Meanwhile, the preachers and church leaders would be preparing the camp ground. They chose a grove of large trees where there would be a maximum of natural beauty, because charming vistas and forest seclusion were vital for the high moods to be cultivated. Of almost equal importance, especially in Texas, was shade. It must be as near solid as possible. Remote depths of jungle were penetrated by the ministers in their search for protection from the sun. Coolness was essential, for the worship would wax warm.

Another prime consideration was water, both for drinking and for baptism. The vast crowds that gathered could consume thousands of barrels, especially as the climactic Sabbath approached and the Holy Ghost descended amidst throat-taxing shouts of "Hallelujah" and "Glory to the most high God!" Practical-minded leaders also saw to it that there would be adequate pasture land for the oxen, mules, and horses of the assembled adorers.

The camp ground had to be level, or nearly so. If sloping, it should rise toward the south, so that the preacher's platform could be placed on the north and the sun would be behind the congregation, for absolutely solid shade could not always be found. Lumber for the platform and seats, and slim trees for tent poles must also be obtainable.

Throughout the camping grounds the trees were trimmed up to a height of ten or twelve feet. All underbrush and weeds were cleaned away beneath them. The tents were arranged in a large oval, each tent facing the center of the grounds. The area within the oval was spaded until all ridges and knolls were gone. Low posts were driven in rows across the area and broad planks were laid on them for seats. Extending down the center of the oval from the preacher's platform to the rear tents was an aisle, usually about seven feet wide.

The daily exercises combined the delight of outdoor picnics with the uplift of continuous concentration on heavenly values. All rose at five or five thirty in the morning, to breakfast about sunup amidst family prayer and thanksgiving. Then came general prayer, led by the ministers. At about ten thirty the preaching began, often heralded by the clarion call of a trumpet, bugle, or home-made hunting horn. Then there would be hymns and spontaneous prayers. Dinner was spread on wide cloths before the tents about twelve thirty. A second series of sermons began about two o'clock in the afternoon and lasted till about sundown. After supper, services would be resumed and would continue sometimes till almost midnight.

The preachers hailed from among the Methodist, Baptist, and Cumberland Presbyterian churches of the area. The sermons were always dramatic, highly colored with flowery language, illustrated by graphic metaphors, and animated by strenuous gestures. Although tears and wailing revealed the intensity of emotion aroused, the ultimate message was primarily one of joy. Sinners were warned against the consequences of persisting in their wickedness, but the emphasis was on the glorious rather than the gloomy side of the Christian faith. Christ's kindness rather than God's severity was the principal inducement to conversion. Covert jibes were leveled at the more conservative sects brought over from the Old World aristocracy: the hard-shells, the Puritans, the lily-fingered gentlemen who deplored proselyting among the common herd.

The generous-hearted preachers of this new creed wanted hope for every living soul. Theirs was a democratic God, and hence a democratic mode of adoration. They naturally resented the cultured prelate trained in high-brow schools to which they had no access. They took pride in laboring with their own hands and using the farmers' vocabulary.

The camp-meeting hymn tunes combined the most beautiful melodies known to the farmers with a swift tempo and rousing rhythm. Their verve conspired with the forest environment to revive deep instinctive chords of communal ardor. The music was accompanied by invitations for sinners to step forward and declare their redemption by shaking the preacher's hand. After the hymns there were prayers designed to help these victorious individuals along their newly chosen paths of virtue. Ministers and church leaders would form circles in the aisle around the novices, pouring forth shouts of gladness at their new resolve, imploring mercy from aloft on their behalf. The spiritual enthusiasm often excluded all attention to physical needs and discomforts. A shower caught one camp-meeting in the midst of a sermon, but the congregation never moved. Drenched in rain, they continued their worship as if the sun were shining.

The Sabbath apogee was often punctuated with some dramatic stunt. Presiding Elder Francis Wilson thought of a masterpiece in 1843 at a camp meeting on Crow Creek near Corsicana. After a week of increasing enthusiasm, the Sunday-night service had closed with a worthy conclusion and dozens of converts fully confirmed. The lights were out, the prayers ended, the woods tranquil. The only sounds were of the breeze among the leaves and the deep breathing of the people asleep in their tents. Everybody thought the show was over.

At twelve o'clock Reverend Wilson had the fires rekindled and a fresh supply of pine knots heaped upon them. The flames leaped high of a sudden. The woods vibrated with the trumpetlike sound of a hunting horn. The people jumped from their beds and rushed out of their tents to see what was the matter. They saw the Reverend Wilson in flowing black robes, his gray hair falling in waves around his shoulders, his Bible in his hand, mounting the platform in the red firelight, reading: "And at midnight there was a cry made. Behold, the bridegroom cometh. Go ye out to meet him."

Thereupon, through speech and gesture, he enacted the great scene of judgment for the sleepy, half-dreaming multitude. He described Christ's second coming: how He would leave His place as mediator and ascend the judgment seat; how an angel would sweep across the heavens and blow out the sun; how the living would cringe, the graves would open, and the dead would rise; how the east would be bathed all at once in a new light brighter than a thousand suns; how Christ's throne would hang suspended in the sky, surrounded by throngs of flying angels; how all heaven and earth would exclaim: "He comes! He comes to judgment!"; how the wicked would plead in vain from dark depths below; how mountain rocks would fall on them, crushing them, smothering their shrieks, and hiding them from the face of Him that sat on high.

Eyewitnesses avow that the tones of Reverend Wilson's voice penetrated and froze their very bones. Moans from the camp ground matched the groans and wails of those doomed sinners whom he so movingly described. Homer S. Thrall, who was at the meeting, says: "The screams of the people drowned the preacher's voice and hundreds fell as though they had been shot. Many of these when they arose were rejoicing in the consciousness of the Savior's love."

Camp meetings continued in Texas until after the turn of the twentieth century, serving farmers primarily, but also drawing large groups from the towns. The extent of their influence is beyond measure. Many members of the older generation now living in the state had their philosophy molded at camp meetings during their childhood. Periodic revivals and regular Sunday worship keep the fires of faith victoriously ablaze today. The Baptists and Methodists lead all other Protestant denominations, but the Roman Catholic Church has not given way to their competition. It ministers not only to the original Spanish and Mexican citizens, but also to Irish groups brought in as settlers and railroad laborers, French farm workers who have moved into East Texas from Louisiana, and recent Anglo-Texan converts.

All the major threads of development in the texture of present-day Texas—Mexican relations, the Negro problem, railroads, ranching, and oil—have affected and been affected by the state's religious life. Where Anglos and Latins live side by side, the Roman Catholic loyalty of most Latins and the Protestantism of most Anglos accentuate the racial and economic lines of cleavage between them. The Negro problem has been affected differently because the pre-Civil War slaves were forced to abandon their original religions. Although both the Baptist and the Methodist denominations were split into northern and southern camps over the slavery issue, the southern branches opened the doors of salvation to souls both black and white, and the Christian ideal of universal brotherhood has done much to salve the wounds of the Civil War ordeal.

The vast majority of farmers brought by the railroads into North, Central, and West Texas were devout church members, mostly Protestant. Of course, the railroad companies had no announced policy of giving preference to any particular religious faith, but since they were financing the new farms, they endeavored to select honest folk of steady, abstemious habits who would be sure to meet their payments on the land. Protestant Christianity and the American distribution of peoples being what they were, those who most successfully met the railroads' standards and who could most easily emigrate were the religious farmers of the middle west: those same jay-hawkers who had earned the lasting hatred of trail-drivers. Like the earlier pioneers, these new Texans looked askance on gambling, strong drink, dances, and secular music of any kind. They forbade every exposure to temptation but did permit their young people to meet at "play parties" and hold hands while dancing around in circles to the chant of simple rhymes. Hence the youth of these areas, like those of the older communities, had no chance to participate in the artistic achievements of their European ancestors. Their access to those achievements was cut off both by space and by theological decree. They were limited to the most elementary form of ballad and the most prosaic, unadorned manifestations of visual beauty, for any kind of decoration, besides being economically unfeasible in these western wilds, was considered spiritually dangerous.

Moreover, as in the case of older Texans, their faith was bolstered by a strong equalitarian outlook. They scorned all aspirations to identify themselves with the self-styled elite by cultivating a fondness for deliberately complex musical, artistic, and literary patterns. Their basic philosophy prevails to this day, coloring the political and cultural life of the state. Their blanket endorsement of plain labor and their suspicion of all exclusively intellectual activities are well depicted in the answer that one West Texan gave when I asked him whether his town had produced any successful artists, writers, actors, or musicians. "No, sir," he said. "None ever had time for such things. All have tried to work and make an honest living."

The exigencies of ranch life have always hindered regular religious worship on the part of cattlemen. Cowboys ride too far and engage in too many tasks of unpredictable duration to be able to conveniently attend Sunday services. There being a scarcity of women on the old-time range, however, the spirits of Texas herdsmen have been softened more than once by marriage to the daughters of the religious farmers brought in by railroads. Thus have old antipathies been salved in a pleasant combination of feminine charms and Puritanical pulchritude. It is hence not surprising that there have been some intensely religious Texas ranchers. Christopher Columbus Slaughter, of North Central Texas, was among the state's most noted Baptists. Charles Goodnight, of the Panhandle, was another extremely pious Texas range man.

But as a general rule, the range man's attitude toward churches, like his attitude toward farm communities with their land taxes, oscillates between mute contempt and tentative, conditional acceptance. Rich ranchers, especially when their benevolence is lubricated by oil discoveries, have often made generous donations to the Christian cause without ever joining a church themselves.

Shanghai Pierce once built a church in his vicinity and engaged a preacher to come and dedicate it. But the preacher got his dates mixed and was absent on the Saturday appointed for the ceremony. The crowd assembled around the new church, and old Shang was there dressed in his Sunday best, but nobody knew where the minister was. They waited until the sun began to sink. Many of them had traveled miles on rugged roads to see the building dedicated. To avoid disappointing them, Shang finally got up and said a speech and dedicated the church himself.

The preacher came on the following Saturday, but there was no crowd. After lingering awhile around the empty building, he drove over to the Pierce estate and inquired what the matter was, saying that he had come to dedicate the church.

"The church?" said Shanghai. "Oh, that's already done. I dedicated it last Saturday."

"*You* dedicated the church, Mr. Pierce?" asked the preacher, astonished.

"I dedicated it," said Shang.

The clergyman then whispered that softly solicitous question which is so often on the lips of ministers: "Do you belong to the church, Mr. Pierce?"

Shanghai bellowed back: "Hell, no! It belongs to me."

Texas's religious institutions have profited much from

Oil-pumping derrick near McCamey, not far from the Pecos River in Upton County.

Humble Oil and Refining Company's Baytown Refinery, Baytown.

oil, not only through donations by rich constituents but also through direct ownership of property. The Merriman Community Baptist Church near Ranger happens to be located in the center of a large oil pool. During the Ranger boom some of its members sank wells in its two-and-one-half-acre lot. All proceeds went to the church, 85 per cent being contributed to the Baptist General Convention of Texas, and the other 15 per cent being retained for a new building on the premises. After the building was completed, $5,000 was given to the Southwestern Baptist Theological Seminary in Fort Worth and another $5,000 went to the Buckner Orphans' Home in Dallas.

But when it came to drilling in the cemetery, the church balked. One million dollars was offered in vain for drilling rights on this property. The church's firm refusal inspired a long poem by Will Ferrel. The Reverend W. T. Hamor and his congregation were described heroically "standing guard above the gravestones in a lot that's not for sale." Reverend Hamor declares that he could not legally have done otherwise, the donor of the cemetery having deeded it to the dead. Whatever the legalities, oil was never lifted from among the Merriman graves.

Much of the higher education in Texas stems from religious institutions. Among the leading Catholic schools are St. Mary's University, Our Lady of the Lake College, and the Incarnate Word College, all in San Antonio, and St. Edward's University in Austin. The Methodist Church has been connected with as many as eighty-two Texas schools, although only ten of these were operating in 1950, the most noted being Southern Methodist University at Dallas. The Baptists control eight Texas universities and colleges, of which the largest is Baylor, with a main campus in Waco and branches in Dallas, Belton, and Houston. Named for Robert Baylor, outstanding pioneer magistrate and preacher, and opened in 1846, it is the oldest institution of higher learning in Texas.

Dances are prohibited on its premises, and its women students are not allowed to smoke.

Shortly after Harry S. Truman took office as President of the United States in 1945, he was offered an honorary degree from Baylor as fortification for the formidable job of running the country and in celebration of the fact that another Baptist had made good. But Reverend L. L. Roloff of the Park Avenue Baptist Church in Corpus Christi preached a sermon on the subject, pointing out that Mr. Truman, despite his praiseworthy attainments, had been known to take a drink of intoxicating liquor now and then when tempted at social gatherings. Roloff deplored the fact that a Baptist school would even think of offering a degree to a drinking man. Other Texas ministers took up the cry.

The habits of Baptists who had previously received the degree, notably John Nance Garner and the Houston philanthropist Hugh Roy Cullen, had not been called into question, but in Truman's case the atmosphere became ominously hostile. At last the President wired his regrets that he could not go to Texas to have the degree conferred, but would have to take it *in absentia*.

Gambling, defined so as to include bets on such contests as horse-racing, is illegal all over Texas. Hence, while the King Ranch has produced some famous race horses, they must win all their laurels outside the state. Saloons selling anything stronger than wine at their bars are forbidden by state law, though hard liquor can be bought in package stores. The result is that clubs wishing to enjoy fine drinks in their exclusive skyscraper retreats must pay twice for their beverages: once in package form, then again at the table to reward the waiter who serves them.

On April 1, 1953, the Texas senate unanimously passed a bill outlawing "the display . . . of nude or partly denuded female figures in compromising and obscene poses," making the offense punishable by six months in jail or a $1,000 fine or both. The moral conscience of the state is thus shown to be as strong today as when it was first propagated by the Protestant enemies of Santa Anna, the competing representatives of the Roman Church, and the carefully selected recipients of railroad land.

The camp-meeting spirit is also apparent in the recreational activities of the Texas people. The forty-odd public parks under state control are equipped more for camping and picnicking than for the combination of landscape and night club which characterizes the world's famous playgrounds elsewhere. A salient example of how the state's natural recreational assets are affected by its religious principles is the way a primitive retreat in the shadow of the southern Gulf Coast's booming industries has been used by Texans.

Running parallel with the shore from the southern edge of Corpus Christi Bay to Port Isabel near the mouth of the Rio Grande is a sausage-like island, varying from a few hundred feet to more than two miles in width, named Padre after a Spanish priest who found refuge there from Mexican revolutionists in the early nineteenth century. Fronting the Gulf with 116 miles of almost solid hard-sand beach—the longest in the world—Padre Island is an exposed sand bar. The wind has done the same thing to its sand that it does to the Gulf water: rolled it up in waves. The sand waves are desert dunes, moving much more slowly than those of the Gulf, but always moving just the same, being swept sometimes gently, sometimes severely, sometimes brutally, by the everlasting trade winds. The sand is fine-grained and pure. Under the midday sun it sparkles, but in contrast to the foam caps and the clouds it is a creamy yellow which becomes first golden then gray as the sun sinks.

Arid and wild, Padre Island is never the same from one day to the next. Every wave, every gust of wind, gives it new contours, new æsthetic effects. Sometimes its low spots are covered by water, so that it becomes two islands, or three, or four. Then a fresh breeze will blow the water away and the island will become whole again. Sometimes a cluster of tough grasses will anchor the sand of a dune for a while, and the free dunes will bend around it or bank up against the grass until they cover it. There is no certainty here, no security, no hope of permanence. All is changing and unpredictable. The only thing you can count on is that there will be more change, more sun, more wind, more violence.

But the island's very aridity, poverty, and primitive insecurity give it a value all its own for Corpus Christi and the lower Rio Grande Valley. Two new causeways, one at each end of the island, make it possible for citizens to go there any time they wish. Travelers and natives can revert to semi-savagery there. A working girl, having slaved for weeks in the service of civilization, can bare her body to the lashing of the briny waves and the reviving ultraviolet of the sun. Under the velvet of freshly created clouds, glittering like the sea foam in the sunshine or tinted with amber and silver by the moon, she can become a cave woman again for a day, or an evening, or a night. She can live for a few hours as Eve lived before the serpent tempted her with the knowledge of good and evil. Working men can take their wives and children to go temporarily wild in the sand and sun.

Many attempts have been made to tame and develop Padre Island, to plant civilized settlements there. All have failed. If you set out domestic trees or palms there, the sand will starve their roots, the sun will suck out their sap, and the wind will blow them down. Hotels have been built between the Gulf shore and the dunes of Padre. The breakers have risen without warning to crash against their walls. Their joists have swollen. Their rafters have expanded and cracked in the damp air. Their roofs have caved in. They have been condemned.

Perhaps the man who understands Padre Island best—certainly the one who writes most beautifully about it—is a small, thin-faced, leather-tanned adventurer named Cash Asher. Cash is the public-relations director for the causeway and parks at the island's northern end and has filled a small museum on Padre with the odds and ends that he has found along the beach. In 1950 Cash had big ideas about Padre. He visualized it as a kind of Texas Miami Beach or Coney Island, with swanky restaurants and amusement halls of every variety. Carnival attractions, including a Ferris wheel, were set along the island beach at his suggestion. Plans were made to set up a tourist city on Padre. Five thousand acres of island land were put on sale. The county began building a park. The dunes were leveled. Buildings were erected. Three hundred and fifty thousand dollars was spent, but the returns were expected to make many promoters rich and pay for the new causeway in addition.

A festival for the opening of the causeway on June 17, 1950, was widely advertised. Expensive ceremonies were instigated. Rivers of people flowed in glossy cars across the causeway. For a while it looked like a success. The old island, which had foiled all efforts of the Indians, the Spaniards, and even the pirates of Jean Lafitte to inhabit its shores permanently, seemed to have succumbed at last to the advance of civilization.

Twelve thousand people crossed the causeway, but only about five hundred of them entered the new park. The Ferris wheel stood still and empty. Nobody registered at the little new tourist cottages that looked so promising to the promoters. The people did not eat much at the restaurants because they had brought their own lunches along. They scattered up and down the beach and camped.

Cash Asher could not stand to think of such great investments being wasted this way, of the food spoiling in the café kitchens, of the Ferris wheel standing so lonely, so motionless, so empty in the wind against the empty sky. So he asked the owner of the wheel to let him try an experiment. If he could have a hundred tickets to give out among the youngsters, perhaps this would start them to riding. Then others might come and pay. At least the wheel would turn for once. Cash handed out the tickets with a generous, anxious smile. Some of the children accepted the gifts politely, then passed them on to their friends, who passed them on to other friends, who tossed them into the water to see how long they would float.

Ferris wheels and carnivals were available everywhere else in Texas. On Padre the children wanted what they could not find in their home towns: a wild island beaten and carved by the waters and winds, like the one Robinson Crusoe lived on, where they could be pirates or warriors or whales and roam and swim at will over the billows and dunes. The Ferris wheel and the carnival attractions vanished, as have all those other things that once aspired to survive on Padre.

Large investments are now being made in the southern end of the island, both by private interests and by the lower Rio Grande counties of Cameron and Willacy. Plans for future development include picnic sites, fireplaces, tables, platforms, and other camping conveniences as well as more elaborate beachside establishments. Eventually, if muck can be dredged from the Gulf and spread over the sand, tame trees and palms might be made to grow on Padre. Such an undertaking, however, would involve a lot of money, possibly more than the people of Corpus Christi and the lower valley, and the tourists whom these places attract, would ever pay.

Possibilities for a tourist resort on Padre to rival those of Florida and New York are limited mainly by cultural factors. The strong religious piety of Texas prevents the sort of all-out pleasure-seeking which big-city spenders prefer for their vacations. Operating through the Texas legislature, this religious spirit has specifically forbidden the big-time sprees that opulent easterners look forward to on their vacations. Nor do the majority of Texas folk want this brand of recreation. Nor do the outlanders who seek vacations in the Rio Grande Valley and along the Texas Gulf Coast. Florida and Coney Island are situated to draw Wall Streeters, Washington big shots, and aspiring white-collar workers who save for years to have a one-week splurge. Texas is nearer and more attractive to the midwestern farmers of the Hamlin Garland stamp: frugal, close-fisted lovers of the great outdoors. Some of the more sociable Texas tourists, if in a sociable mood, will consent to shuffle-board or maybe even a little dancing, provided the music is suitable, an old-time fiddler and guitarist from among their own number being preferred. The dancing will be square, of course, possibly with a few Latin steps mixed in out of defer-ence to the locality. But most of those who come to Texas prefer the comparatively sinless and more invigorating pur-suits of swimming, fishing, and camping under God's wide-open sky. Padre Island, with its beaches facing both the Gulf's great breakers on the east and the smooth waters of the Laguna Madre Bay on the west, with its 272 different kinds of fish, with its continuous resistance to all efforts at permanent de-velopment, with its stiff winds from the Gulf Stream and its stiff laws from the state capital, suits them fine.

<><><><><><><><><><><><><><><><><><><><><><><><><><><><><><><><><>

4. *Politics and Flour*

THE IMPACT of religious convictions on Texas politics has been most incisively implemented by the appalling career of Wilbert Lee O'Daniel, a flour-salesman from Ohio who went to Fort Worth in the latter 1920's. His success stemmed from five main sources: first, radio, a new tool of communication for which his personality was peculiarly fitted; second, his ap-peal to deep-seated human urges; third, his own background and religious convictions, which harmonized with the precon-

ceptions and tastes that rural Texans had acquired from a
rigidly limited background of intellectual and artistic experience; fourth, his brilliant showmanship; fifth, the trend toward
industrialization brought on by the fuel-oil era.

Texas had known skillful politicians before O'Daniel's
time. There was "Farmer Jim" Ferguson, who, after being im-
peached on nine different charges, succeeded in getting his
wife elected to the state's highest office and exerting his will
through her, thus giving Texas "two governors for the price
of one." There was Archie Parr, who, by voting illiterate Mexicans in Duval County of Southwest Texas, erected and be-
queathed to his son a regional machine which functions to this
day. Texas has also produced many high-caliber statesmen
who have played major roles in the national arena, notable ex-
amples being John Nance Garner, Sam Rayburn, Tom Con-
nally, and Jesse Jones. More recently, Oveta Culp Hobby, wife
of an elderly ex-governor, has become a member of President
Eisenhower's cabinet. But none can match O'Daniel in evok-
ing the old camp-meeting spirit and profiting from the suspicious attitude toward specialists which it has engendered. Nor
have any of them changed the political picture within the
state the way O'Daniel has.

O'Daniel was a super-salesman, with all the super-salesman's brilliance, alertness, boundless energy, dauntless audacity, keen social sense, flair for showmanship, aptitude for spontaneous speechmaking, and proneness to jump at snap conclusions. Before he entered politics, his entire experience was
in selling flour, a product that everybody needs, but which affords almost no variation in quality. Flour is flour, no matter
what the brand or source. As long as the wheat is fresh and the
mill clean, it will make edible bread.

In peddling such a commodity on an open market, the personal charms of the salesman are of prime importance. All
other criteria for choice being absent, the customers will prefer the brand connected with the most attractive countenance.

They cannot be blamed, since there is nothing else on which they may base their selection. Competing advertisers can insist with equal vanity on the excellence of their respective brands. Success will go to him who does it in the most affable fashion, whose voice is the most pleasant, whose approach is the most varied and spectacular, whose statements are most in harmony with the customers' preconceived ideas.

In voice, affability, appearance, and personal tact, O'Daniel excelled all. His voice was clear and rich. It covered a vast range of inflections and pitch with captivating naturalness. He was of average height, firmly built, thick in the chest, and tending toward a robust plumpness. His face was smooth, handsome, and hardy-looking, with round cheeks and large, frank eyes.

An example of his skill at seizing every chance to capture public applause is his manipulation of his own names, Wilbert Lee. In Ohio and Kansas he had used the first name only, but on coming to Texas he reduced it to an initial and let the limelight fall on the second name, Lee, which might remind some southerners of their great Confederate general. To help their memories, he told a touching story. His uncle, a northern soldier, was wounded and lost in the War between the States but subsequently adopted and nursed back to health by a southern family. Impressed with this hospitable act, the flour-salesman's mother had christened him Lee out of reverence for the immortal Robert E.

In 1930 O'Daniel's peculiar aptitudes had gained him the position of sales manager for the Burrus Mill and Elevator Company in Fort Worth. At that time a group of hillbilly musicians was advertising Will Ed Kemble's furniture store over a local radio station. The arrangement was fortunate because Kemble also sold phonograph records. These gave the musicians access to new tunes. They practiced regularly at Kemble's store, learning the ditties from those records which enjoyed the widest sale.

When the abilities, ambitions, and financial needs of Kemble's troubadours outgrew his resources and advertising needs, they asked the Burrus mill to sponsor them. Sales manager O'Daniel approved their program among sundry other publicity schemes and paid them little attention until they began to garner fame. When the popularity of their music caught his attention, he decided to supplement their radio programs with tours of the state in a sound truck. Later, when other duties called the regular announcer away, O'Daniel began announcing the program himself and captivating the audience with his agreeable personality. Since the Burrus mill had named its product "Light Crust Flour," the team called itself the "Light Crust Doughboys," and many a Texas home soon rang daily with the rousing announcement in O'Daniel's excellent radio voice: "The Light Crust Doughboys are on the air!" The concluding words of this high-spirited greeting blended with a mellow, melting grace into the lilting tones of a fiddle and several other string instruments playing a swift series of simple melodies mingled with blues songs, recent popular hits, hillbilly ballads, hymns, and old-time play-party chants.

O'Daniel had never lived in the hills, but this did not hamper his becoming a first-class hillbilly. He had grown up in a poor and humble family of common folk. His highest schooling had been at a business college. He knew how country people felt and what they liked. He had come to the cities when still young, but, like many a Texas city man, he had never lost the spirit of the country boy.

At the beginning of the 1930's there were still eight times as many people working on Texas farms as in the young fast-growing Texas factories. Even those who had come to town were not yet acculturated to city life. Most Texas cities were little more than mushroom accumulations of freshly acquired and still largely unassimilated rural folk. Money from oil and sudden industrial growth had drawn these farm boys away from their old stomping grounds, but they had brought with them all the habits, customs, tastes, vocabulary, and views of their former life. Electric streetlights were still the supreme wonder of their lives. Big business, for which they toiled with untainted faith, was still the idol of their secular dreams.

Bolstered by the Doughboys, O'Daniel made a hit with them. He played no musical instrument, but he loved to whistle simple tunes and set them to the advertising slogans which were constantly popping into his fertile mind. As his poetic urge grew, he began composing tunes of his own and setting them to the rhymes that kept coming to him constantly. Having been originally introduced by his mother to the Church of Christ, he soon sensed the radio powers of the old-time religion and had his boys sing: "It was good for Lee O'Daniel and it's good enough for me."

Neither O'Daniel nor his Doughboys, he declared, expected to go down in history as originators of great music. Indeed, it was the music's lack of originality that made it popular: it followed the patterns with which everybody was familiar. The same is true of its literary content and the homespun philosophy which O'Daniel soon began weaving into the programs.

One of his most successful stunts, many times repeated, was to initiate some crusade favoring a cause which everyone could endorse, regardless of specific political views, and which no sane man would think of opposing. For instance, he organized a statewide safety association for children, sending out badges to all members. The one rule of the organization was that every qualified member should walk on the lefthand side of the street so as to face approaching traffic.

Who could object to such a crusade? And who could refuse to buy flour from this benevolent man who saved the lives of so many innocent little ones? Those who had children, particularly, insisted on biscuits made with O'Daniel's flour.

All families did not have children, but O'Daniel soon hit

upon a way to remedy that. Over the ether waves he urged that all childless couples adopt babies, thus relieving the congestion in orphan asylums and blessing their homes with an essential element for complete happiness. The response was so tremendous that the demand for orphans soon exceeded the supply, and O'Daniel himself had to go out on a hunt for adoptable babies.

The O'Daniel compositions, sung by his radio troubadours, touched the same wholesome, deep-seated, generally approved universal human drives on which his crusades were based: local pride, conjugal love, sympathy for the unfortunate, and the desire for economic betterment. Some of their titles are self-explanatory in this respect: "Beautiful Texas," "Sons of the Alamo," "In My Garden," "Human Blossoms," "Your Own Sweet Darling Wife," "Our Baby," "Marvelous Mother," "The Boy Who Never Gets Too Big to Comb His Mother's Hair," "The Orphan Newsboy," "That City for Shut-Ins," "Your Ship is Coming In," "Your Pot of Gold," "My Million-Dollar Smile."

O'Daniel was alive to every event that gained nationwide attention, and he versified his feelings about each happening at the apex of its popularity. In addition to expressing his joy or grief over these momentous occurrences, this practice turned out to be another highly successful publicity technique, because at each of these intensely emotional moments everybody felt exactly as O'Daniel did. When the New Deal first came in, he composed "On to Victory, Mr. Roosevelt" in exhilarating march rhythm. When the Lindbergh baby was kidnapped, his musicians agitated the ether with a sympathetic creation of O'Daniel: "Please Bring Back My Daddy to Me." The tune resembled the well-known air of "My Bonny." When Will Rogers was killed, the O'Daniel singers wailed: "Someone in heaven is thinking of you; someone who always was loyal and true; someone who used to be close by your side;

laughed when you laughed and cried when you cried." The song was dedicated to Mrs. Rogers.

In the summer of 1935 O'Daniel grew weary of working for others. There was no reason why his magnetic selling power should all be traded off for a hired man's wage. Besides, his children were becoming older and more musical every day, and they could use jobs on the air. Mike played the fiddle with the dexterity of a real old-timer, and Pat had grown proficient on the banjo. Molly had taken to the accordion and loved to be heard on the radio.

So O'Daniel abandoned Burrus and the Doughboys to set up business for himself. He had no mill of his own, but he did not need one any more than he needed hills to be a hillbilly. He bought ready-made flour from various mills, had it packed in ready-made bags, and composed the following stanza to be stamped on each bag under a big picture of a billy goat:

> Hillbilly music on the air,
> Hillbilly flour everywhere;
> It tickles your feet—it tickles your tongue.
> Wherever you go, its praises are sung.

Beneath this rhyme in glaring black capitals appeared that famous word so long a favorite among faithful salesmen: "GUARANTEED." Printed in red at the bottom of the sack was the slogan: "Please pass the biscuits, Pappy."

Most of the flour was manufactured and packed in Wichita Falls at the plant of General Mills Incorporated. To advertise the gaily adorned flour sacks, O'Daniel organized a new group of musicians with his own children as star members and called them the Hillbilly Boys. To improve the program's domestic atmosphere and further magnify his offspring's glory, he gave his sons pet names over the radio. Pat became Patty Boy and Mike became Mickey Wickey with his fiddledy-widdledy. Their theme song was:

I like mountain music,
Good old mountain music,
Played by the real hillbilly band.
I like bread and biscuits,
Big white fluffy biscuits—
Hillbilly flour makes 'em grand.

Their success was phenomenal. Orders poured in from every nook and cranny of Texas. Milling concerns soon learned that the surest way to sell their product was to let O'Daniel put it in hillbilly sacks. Practically every home with a radio had to have a supply of the flour that made those "big white fluffy biscuits."

As O'Daniel's business grew, the multiplicity and audacity of his selling schemes increased. No undertaking was too great as long as it would impress his name and his billy-goat trademark more indelibly on the public mind.

As the elections of 1938 drew near, he noticed that the twelve candidates for the state's highest public office were often in the limelight, so he decided to add his name to the list and make it a baker's dozen. On Palm Sunday he remarked over the radio that many of his friends and admirers had urged him to offer himself as candidate for governor. "I want all you folks to tell me what you think about it," he said.

Of course he was deluged with letters begging him to run. He waited until he had an impressive pile and announced on May 1 that he would be a candidate "at the request of 54,499 common citizens who have written me." Then he added: "I have not been approached by any clique or organization or their representatives. . . . I have no campaign manager, no political adviser, and no attorney to tell me what to do. Perhaps those experienced in these matters are scoffing. Perhaps their scoffing is justified. Perhaps they are like those who scoffed at David when he faced Goliath. . . ."

But where was the Goliath whom this flour-selling David

proposed to slay with his slingshot of homespun wisdom and swingtime country tunes? Now that the depression had been overcome, there was no likely villain in sight, but this did not hamper the super-salesman from Ohio any more than the lack of hills and a mill had hindered his becoming a first-class hill-billy miller. There were always those whom the camp-meeting-trained country folk viewed with distrust, whose special education they questioned, and whose pretensions they resented.

Who, then, would play this role of giant for the redoubt-able young hero? Who but that same lily-fingered gentleman whom the preachers of old condemned: that school-nurtured priest, now wearing the statesman's derby rather than the cler-gyman's cloth and carrying cigars instead of holy incense? The radio warrior thereupon resolved to wage a fierce and won-drous fight against "professional politicians."

A party platform was also in order. The other candidates for governor had studied the plight of Texas and carefully out-lined their recommendations, so the people would know what to expect if they should get elected. The strongest among them was Ernest O. Thompson, a highly educated lawyer and a gifted, convincing speaker. Thompson pointed out all the mistakes that had been made in the past and described how he would correct them. He drew large crowds of serious citizens from all walks of life. They came by tens of thousands to weigh his words and ponder his possibilities.

O'Daniel had no training or experience which would qual-ify him to compete with such a candidate. All he had was his quick wits and his salesman's instinct, but as usual these served him well. When people asked him what his proposals were, he provided a platform which no man could oppose in this Chris-tian world, and which not even Thompson could surpass: the Ten Commandments. When his listeners insisted that he be at least a little more specific, he came forth with a motto: the Golden Rule, and a slogan: "Less Johnson grass and politi-cians, more smokestacks and businessmen." Here were graphic phrases which aroused meaningful images instead of the be-wildering statistics so often on the lips of candidates.

In 1938 Texas was an economic colony. Great corpora-tions of the north and east were draining off her oil and gas. Rich sulphur deposits had been discovered along the Gulf Coast. Pipelines and freight trains carried the precious wealth away, leaving little more than the smell for Texas citizens. The state government was more deeply in debt than it had ever been before. Its expenses for the year had amounted to $157,-747,877.57: a staggering sum in the eyes of the average Texas farmer. The deficit had reached a new peak of $19,182,838.

Yet social security was in the air. The people had voted overwhelmingly for old-age pensions under the previous ad-ministration, but the legislature had blocked the full fruition of the plan.

O'Daniel picked up these cues with his usual alacrity and made recommendations which were more practical as sales devices than as actual remedies for Texas's ills. They held out pleasing hopes to both the native and the absentee owner, both the exploited and the exploiter. Bring more factories to Texas, he preached, and buy more goods made at home, in-cluding Hillbilly Flour. He plugged "good business methods," coupling them with more home industrialization. The govern-ment was in debt, he said, because its officials were not busi-nessmen. It must be put on a business basis. By running it more economically, he could lower taxes and thus attract more capital into the state. Texas would be run for big business, and big business would make it great. All persons more than sixty-five years old would get thirty dollars a month for the rest of their days.

Practically all the other candidates were advocating almost exactly the same things, but they were operating under several grave disadvantages. They had no hillbilly band. They did not compose songs. They never mentioned the Ten Command-ments. Their choice of words did not arouse clear-cut pictures in the minds of their listeners. They could point to no previous business experience, such as flour-selling, which would qualify them to run the state government in a businesslike manner.

Also, O'Daniel stressed industrialization and tax cuts more than did the others. "Let businessmen have a chance to establish a bigger and better Texas," he cried. "Let the state encourage business—advertise the advantages of Texas—bring new factories here—do something constructive for the Texas businessmen rather than abuse them and tax them. All's going to be well with Texas if we have a business administration instead of a professional political regime."

While his opponents filled their listeners' ears with abstract figures and statistics, he declared: "Not long ago I spoke in Jacksonville, the heart of the tomato country. At that time tomatoes were rotting in the fields without a market. Yet on the dinner tables in their local eating-places were bottles of catsup made from tomatoes hundreds of miles away in another state. This same situation holds true all along the line. We can and should be more self-supporting." Other candidates were vague about just how much pension the old people would get and just who would get it. O'Daniel offered thirty dollars per month to all alike, worthy and unworthy, rich and poor.

With these firm planks to sustain him, O'Daniel set out rather late in the campaigning season of 1938 to win the race for the governorship. He left his wife in Fort Worth to receive his mail and manage his headquarters. Taking his three teenage children, Pat, Mike, and Molly, to help the other hillbillies, he sallied forth in a big white bus which had a platform and microphone on top and "o'DANIEL FOR GOVERNOR" painted across the side. He composed a new song, "Them Hillbillies Are Politicians Now," to ring down the roads as the bus roared along.

The Texas electorate responded in concert to the flour-merchant's apparently magic drawing power. Over the vast waves of prairie, from among the flat-topped western hills, and out of the deep East Texas forests, voters converged to hear the new candidate and his troubadours atop the great white bus. The campaign surpassed anything that the most ambitious aspirants to public office had ever before dared imagine. Crowds of twenty, thirty, and forty thousand jammed the highways, sometimes waiting three, four, and five hours to get a firsthand glimpse of the famous radio salesman. They forced him to speak in towns where he was not even scheduled to stop. Their devotion had in it a touch of reverence: some of the love that can make men follow a leader to the door of death; some of the faith that can make mountains move.

Like the camp-meeting preachers of the previous generations, O'Daniel cut across all lines of local authority. His bus rolled into the towns without the consent or co-operation of city and county officials. Former campaigners had always been careful to have their speeches prefaced with flattering prearranged introductions from community leaders. O'Daniel needed no such regional recommendations. Radio and highway transportation were rubbing out those ancient vestiges of petty principality and ushering in a new brand of over-all democracy. Also, like those camp meetings of old, the flour-salesman's rallies were out in the open, under God's sky, in the bare light of heavenly bodies.

The O'Daniel rallies appealed to the same deep human instincts and provided the same emotional outlets which the camp meetings formerly offered. Here again was a chance to enjoy the thrill and glory of a martial movement without risking any physical bloodshed. Christ was still the hero and Satan still the enemy, but both had new mouthpieces now. Christ's good, which had previously radiated from the camp-meeting preacher, was now represented by the flour-salesman. Satan's evil, previously attached to that abhorred aristocracy which had been the pioneer's European superior, was now

found to reside in the professional politician. Roles, stage setting, and costumes were changed, but the plot of the drama
was the same.

The O'Daniels were a model family, and it must have been
great fun for them. Old-time fiddlers gaped at the nimble fin-
gers of Mickey Wickey with his fiddledy-widdledy. Banjo experts acknowledged their master when Patty Boy stepped up
to the microphone. The musicians not only attracted and entertained the people, but were also always on hand to distract
their attention when somebody asked O'Daniel exactly how
he planned to cut taxes and at the same time pay the old-age
pensions. The candidate's standard answer to such embarrassing questions was: "All right, boys! Strike up a tune!"

Persistent inquiries would be met by the flour man's million-dollar smile and indomitable optimism: "If we can attract
ten factories where one now exists, the increased taxes would
not only provide enough money to run the state and probably
permit a reduction of tax rates, but the unemployment problem would be solved."

O'Daniel initiated another new practice in politics which
was again reminiscent of the camp meeting. He took up collections at his rallies to finance his campaign. Besides raising
money and obliquely associating his campaign with the everlasting fight against Satan, this practice impressed the people
with the idea that it was their fight and that no large hidden
interests were supporting or controlling their leader.

"The only thing," he said, "that can prevent us from winning is lack of sufficient campaign funds. If you want me to
run the race on a bicycle while the other candidates have high-
powered racing cars, that's up to you. . . . I say to you in all
sincerity . . . you had better take that old rocking chair down
and mortgage it and spend the money in the manner you think
best to get your pension. . . . We have not one dollar in our
campaign fund." Note the graphic phrases again: "a bicycle,"
"high-powered racing cars," "the old rocking chair," "the pen-

sion." A contribution to O'Daniel was not a gift, but a purchase of future security.

He obtained some small wooden kegs, cut money slots in them, and labeled them: "FLOUR; NOT PORK." At the climax of each rally, he would have his hillbillies carry these among the crowd to be filled with dollars, dimes, and nickels. "It's your campaign, not mine," he would proclaim into the microphone. "The boys and girls have some little flour barrels they're going to pass around. If you want to put any money in them, you shall have the opportunity. . . . But don't go away from here and say that W. Lee O'Daniel asked you to put any money in. I'm just giving you the opportunity, if you want to join the people's candidate against the professional politicians."

Here was the super-salesman at his best. The customer was offered not an ordinary commercial transaction, but an opportunity. He was invited not merely to spend his money, but to become part of a glorious movement.

While campaigning in Wichita Falls, O'Daniel found a twenty-dollar bill in one of the barrels. Waving it aloft, he shouted: "Who put in this twenty?"

When the donor stepped forward, O'Daniel declared: "I don't want such large contributions. A dollar is enough." He gave the man nineteen dollars change.

This brought him closer than ever to the hearts of those thousands who had each given a dollar or less. How could they doubt that he was their man, after such a show?

O'Daniel himself usually climbed to the top of the bus rather late in the rally, after the songs and music had set the proper mood. Once there came a shower at an appointed place and time, and a crowd of over twenty thousand stood waiting several hours in the rain, just as their ancestors had worshipped at camp meetings rain or shine. At last the great white bus appeared like a ghost amidst the haze of raindrops. The crowd's cheering surpassed the thunder of the black clouds overhead both in volume and in duration. With a broad umbrella to protect their instruments and the microphone, the Hillbilly Boys whipped up all spirits with such appropriate airs as "I Get the Blues When it Rains."

Then O'Daniel mounted the bus, wrapped a handkerchief around the microphone to keep its insides dry, took the umbrella down, and shouted: "If you folks can stand in the rain and listen to me, I sure can stand in the rain and talk to you."

The splatter and whirl of raindrops was drowned in a deluge of clapping, whistling, and shouting. In the light of such performances, no discerning observer should have been surprised to see this flour-peddler drawing huger crowds in thunder storms than others could attract in fair weather. His connection with flour made him far more than a mere candidate for public office. He was a provider, closely associated in the public mind with the very staff of life. Moreover, the humble flour sack kept the public eye focused on him as an average man, proving by his success that the same achievements are open to all. His election would commit him to the task of conserving those conditions which would enable other average men to grow in wealth and fame. Thus he was a symbol of God's democratic goodness, the land's bountifulness, and every man's hope, all rolled into one.

This being the happy position in which his particular skills plus a lucky combination of circumstances had placed him, he could not lose. Even if he should fail to attain the governorship, the publicity he gained would boost Hillbilly Flour sales beyond all former stunts. He never denied that a prime aim of his campaign was to sell more flour. The race, he said, was "sure good for business." Trainloads of flour in Hillbilly sacks, hurrying to all parts of the state, testified to his success. Every speech he made was accompanied by a plug for Hillbilly Flour. The advertising was free, because the voluntary contributions were more than paying for the campaign.

In the midst of all this glory, somebody discovered that O'Daniel had forgotten to pay his poll tax. He was not even a qualified voter. "He can't even vote for himself," sneered the *El Paso Post*, "yet he comes before us asking to be made governor of Texas. He has a crust all right, and it is not a light crust."

O'Daniel retorted that no professional politician was worth the $1.75 poll tax. "I didn't pay my poll tax," he explained, "because I was fed up with crooked politics in Austin and hadn't intended to vote for anyone this year. I didn't know I was going to be called on to run." He later added that he thought the poll tax ought to be abolished anyhow.

That was an easy one compared to the attack of William McCraw, a rival candidate bent on slinging mud. McCraw came forth with the revelation that O'Daniel had been born in Ohio and reared in Kansas. He was not a native Texan, but a Yankee: a carpetbagger. For an ordinary demagogue, such a disclosure might have been fatal, but not for O'Daniel. He simply remarked that there were 750,000 people from other states living in Texas. Unfortunately for McCraw, President Roosevelt had just unveiled an American symbol of peace eternal at Gettysburg, before two thousand cheering veterans of the blue and the gray. O'Daniel said that McCraw was trying to "burn anew the flames of sectional hatred, and just after the final beautiful peaceful reunion at Gettysburg!"

A letter to the editor of the *Dallas Morning News* shows how utterly McCraw lost this bout in the eyes of at least one serious-minded citizen: "Until within the last few days, I had not made up my mind as to which of the candidates for governor I would support, but since a few of the self-styled 'leading candidates' began their cheap campaign against another candidate by calling him a Yankee carpetbagger, a flour peddler, a showman, a tax dodger, I have had no difficulty in deciding whom I would support."

Another writer exclaimed that O'Daniel's "high ethical standards have outlawed mudslinging in politics."

Fortunately for the flour-salesman, he did not need to lambast Thompson and McCraw. This hatchet work was done for him, unwittingly no doubt, but effectively just the same, by Karl Crowley, another gubernatorial candidate, whose antagonism toward Thompson and McCraw probably weaned hundreds of voters away from them. Instead of voting for Crowley, however, these recruits gavitated toward the more soft-spoken O'Daniel. Such combinations, often unintentional, have occurred many a time in Texas politics. When a candidate is discredited, the votes seldom go to the man who does the dirty work, however necessary it may have been.

As O'Daniel's crowds grew bigger, his opponents waxed bitterer, until some of them forgot their positive platforms and concentrated a barrage of invective on him. Unable to find any significant skeletons in his closet, they endeavored to vilify him with derogatory words, but his genius for turning every apparent adversity to an advantage never abandoned him. Their abuse merely gave him a chance to identify himself with the Saviour's chosen by quoting scripture. "Blessed are ye," he intoned into the microphone, "when men shall revile you and persecute you and say all manner of evil against you falsely for my sake."

Seeing that they could not smear him out of the race, O'Daniel's rivals tried, timidly at first, then more overtly, to imitate him. They adopted his folky expressions, strove to make their language more concrete, and later even hired hillbilly bands. The saying went abroad that "the politicians are hillbillies now."

But there was one important lesson that they never learned: O'Daniel did not resort to personal mudslinging. If attacked, he would defend himself, calling his assailant by name, but he presently returned to the discussion of policy.

He lambasted "professional politicians," but he never spent his time trying to dig up dirt from the past careers of individual opponents. Nor did he fail to remind all citizens of this virtue at the end of the race, when he won by a landslide, getting a total of 573,166 votes from a statewide tabulation of 1,114,885. This gave him a clear majority: 31,447 votes more than all the other candidates put together. When the news of his victory went out, he declared:

"I am happy in the thought that I indulged in no personalities during the campaign and have no bitterness in my heart toward any man, woman, or child. I am not of the disposition to gloat over victory. I humbly bow to the will of the people, accept their mandate, and with the help of God and the cooperation of my good friends and the citizens of Texas, we shall march onward and upward to happier days. . . . I bear no ill will toward those who did not vote for me. After all, I didn't vote for myself, so I couldn't hold that against them."

Like the prophets of yore, he proclaimed a new day: "The old order of politics has been that when the victor was crowned, the show was over, the lights were turned out, and the crowd went home for two more years. This next administration is not going to be ME AND GOD—It is going to be BY GOD, THE PEOPLE, AND ME. Thanks to radio."

But he did not presume that all would be easy for him. "I intend," he declared, " to study the job and work at being governor of Texas just as hard as I worked in selling flour. To me, it's just another job."

Thereupon, he published his campaign account:

Contributions $6,586.00
Expenses 5,789.00
Profit . . . .$ 797.00

A few tardy dollars must have subsequently drifted in, for on August 8 he gave $801.30 to the Red Cross, this being "the amount the people donated above my expenses in the race for governor."

An advertising agency offered him $2,000 a week to go on the radio for them, but he refused because he needed all his time to study "for the job of being the best governor Texas ever had."

For the flour business, the race proved profitable beyond all previous hope. Sales of Hillbilly Flour doubled during the campaign and rose faster than ever after the election. The new governor turned this booming business over to his oldest son, Mike, making him president of the O'Daniel Flour Company.

Not only had O'Daniel won by an overwhelming majority without spending any money, boosting his individual fortune all the while; he had done it without committing himself on any controversial issues of lasting importance. As one observant citizen pointed out: "He did not tell us whether he was a Jeffersonian or a Hamiltonian . . . whether he believes in a constitutional government or a pure democracy . . . whether he is an individualist or a collectivist . . . whether he is a wet or a dry . . . whether he believes in sit-down strikes or . . . property rights. He made war upon the professional politician, but he did not tell us the difference, in his opinion, between a politician and a statesman."

His endorsement of the Ten Commandments and the Golden Rule had so excited the voters that they had forgotten to ask him about these other matters. In North Central and Northwest Texas especially, the religious appeal was most apparent in the jubilation of his supporters. Through their comments runs the strong equalitarian strain of the cosmic democracy extolled by their old camp-meeting preachers. God is described as speaking not through specialized governmental or clerical authorities, but through the spontaneous wisdom of the common folk. "The people have spoken," runs one letter to an editor, "and the voice of the people is the voice of God."

Another rejoiced as follows: "I interpret this as the voice of the majority of the people approving the Ten Commandments and the Golden Rule as a vital force in the government of Texas to be reflected in its laws and the public policy of the state for the general good of the people."

Said another: "Texas voters still believe in the truth of these Commandments and accept them as a good standard for all people to live by, even men who seek and hold public office."

And another: "The people have spoken. O'Daniel is the new Moses in Texas. Every patriotic heart must hope that he confirm the faith of the people and put no stumbling block before him and help him to meet the need of the hour, the need of the people, and the need of the state."

That his folky style also bore fruit is revealed in many comments to the effect that: "We have our friend for a governor. No one is a stranger or an enemy to him. He knows each and every one of us," and: "He is not a radical, but a simple, common, and humanly understanding man. A man who is not afraid to place himself on the level with his most common fellow man."

His pension promise was another important item. Scores of aged aliens from Mexico and elsewhere, who had been illegally in the state for over five years, applied for citizenship in order to qualify for the O'Daniel pension.

Business leaders were happy too, for he had promised not to tax them. In Fort Worth they gave him a white gold watch with inlaid diamonds and the inscription: "Hon. W. Lee O'Daniel, who made a miracle of time."

Since Texas politics has traditionally been a one-party affair, the actual choice of state officers rests in the Democratic primary. Whoever gets nominated in the primary is automatically considered the state's choice, for no Republican has ever made much showing in the general elections for state posts. Nomination in the primary requires a majority of all votes cast.

If no candidate attains such a majority, there is a run-off contest between the two leading aspirants.

A few weeks before the primary, O'Daniel coined a song and had his Hillbilly Boys disseminate it through the ether: "There ain't gonna be no run-off; there ain't gonna be no run-off; we did away with run-offs when O'Daniel came to town." In his own case, this was true, but the candidates for minor offices did not fare so well. Just before the run-offs for the final choice of these, O'Daniel read over the radio the names of the men with whom he said he could work best, asking the people to elect them, saying this was the way things were managed in business, and therefore it ought to work well in government. This brought widespread criticism, not only because it smacked of dictatorial methods, but also because many of the men whose election the new governor requested could be regarded as professional politicians: those wicked authors of all social ills whom the fair-haired boy had sworn to exterminate. Now he was recommending them; even begging his supporters to elect them!

Several of these politicians, though they had scored second in the original primary, moved up to the lead in the run-off. Their victory was thus an obvious result of the O'Daniel nod. Notable among them was a slow-spoken, pipe-smoking ex-goat-rancher named Coke Stevenson, for lieutenant governor.

O'Daniel was quick to learn from his critics, however. Never again did he recommend by name any candidate for other state offices. In all subsequent speeches he merely urged voters to select whoever agreed to support his program.

His zeal to eliminate all "professional politicians" ebbed fast after his first inauguration. Moreover, although during the campaign he had opposed the sales tax as a tax on poverty, when he came to grips with the ghastly task of finding money for the old-age pensions he had promised, the only proposal he could offer was a "transactions tax." His critics cried that a transactions tax was a sales tax, but he answered that his plan taxed all exchanges, whereas the sales tax had been limited to retail sales. However, the legislature rejected his scheme, thus failing to provide the thirty-dollar-a-month pension for all persons over sixty-five years old. Yet in his second race for the governorship O'Daniel got 645,646 votes: 72,480 more than he had polled in the first election.

Again, religion was an important source of his success, but of much value also was the business background which put him in step with the general post-New Deal drift toward a fresh exaltation of free enterprise. The drift was accelerated in Texas by her recently developed natural resources and her consequent industrial prosperity. Thus O'Daniel got credit for all the multi-million-year-old opulence that was flowing from the Texas earth. All criticism of him fell on deaf ears. The cry that he was out to "save the poor man's soul and the rich man's cash" was greeted by deadpan indifference.

Again, his religious position and business experience were bolstered by his showmanship: his animated spontaneity, his million-dollar smile, and his graphic diction. Instead of reducing that abstract something called a budget by a haze of prosaic figures, he "got the biggest blue pencil I could find in Austin and began paring down the big, juicy pie that the professional politicians were getting ready to eat." His big white bus was adorned in the second campaign with a huge capitol dome above the microphone. In answer to snide remarks about its probable cost, he described it as "just a common, ordinary used car that will go back to the dealer as a used car when the campaign is over. You probably will see it hauling cotton and potatoes on the highways of Texas before the end of the year."

While he still refrained from singling out individuals and digging up dirt about their past, his second campaign included dramatic attacks on a few selected governmental agencies. He bombarded them with bizarre accusations and held them up to public scorn. The victims of the attacks usually failed in their efforts to defend themselves because their replies, however convincing, never achieved the wide dissemination enjoyed by the governor's famous radio voice.

O'Daniel's vociferations against the "professional politician" carried less conviction now. He must find another Goliath: another target for his crusading zeal. As usual, his quick eye perceived a likely antagonist: "labor-union leader racketeers." In general, the choice might not seem appropriate for an avowed champion of the common folk, but considering the time and place, it was masterful. Back in 1930 organized labor had been a genuine underdog throughout the United States, but with the protection of the New Deal many a labor leader had grown overconfident and committed abuses which the public could not soon forgive. Being still predominantly a farming community, dazzled by the O'Daniel personality in which deep-seated religious convictions were identified with big business interests, Texas was particularly suspicious of these labor leaders.

In 1941, when his second term as governor was well under way, O'Daniel submitted to the legislature a law governing labor-union activities. According to this law, if a picket used violence to prevent a strike-breaker from entering a plant, he was subject to a two-year penitentiary sentence. Yet there was no such punishment for strike-breakers who committed violence. Labor unions over the state protested that this would weaken the worker's only weapon without imposing any limitations on the activities of the employer. But such protests had little effect against the super-salesman's magic. Over the radio he proclaimed:

"We have plenty of idle hands in Texas anxious for jobs, enough of those idle hands to keep all the wheels of industry turning twenty-four hours per day, and seven days per week, if necessary, and we intend to keep the wheels turning, and if any of these wild-eyed labor-leader agitators drifting into Texas from other places think for one minute that they are going to take charge of Texas and stop our industries from

running, they have another guess coming. We have 75,000
acres of state prison farms, and that will take care of a lot of
that kind of racketeers, and that is where they will find themselves, picking cotton, if they come down here and violate our
laws."

Here again was a crusade in which all good Texans could
participate with exhilarating enthusiasm, especially in times
when a prolonged strike could seriously cripple the European
war against fascistic dictatorships. The "wild-eyed labor-leader
agitators" were labeled as foreigners "drifting in from other
places." They were threatening to "take charge of Texas" and
"violate our laws." Their proposed imprisonment, besides being a flattering proof of Texas power, promised work for the
"idle hands" of those who needed jobs. Thus was local pride
combined with economic and wartime needs to exalt the hopeful egos of the salesman's disciples.

This speech of O'Daniel against foreign labor transgressors
was broadcast over Station XEAW, just across the Rio Grande
from Hidalgo. Being in Mexico, XEAW was not subject to
United States regulations regarding the maximum power used
by individual radio stations. It could therefore drown out all
stations in South Texas whose frequency approximated its
own, and it had an inequitable advantage over all others.

O'Daniel's law was passed by a big majority in the legislature. It initiated a long series of anti-labor laws in Texas. A
relatively mild act was enacted in 1943. Then came nine more
stringent measures in 1947, when the removal of national price
controls had precipitated a series of telephone strikes and Taft-
Hartley was in the national air. Finally, an act passed in 1951
heavily penalizes any person or organization agreeing to hire
workers in accordance with their membership in unions. This
outlaws, among other things, the hiring-hall.

The Texas laws forbid any contract which ties a job to
union membership. This outlaws the closed shop, the union

shop, and maintenance-of-membership clauses. "Secondary boycotts"—that is, mutual agreements among two or more persons to withhold their trade from a picketed plant—are illegal. Public officials may not recognize any union as a bargaining agent for public employees, nor may public agencies be picketed. Public utilities may not be picketed if it will interrupt their service to consumers. Under certain conditions— for instance, a strike in breach of contract—the union is held responsible for the acts of its individual members. Picketing may never be carried on by groups of more than two persons each. No two of these groups, or pairs, may be less than fifty feet from each other, nor may there be more than two persons within fifty feet of an entrance to a plant. Labor unions may not contribute money to candidates for public office. All local unions must file their financial statements and constitutions with Texas's secretary of state. While the proponents of these laws are sure that they constitute a fair price for industrial peace, their effect has often been to impede sincere efforts to win better salaries and working conditions.

Texas also has the usual statutes protecting workers against dangerous or unwholesome conditions and providing for unemployment compensation. These were already on the books when O'Daniel came to power. In fact, most of them were enacted about the beginning of the twentieth century. They therefore deal with obsolete machinery and do not cover such recent perils as those occurring in oil, chemical, and metal plants. Moreover, their enforcement is handicapped by the lack of a state labor department. The Bureau of Labor Statistics handles complaints concerning their violation, but its authority is limited. Another deficiency in the Texas labor picture is the lack of any legal machinery whereby the employees of a purely Texas enterprise which does not directly affect interstate commerce may demand and obtain recognition for their union as a bargaining agent. The owners of

hotels, retail stores, and taxicabs, for instance, may successfully refuse to bargain with any organization of their employees.

Since about the beginning of the century, Texas laborers
have been protected against tardy pay checks, blacklisting, and
discrimination by corporations on account of previous participation in strikes or membership in unions. Corporations
and their agents must keep their employees fully informed of
all statements made about them to prospective employers.
Any discharged person has a right to a full written statement
of the reasons for his discharge. If he leaves a plant voluntarily,
he may demand a statement to this effect. Of course, such
statements may not be used as a basis for libel suits. Since
these rules apply to corporations and their agents only, they
are sometimes circumvented by a corporation's having a contractor to do its work. The contractor, being an individual, is
not subject to so many limitations in the treatment of his
laborers.

On April 9, 1941, just eight days after O'Daniel's speech
from Mexico initiating the state's labor-control legislation, the
national capital was stunned by the death of United States
Senator Morris Sheppard, sixty-five-year-old Texas Democrat,
father of national Prohibition and chairman of the senate
military-affairs committee. His physician said that he had
died from overwork; the load on the committee had grown
steadily heavier since the outbreak of World War II. National
defense demanded that the governor of Texas immediately
appoint a competent senator to fill the vacancy left by Sheppard's death. Local pride demanded that this ad interim appointee be a credit to Texas. Governor O'Daniel heeded
neither of these demands.

The law required that once a good man had been appointed to meet the emergency in Congress, the governor
should announce a special election for a successor to complete
the term of the deceased. There were many Texans who would

Dallas.

Senator Lyndon B. Johnson

W. Lee O'Daniel (left) and Coke Stevenson (right)

have made worthy successors to Sheppard. Ex-Governor Dan Moody, a successful oil attorney, was experienced, competent, and energetic. Ex-Governor James V. Allred, at that time federal judge for the southern district of Texas, was favored by President Roosevelt. But Governor O'Daniel showed no sign of haste either in providing the needed man for the war-time situation or in announcing the special election. Malicious whispers had it that the governor wanted to be senator himself, and that the appointment of an able statesman, even to bridge the interim between Sheppard's death and the special election, might jeopardize his chances. The vacancy remained unfilled until April 21, 1941.

Now for all good Texans, April 21 is a holiday second only to Christmas. It is the day when Sam Houston defeated Santa Anna at San Jacinto and thus won Texas independence from Mexico. Patriots from all over the state converge at the San Jacinto Battle Ground, on the shores of the Houston Ship Channel, to revere the immortal heroes of that victory. The San Jacinto Monument is the center of attention. It is shaped like the Washington Monument except that it is fifteen feet higher and has a huge single star at its summit. At its base is a square building measuring 125 feet on each side. It houses a historical museum and an auditorium where the multitudes gather to hear patriotic speeches and sing patriotic songs on San Jacinto Day. Patriotism among Texans, of course, means reverence for Texas. Besides being audible to the gathered patriots, the programs are broadcast over a statewide radio network.

To this shrine went the super-salesman from Ohio on April 21, 1941, dressed in a brown business suit with the trouser legs stuffed into elaborately decorated cowboy boots. As always, of course, he was welcomed by an enthusiastic ovation, and his position as governor naturally gave him the privilege of interrupting the festivities at any time. Apparently he was not interested in listening to any of the regularly scheduled speakers on the program; he loitered around a nearby filling station until the time when, according to last-minute arrangements, he was to speak in the auditorium. Then at three o'clock in the afternoon, while a drizzling rain fell outside, he clumped down the aisle of the auditorium and took charge of the microphone to further glorify Sam Houston's memory.

His message was a big surprise. Sam Houston's only surviving son, Andrew Jackson Houston, was to be senator. "As governor of the state of Texas," said O'Daniel, "I have wished to recognize the useful life of Andrew Jackson Houston and to pay another tribute to the immortal memory of his father. . . . I have today, therefore, by virtue of the authority vested in me by the constitution and laws of the land, appointed Andrew Jackson Houston to the high position of United States senator from the state of Texas to serve until the vacancy caused by the untimely death of the late Senator Morris Sheppard shall have been filled by election, as provided by law."

The governor exerted the full force of his fine salesmanship in advertising his appointee's merits. "Even as his father brought fame to him, so has Andrew Jackson Houston, in turn, honored his father by being diligent in the service of society, devoted to his native state, and dedicated to the highest principles of public and personal virtue. He has carried the banner of Houston high and has added luster to an already ennobled name."

The new senator's abilities came in for extravagant praise. "Despite the strain of the busy, purposeful, and successful life which he has lived, he is still a close student of the trend of the times. I have heard him speak with great fervor on moral issues which demand the attention of our society. I have known of his work as a civic leader from every community in which he has lived. His literary skill, his ability as a lawyer, and his charming talent as a painter are well known."

Indeed, Andrew Jackson Houston had graced the state

with a series of impressive achievements. After attending
Bastrop Military Academy, Texas Military Institute, Baylor
College, and Salado College, he organized the Travis Rifles to
guard the Democratic state legislature in the carpetbagging
days of 1874. In 1876 he was admitted to the bar, and he
served as clerk of the United States district court from 1879
to 1889. He ran for governor on the Republican ticket in 1892,
to be defeated by that great Democrat, Jim Hogg. In 1898 he
headed a troop of cavalry for Theodore Roosevelt's Rough
Riders. In 1910 and 1912 he ran for governor again, favoring
Prohibition and woman suffrage. In both races he ran near
the rear, the winner being O. B. Colquitt. In 1938 he published a lengthy account of his father's achievements in the
Texas revolution, and he was appointed major general of the
Texas National Guard in 1939. Thus his selection as United
States senator by Governor O'Daniel in 1941 crowned a long
line of honors. As the governor put it in his speech to the San
Jacinto crowd, Andrew Jackson Houston's "own high intellectual attainments, his long, useful experience, his patriotic
service to his state, distinguish him as a great son of Texas and
make it particularly appropriate that he should receive, to
climax his career, the highest honor in our power to bestow."

About General Andrew Jackson Houston's long experience there could be no question: he was eighty-six years old.
The dimness of his eyes and the thinness of his face indicated
that his best days were behind him. Most of the flesh had
wasted away from his cheek and jaw bones, leaving the skin
loose upon them. Very little hair was left on his head, and very
little vigor in his movements. His steps were unsteady, his mustache gray.

He was not present at the San Jacinto assembly where the
flour-selling governor had come to heap such praise and unexpected honor on him. Illness and old age kept him away.
The news of his senatorial post had sent him to bed, and a
guard of highway patrolmen had been set up at his cottage to

keep visitors from molesting him with congratulations and
questions of state.

Like all other seeming misfortunes, the rain which fell on
that San Jacinto day was transformed to an asset by the
O'Daniel magic. He told in touching terms how, when he
drove up to General Andrew Jackson Houston's humble home
near La Porte and informed him of his appointment, the
clouds parted momentarily, as though God were drawing aside
the heavenly curtains. "Just as I broke the news to him of his
appointment," declared the governor, "the sun suddenly shot
through the dark rain clouds in such a fashion that it appeared
dazzling. I said: 'General, do you know what caused that sun
to suddenly burst through those dark and heavy clouds? It
appears to me as if our great and good loving God had just
spread the clouds apart so the spirit of your illustrious father
could smile down upon his son on this particular scene and
see the big smile on your face.'"

The applause was thunderous.

"What could bring such joy to the heart of General Andrew Jackson Houston," intoned the governor's best radio
voice, "than to walk into the senate of the United States and
to occupy as a senator from Texas the same seat which his illustrious father occupied March 30, 1846, as one of the first
two senators from Texas? What could be more inspiring and
encouraging to the other ninety-five United States senators, at
this crucial time in world history, than to sit in session with
the son of that great general who in days of crisis a hundred
years ago played such an important role in the history of this
state and nation? And, last but not least, what a contribution
General Andrew Jackson Houston in his own right can make
to our cause of freedom and democracy! He receives this hon-
orable appointment not alone as a tribute to the memory of
his distinguished father, but also because he is eminently
qualified for the place."

Andrew Jackson Houston took the oath of office on June 2

and held the senatorship for the last twenty-four days of his life. Needless to say, there was no danger that he might spoil the hopes of any other man who chose to run for his post in the special election. After barely surviving the trip to Washington, he appeared three times on the senate floor, attended one committee meeting, underwent a stomach operation, and passed away in peace at the Walter Reed Hospital. He had the undisputed distinction of being the oldest man who ever entered the United States senate.

Shortly after Houston's appointment, Governor O'Daniel was asked whether or not he planned to run for the senate. He merely smiled his million-dollar smile and remarked: "I've got a job."

He was then asked whether he would yield if the usual deluge of letters, telegrams, postcards, and telephone calls should pour in upon him, urging him to run. Again came the O'Daniel smile and the reply: "You've got a senator."

The deluge of requests came through in good time, and the governor gracefully acquiesced.

At this time Texans and other Americans were seeing and applauding two very popular movie productions. The earlier of these was entitled *Mr. Deeds Goes to Town*. In it, Gary Cooper played the part of a tuba-tooting hick who suddenly got rich and was lured into the wicked city. Hypocrites and slicks gathered around him. When he determined, in spite of them, to give his money away, they harried him into court for insanity, but of course he emerged victorious in the end.

This picture was so successful that another with the same romantic suspicion of the city soon followed: *Mr. Smith Goes to Washington*. In it, James Stewart began as an honest innocent from the sticks and wound up as the only upright man among the capital city's unprincipled politicians.

Here was another lucky break for O'Daniel. Those of his followers who saw the movie lost no time in mentally identifying Mr. Smith with the flour-salesman. They saw Mr. O'Daniel

as Mr. Smith in a real-life Texas drama which paralleled the
motion picture. Announcements advertising the movie were
obtained. The name of Mr. Smith was marked out with two
lines which left it still legible, and that of Mr. O'Daniel was
placed above it. These changed announcements were used as
auto windshield stickers all over the state. Thus all the emotion which James Stewart's histrionic talent had aroused was
deflected into the Texas governor's race for the senate. This
was exactly the kind of situation which O'Daniel was an expert
at exploiting. He slipped into the role with all his wonted
skill.

"I have twisted the politicians' tails in Austin," he proclaimed, "and I can twist their tails in Washington. And you
bet your life I'll twist 'em too until we get the job done, no
matter how loud they bellow or how many are in the herd."
He began the campaign by letting his children tour the state
in the sound truck and play recordings of his speeches on the
phonograph. His duties as governor, he said, kept him busy in
Austin. Later, however, he took to the road himself.

But the O'Daniel glory was beginning to wear thin. His
crowds were smaller now. In Houston only forty-five hundred
came to hear him, as compared with tens of thousands in his
earlier campaigns. He won the election by a narrow margin,
polling 451,359 votes while his Roosevelt-backed opponent,
James V. Allred, got 433,203.

In Washington, O'Daniel essayed to give the nation the
same kind of labor laws that he had initiated in Texas. His
most pressing mission was to agitate for the repeal of Roosevelt's Fair Labor Standards Act, which required all employers,
in Texas as well as elsewhere, to pay time and one half for all
work done above forty hours per week. His efforts in this direction met with abject failure.

In 1942 he ran a second race for senator. It was more
barbed with ugly insinuations and insults than any of his
former races. He made personal attacks on his two opponents,

Allred and Moody, nicknaming them "the gold-dust twins."
He implied that Allred had been bribed by labor leaders to
quit his $10,000 judgeship and make the race for senator. He
assailed the press repeatedly. Especially ironic was his attack
on the *Dallas Morning News,* one of the state's most strongly
anti-labor papers.

"The filthy money of the labor racketeers is keeping the
Dallas News from printing the truth," he shouted. "Money
is being spent like water to prevent my re-election. The Communist labor racketeers, with a billion-dollar slush fund, are
helping finance my opponents. . . . The Communistic labor-
leader racketeers are trying under cover of the war to steal our
American form of government. . . ." He said we had already
lost one of our greatest freedoms: "the God-given right to
work," and predicted that "the creeping menace may extend
to every segment of American life." The phrase "Communistic
labor-leader racketeers" was repeated fourteen times in a
speech at Denton and sixteen times at Tyler.

Businessmen reacted favorably to O'Daniel's stand on
labor and added their support to the thousands of votes already won by his praise of the Christian religion and the Texas
heroes. Thus he achieved his fourth and last political victory,
which put him in the United States senate for six more years:
until 1948.

In 1944 Senator O'Daniel joined forces with a few disgruntled Texas businessmen to rob Texans of their right to
vote for Roosevelt. Their plan was to pack the state Democratic convention with anti-Roosevelt delegates and persuade
them to place "uninstructed" electors on the national ballot.
These electors would thereupon vote for whomever they
pleased. Since their sympathies were Republican, they could
be expected to cast their votes for the Republican candidates.
Thus, the Texas citizen would be entirely disfranchised in the
general election, because if he crossed out the names of the
Democratic electors, the Republican electors would vote for

Dewey and Bricker; if he crossed out the names of the Republican electors, the Democratic electors would also vote for Dewey and Bricker.

The scheme almost worked. At its May meeting, a narrow majority of the convention in Austin chose a set of uninstructed delegates for the national convention and named a slate of electors who announced that if Roosevelt were nominated at the national convention they would vote for somebody else. The dome of the state capitol rang with indignant shouts from delegates who had not heard before about this well-laid plan. A war was on. Roosevelt was their Commander in Chief. Victory might hinge on their loyalty to him. They might let businessmen bicker about the president's domestic policies, but they would not have their suffrage wrenched from them or their war effort scuttled. Half the convention walked out in a body, leaving the Roosevelt-haters alone in the senate chamber.

On the floor of the house, the pro-Roosevelt forces assembled to organize their opposition against this unexpected conspiracy. Oratory waxed violent in both rooms of the red granite capitol. Dan Moody swung the gavel for the anti-Roosevelt crowd. At the mention of Roosevelt's name, their booing swelled like the bellow of a huge beast. The walls vibrated with angry yells and echoes. From the house chamber came the cry that the party's manipulators would reduce Texas to a voteless principality with no more freedom than a Fascist state. A handsome young lawyer named Herman Jones, stripped to his shirt sleeves for the heat of battle, drenched in sweat by the heat of the spring day, shouted from the house floor that Roosevelt's opponents were lending "aid and comfort to the enemy." His voice went with his listeners back to their respective counties, where they worked throughout the summer to alert their constituents. Nor was the anti-Roosevelt element idle.

In September the convention met again, with the Roosevelt-haters still in control of the party machinery. But the pro-Roosevelt delegates were in the majority and won the day by the skin of their teeth. The anti-Roosevelt leaders, after appealing in vain to the courts, organized a party of their own, called it the Texas Regulars, spent thousands of dollars on political ads in the newspapers, and summoned Senator O'Daniel down from Washington to stump the state on their behalf.

On November 2, 1944, when O'Daniel appeared at the City Auditorium in Houston to speak against Roosevelt, he was greeted by a shower of eggs, tomatoes, and sundry other stale edibles thrown at him by irate Texans. Special police squads rushed to his rescue and escorted him to safety after thirty minutes of turmoil. Daunted but not quenched, he covered the state, favoring the slate of uninstructed electors and explaining that the nation's founding fathers never intended for the people to have a direct voice in choosing their chief executive. His crowds were small and either apathetic or prone to loud booing. In the November election the Texas Regulars got only 135,000 votes as compared with 191,000 for the Republicans and 821,000 for the pro-Roosevelt Democrats. Seeing that they represented only a little over 13 per cent of Texas's voting population, the Texas Regulars officially dissolved their party in the spring of 1945.

Senator O'Daniel's formerly tender heart appears to have hardened somewhat after his return to the District of Columbia. Amidst the housing shortage in 1945, he bought a large apartment house in Washington and converted it into a home for his one family. It had fourteen apartments with fourteen separate bathrooms. The former tenants were driven into the streets, with no roof over their heads, though they were able and eager to pay rent. Many Texans felt that this was carrying rugged individualism and survival of the fittest a bit too far. One ironic East Texas columnist expressed "resentment" at people criticizing Senator O'Daniel for buying a house with fourteen bathrooms, since "he ought to know how many it takes to keep his hands clean."

After this real-estate venture, not much was heard of O'Daniel in Texas politics. He just faded away. Since much of his support had come from farmers and recent ex-farmers in whose hearts the camp-meeting spirit had not cooled, his eclipse may be partly attributed to the rapid urbanization which was taking place all over Texas in the 1940's. Today he owns and runs the W. Lee O'Daniel Life Insurance Company, with an office building and an apartment house in Dallas.

Whatever may have been the causes of O'Daniel's political decline, his influence has outlived his individual popularity. In his career, Texas's multi-million-year-old natural wealth converged with her hundred-year-old religious traditions to crystallize in her people a steadfast moral, political, and economic conservatism which colors her life to this day. He and his successors have given the state a strongly pro-big-business government which has successfully weathered storms of protest from within and without.

This is exactly what might be expected in the light of the anti-clerical sentiments with which camp-meeting preachers, democratic leaders, and frontier conditions have imbued the Texas people. Big businessmen enjoy none of the institutional connections that would make them eligible successors to the despised high-church prelate. They can usually point to childhood difficulties which dramatize their rise to wealth as self-made men. They have no formal training or special authority to set them off from ordinary people. They are just plain country boys who struck it lucky, and the humblest of mortals may embrace them as brothers. Like O'Daniel, they are small men who have grown great by dint of happy windfalls plus their own inborn acumen. By their rise they prove that every individual, however destitute at the moment, has similar possibilities.

Thus basking in the applause of their less opulent fellows, Texas multimillionaires are now reaching out to control the politics of the entire nation. They have poured money into the campaign funds of their favorite Congressional candidates from Wisconsin, Maryland, Connecticut, New York, Maine, Virginia, Missouri, Ohio, Indiana, Illinois, Michigan, North Dakota, Wyoming, Montana, Idaho, Washington, California, Nevada, Utah, Arizona, and New Mexico. Very few of the Texas-supported candidates from these states were actually elected in 1952, however.

The most noted among the successful Texas darlings is Senator Joseph R. McCarthy. In addition to heavy support for his own campaigns in Wisconsin, McCarthy obtained from his Texas friends several large contributions for the defeat of Senator Millard Tydings from Maryland in 1950. One gift to Tydings's opponent, made at McCarthy's request, amounted to $10,000. Half of it came from Clint Murchison of Dallas, half of it from Mrs. Murchison. An item in the Tydings fight was a composite photograph, made by combining one of Tydings with one of Earl Browder. Altogether, Murchison alone has donated approximately $40,000 to various McCarthy projects. These include airplane rides in Murchison's private planes and travel expenses for special trips undertaken by the gentleman from Wisconsin. On September 28, 1951, Senator William Benton of Connecticut made ten charges of dishonesty and unethical acts on McCarthy's part. Since these charges were specific and well documented, Benton had to be removed from the senate. Partly because of large contributions to his enemies by rich Texans, he lost in the elections of 1952.

Texas enthusiasm for McCarthy is not limited to multimillionaires. On his wedding day he received a Cadillac as a gift from Texans of modest means. It had been bought through contributions ranging from one to one hundred dollars, three fourths of the money coming from within Texas.

On April 21, 1954, McCarthy was the speaker at the San Jacinto celebration. His audience, estimated at somewhere between six thousand and ten thousand, was described by the *Houston Post* as being "generally sympathetic," with frequent applause coming particularly from the reserved seats of special guests in the front rows. Unlike that rain-bound festival of thirteen years before, when Governor O'Daniel made his surprise announcement of Andrew Jackson Houston's appointment as senator, the McCarthy event took place outside, with the Wisconsonian speaking from a large bunting-draped platform before the star-capped monument. Airplanes roared over the gathering while the famous red-hunter poured his eloquence into the microphone, and humorous remarks were made to the effect that the noise of the planes stemmed from a deliberate conspiracy to hamper the McCarthy crusade.

When one clipper flew so low that the senator had to pause until it passed, a man in the audience shouted: "Maybe that's one of your red friends!"

Sam Houston's triumph at San Jacinto, said McCarthy, was "perhaps the most outstanding victory ever witnessed on a battlefield since time began." Santa Anna was roundly condemned as a "blood-stained brutalitarian." General Houston was compared with General Douglas MacArthur, but Houston was more fortunate because his orders were not "treasonably countermanded" by politicians in Washington. "If freedom ever dies in this troubled world," declared the senator, "one of the last places in which it will die will be Texas. If Texas were the first to be attacked, I am sure it would be one of the last to be vanquished."

Like O'Daniel, McCarthy chose graphic diction. Persons with Communist records, he said, are being allowed to stand "poised with a razor, if you please, over the jugular vein of this nation." His efforts, he complained, are being "ground to a standstill by the machinations of clever Pentagon politicians."

Now the robe of priesthood, which Texans traditionally distrust, has fallen on the Pentagon. In the days of Sam Houston and Stephen F. Austin it was seen on the genteel clergymen of Europe and the monastic friars of Mexico. O'Daniel placed it on the politicians, first in Austin, then in Washington. Now McCarthy has identified it with both politics and military brass.

With the televising of the McCarthy-Army hearings, Texas's enthusiasm for her "third senator" has cooled. Even Murchison now feels that McCarthy's exaggerations have weakened our case against real Communists. Robert E. Smith, the great independent oil operator and civic leader of Houston, said recently to Charles J. V. Murphy of *Fortune* magazine: ". . . If it came to a choice between Eisenhower and McCarthy, I'd take Ike. . . ."

For the May 1954 issue of *Fortune*, Murphy interviewed forty-four Texas businessmen. Although he found Texas more favorable to McCarthy than any other area except possibly Chicago and environs, considerable criticism was encountered. Houston Harte, who owns a controlling interest in eleven newspapers scattered from West Texas to the Red River Valley and the Gulf Coast, considers McCarthy a cheap demagogue. J. R. Parten, president of the Woodley Petroleum Company in Houston, said: "I am for dealing firmly with traitors but not in McCarthy's way. Our tradition of civil liberties means too much to me to see it sacrificed to catch Communists." Actually, neither Harte nor Parten ever had much use for McCarthy. The *Dallas Morning News*, which endorsed him wholeheartedly for a long time, now supports him only "with reservations."

Much Texas money has also gone into the presidential races. General Douglas MacArthur got heavy support from Texas millionaires when there was a chance of his being nominated for the presidency. After MacArthur lost the nomination, the flow of Lone-Star cash was turned to Eisenhower.

Since the removal of O.P.A. price ceilings, the Texas government has been kept well out of debt, thanks largely to taxes on gas and oil. Strangely, the stringency of Texas labor legislation, while it limits union activities, has not seriously retarded unionization. Some enterprises, such as the Le Tourneau company, making large machinery in East Texas, persist in using cheap labor and keeping unions out by every means available. But in others—for instance, the Bell Telephone companies—Texas happened to have good leaders, and the Texas workers are more highly organized than those of other states. Also, many large companies, such as Sheffield Steel, Sinclair Oil, and Alcoa and Reynolds Aluminum, were already organized on a national scale before they came to Texas. They thus ushered the unions in. A third type of industry in Texas consists of companies which, like the railroad enterprises of the nineteenth century, had already learned before they came into the state that they had better pay good wages and provide good working conditions. By voluntarily maintaining standards on a par with those established in unionized plants, these companies have prevented the suffering, insecurity, and discontent that have driven the workers of other states and other shops within the state to organize. Thus, the salaried laborers of such enterprises—Humble Oil is an example—are enjoying the benefit of reforms achieved by unions already existing in the older industrial regions. Without organizing themselves, these former farm boys have all the prosperity and security they need. They hold their employers in high regard and look with suspicion on the very type of collective action that has made their happiness so easily attainable.

One important factor which tends to prevent unionization is the peculiar nature of the oil, gas, sulphur, and chemical industries on which the Texas economy rests. Being liquid and volatile, these materials can be conducted through pipes and automatic valves with very little physical effort once the plants are built. Large permanent labor crews are therefore unnecessary, and Texas cities consequently have an unusually high proportion of white-collar workers, engineers, chemists, geologists, and physicists. Such persons need join no union to obtain good salaries, since their talents are rare and in constantly increasing demand.

A lamentable characteristic of present Texas politics is the lack of strong representation in her lawmaking bodies. Because of the small salaries paid to senators and representatives, the caliber of the Texas legislature is low and its susceptibility to lobbying is high. Free meals, drinks, and similar favors are liberally thrown in by the lobbyists for good measure. These are welcomed, since legislators receive only ten dollars a day for the first 120 days of each regular session and five dollars a day for the remainder of their stay in Austin, plus $2.50 for each twenty-five miles to and from the capital. Because the normal session lasts 120 days and the legislature meets only once every two years, this amounts to an income of only $600 per year plus the travel allowance. Since no man can come anywhere near supporting himself alone, much less a family, on such low pay, a legislator must have some other source of income. Yet his business must be such that he can leave it when the legislature meets. This seriously cuts down on the number of possible candidates. Lawyers can run for the office only if they have funds to fall back on and partners who can keep their firms alive while they are away. Since the regular sessions begin in January, when cattle and crops need little attention, ranchers and farmers are sometimes elected. Merchants often serve if they own their stores and can leave them with trusted partners or employees.

The fifty-second legislature, which met in 1951, contained seventy-eight lawyers, thirty-seven businessmen with specialties ranging from storekeeping to real estate, twenty-one students mostly of law, eighteen farmers, fifteen ranchers, three military men, and one teacher. The remaining eight had no occupation outside politics. They were largely old men who had retired from their more lucrative life work. The fifty-third legislature, meeting in 1953, had a roughly similar composition. The same has been true of other legislatures for which there is a record. Actually, then, the professional politicians so loudly assailed by O'Daniel have always been a small minority at Austin.

One way to boost the income of legislators is to close the regular session at the end of the 120 days which provide the ten-dollar-a-day stipend, then persuade the governor to call a special session immediately afterward. Pay for the special session is ten dollars a day, as contrasted to the five-dollar-a-day provision for the regular session in excess of 120 days. When the governor refuses to call a special session, however, the prospect of lower pay stimulates the legislature to finish its decisions on important bills within the 120 days.

Since decisions on most bills are made in committees, and since the voting in the sessions is seldom widely published, the activities of legislators in Austin are not very stringently limited by the wishes of their respective electorates. The ranchers, farmers, and businessmen in the legislature can be expected to look after their own interests, and the practicing advocates are more apt to heed their paying clients than to carry out the desires of their voting constituents.

The speaker of the house, who appoints the committees, holds a position far more powerful than is warranted by his responsibility as representative of a single district. By packing the committees with members who have pledged him their support, and by distributing his opposers in minorities on these committees, he can often kill or obtain the passage of any legislation about which he may feel strongly.

In addition to the low pay of legislators and the excessive power exercised by the speaker of the house, Texas politics suffers from a third weakness which, under present-day conditions, has far-reaching and often rather unhappy consequences. This is the one-party system. Many Texans today have sentiments more in harmony with Republicanism than with De-

mocratism, but the Republican party is so weak in Texas that
they dare not support the Republican candidate for fear of
throwing their votes away. The only avenue open for the political expression of their views is the devious one of masquer-
ading as Democrats and endeavoring to divert the Democratic
candidate from his party's generally accepted national platform. Since O'Daniel's time, this has been done with considerable success, but the method is beset with perils. Announced
Republicans and right-wing Texas Democrats would have far
more power if they could work together steadily instead of
spasmodically. As it now stands, a Republican cannot endorse
a right-wing Texas Democrat without being accused of dis-
loyalty to his fellow Republicans. Likewise, a right-wing Democrat, if he favors a Republican, is stigmatized for having
"bolted the party." Besides the fear of this dangerous stigma,
many right-wing Democrats still nurse the traditional dread
of being identified with northern abolitionists. This dread is
perpetuated indefinitely by the strong racial prejudice which
old-line southerners treasure as a part of their heritage. Such
southerners have always been conservative, but with the advent of Franklin D. Roosevelt and Harry Truman, their party
has changed. Since they will not change with it, they are left
out in the cold, cut off from their old allies, yet culturally
unable to form new alliances with those industrialists from
the north whose predecessors opposed slavery when it threatened to compete against their paid labor, but who now find
equally potent reasons for soft-pedaling the race question.

A fourth unfortunate feature of present-day Texas politics
is the poll tax. Originally adopted in 1902, when the Populist
party was threatening the *status quo*, it cuts down on voting
volume among the poor of all races and creeds. In 1949 there
was an unsuccessful movement to repeal it.

A fifth serious weakness in the Texas political system is
the governor's appointive power. Too many of the important
governing boards in the state, which control the schools and

other instruments of public welfare, are appointed by the governor. Their program of rotation is such that in two terms a governor can put his own appointees in the majority on each board. These boards, in turn, can mold public opinion in such a way as to perpetuate in office either the governor to whom they owe their power or his hand-picked successors. This makes it extremely difficult to remove from the government any group of individuals that may become entrenched.

Texas's tardiness in getting rid of these incumbrances is no doubt partly due to the strong influence which her more conservative elements have exerted on the education of her youth. Prior to 1949, textbooks for the public schools were chosen by a politically appointed committee. Members of this committee were often extremely narrow-minded and fearful of change. The same was true of the governing boards for the state's principal postgraduate schools: the University, A. and M., and the Texas Technological College. As governors of Texas, O'Daniel and his successors appointed extremely conservative regents to the boards of these three schools. They got along fairly well with A. and M. and Texas Tech, but their troubles at the University have had lasting repercussions.

◇◇

5. Politics and Public Education

THE MASSES of Texas were boiling with rage in the spring of 1942. A war was on. Pearl Harbor had been bombed. Texas boys were giving their lives at the front to save democracy from the Nipponese, the Nazis, and the Fascists. The national Congress was wasting precious time on long-winded speeches and legalistic quibbles. Capital and labor were squabbling over wages, hours, and extra pay for overtime. Strikes had tied up huge armament plants while Texas boys, in need of guns, were dying overseas.

Although capital and national politics were partly responsible, the public wrath of Texas was largely concentrated on organized labor. For this there were numerous reasons. Strikes and walkouts are more visible and spectacular than the quiet swell of figures on the profit side of big-business ledgers. Newspapers, while they often tried to be impartial, were naturally inclined to capitalize on the drama of the moment and to favor the businessmen who bought advertising space in their pages. Texas, with her relatively small amount of unionization, her anti-labor law, and her fair-haired boy O'Daniel up in Washington spreading the anti-union gospel, could look with smug disdain on the bickerings of big labor leaders in the north and east.

Yet much of Texas's ire was also vented on Washington, that hotbed of professional politicians and academically trained specialists who would not listen to her patriotic Senator O'Daniel. Texas capitalists, eager to escape all blame for the situation and at the same time keep wages as low as possible, did what they could to feed the flames. Here was a chance to agitate with telling eloquence against Roosevelt's Fair Labor Standards Act, with its obnoxious requirement that employers pay overtime rates for all work done in excess of forty hours a week. Front-page editorials bawled out long denunciations of "Washington-as-usual, with its card indexes, its swivel chairs—and its alibis." Phrases in bold-faced print created the impression that the Fair Labor Standards Act prevented men from working more than forty hours per week. Washington's politicians were featured as "rebuking" the people for "getting too much in earnest about an all-out working week for an all-out war." The swivel-chair gentility, cried the *Dallas Morning News*, "means only all-out for forty hours a week."

The response was so tumultuous that the *News* devoted whole pages to letters from its readers which echoed in righteous, self-congratulatory indignation: "I don't see how a war can be won . . . with a forty-hour week. . . ." "All of us should work as long as is necessary to get the job done. . . ." "Hours don't enter the mind of a farmer." "All the farmer asks is an opportunity to do the job."

In March 1942 the *Congressional Record* printed 128 telegrams to O'Daniel, bearing thousands of Texan signatures, urging him to push anti-strike legislation and, above all, to combat the forty-hour week. The uniformity of these telegrams and the sentiment expressed at scores of indignation meetings held over the state indicate that their encouragement and direction on the part of labor's enemies was adept and vigorous. The anti-forty-hour-week messages to O'Daniel grew so voluminous that the government printing office complained about the unprecedented cost of incorporating them in the *Congressional Record.* O'Daniel suggested that it was the import as well as the quantity of the telegrams which alarmed the "gentlemen."

On March 17 the *Dallas Morning News* devoted all of page 13 in section one to an important announcement. In the upper lefthand quarter of this page appeared a picture of soldiers at Bataan, poorly equipped and under enemy fire. The upper righthand quarter portrayed factory buildings closed because of strikes, the forty-hour week, and holidays. Between these drawings was a two-inch space labeled "The Pacific Ocean (not as big as it used to be)."

The remainder of the page carried several strongly worded paragraphs in large black type. One of them said: "Factories which can turn out 1,000 instruments of war a week are only turning out 500. Why? Because there is a law which says a man should work only 40 hours per week! A law indeed! 40 hours of work! *Is there a law which says our sons must fight only 40 hours a week or die only 40 hours a week?"* The italics are from the original.

A concluding paragraph read: "WHAT CAN YOU DO ABOUT IT? PLENTY! Find out by attending the giant WE WANT ACTION mass meeting next SUNDAY at 3:30 p.m. at Fair Park AUDITO-RIUM, Dallas." At the bottom of the page were listed twenty-six names of Texas mothers whose sons were in the armed forces.

Karl Hoblitzelle, slender, handsome president of Interstate Theaters, was chairman of the committee which sponsored this mass rally. A front-page story in the *Dallas News* quoted him as saying: "The main object of the meeting is to offer every citizen an opportunity to express his sentiments concerning the important issues now before Congress."

The turnout for the meeting was tremendous. The Fair Park overflowed with cars and pedestrians. The auditorium was packed, and a sea of citizens stood outside. A loudspeaker conveyed the voices of orators to these latecomers. The fair grounds were redolent with huge signs reading "WORK OR FIGHT," "IT'S NOW OR NEVER," "WORK WILL WIN." Parents of fighters overseas were honor guests, occupying seats on the speakers' platform inside the auditorium.

Standing beneath a huge United States flag and a sign in red, white, and blue which read: "LET'S START WINNING THIS WAR," Hoblitzelle declared that patriots probably predominated in labor groups, but that all organizations had had false and selfish leaders.

The star speaker was Dr. Umphrey Lee, president of Southern Methodist University. "No man worth his salt," he said, "wants any man to make a fortune out of this war. We must say to our representatives in Congress that they must not support any measure that will let any group or individual line their pockets."

A printed petition was adopted by a rising vote and signed

by hundreds. It demanded a "War Law" which would command 100-per-cent co-operation by both management and labor, prohibit all lock-outs and strikes, and lengthen the standard working week to forty-eight hours.

"This would not lower the basic wage under the present law," said the petition, "nor prevent overtime bonus beyond 48 hours. It would not bar higher wages, based on merit or justified by the cost of living. But it would let our millions of patriotic workers do more for their country, and still get pay at standard rates for the additional hours of work. . . ."

Somebody shouted from the audience: "You're hearing only one side of this!"

Another man called several times for recognition but did not get the floor.

Present also were four representatives of that intellectual elite which Texans had learned long before to look upon with diffidence. They were economics teachers from the University of Texas, that great secular institution at Austin which had been established in 1887 and enriched in the 1920's by West Texas oil. These teachers had written the *Dallas News* on March 19, calling attention to the erroneous remark in the announcement that there was "a law which says a man should work only 40 hours a week," and asking for a place on the program at the meeting where they could correct the error by explaining the true provisions of the Fair Labor Standards Act: that it did not prevent employees from working as long as necessary, but only required employers to pay time-and-one-half wage rates for work done beyond forty hours in any given week by one individual. The *News* referred the teachers to Chairman Hoblitzelle, but no time was allotted them on the program.

They went to Dallas on the day of the rally and spoke with the chairman a few hours before the meeting, requesting permission to address the crowd for two minutes. The permission was refused.

The teachers attended the rally, but made no further effort to speak. After it was over, they took a written statement to the *Dallas News*. The *News* did not print it verbatim, but incorporated it in a longer story of the meeting. It averred that the gathering had not been spontaneous but was well organized, that volunteer speakers had been refused, that the scheduled speakers were not representative but chosen "on a basis of previously assured viewpoint, and that while all sides were condemned, labor was branded in particular." The teachers signed their names: Valdemar Carlson, J. Fagg Foster, Wendell C. Gordon, and W. N. Peach.

Shortly after this statement was published, Judge T. W. Davidson of Dallas wrote to the governing board of the University of Texas, complaining that its teachers had departed from "true economics." The University's governing board consists of nine regents appointed by the governor of the state and confirmed by a two-thirds majority in the senate.

The teachers finished their current contracts at the University. Then Carlson returned to another school where he had formerly been teaching. Foster, Gordon, and Peach, being in line for reappointment, were asked by the regents to apologize in writing for their statement about the Dallas meeting. They refused.

Although recommended by their department and the University administration, they were not re-employed. The reason given for the termination of their services was that they had failed to show "a generous respect for the rights, feelings, and opinions of others," and had hence violated the University rules. The board's action was condemned as an infringement on academic freedom by both the American Association of University Professors and the University's forthright, outspoken president, Homer Price Rainey.

In January 1943 another unfortunate rift between the state's traditional standards and the more recently imported culture of its leading educational institution was publicized by a sudden action of the board. As was the case with the economics instructors, the leading regents in this action were appointees of ex-Governor W. Lee O'Daniel and his protégé, Governor Coke Stevenson.

There was on the reading list of a University English course a book entitled *U.S.A.*, by John Dos Passos. Hailed by the *Saturday Review of Literature* as one of the nation's five best contemporary books, *U.S.A.* had been placed on reading lists in sixty-eight other American institutions. The book seemed intellectually stimulating to the University's lily-fingered liberals but could not be other than obnoxious to Texas's God-fearing farmers and mushroom industrialists. In addition to some stylistically admirable writing and some exquisitely touching scenes, it gave a swift, graphic picture of life in the big cities, portraying the United States as a vicious financial oligarchy where no man might succeed and "think" at the same time, and where the best of women were prone to excessive blushing and sleeping with men whom they had not married. In response to criticisms from parents and other professors, the teachers of the course had agreed to drop the book at the end of the semester.

Then the regents found out about it. On January 9 they met and conducted a two-hour examination of the committee which taught the course, saying repeatedly that they wanted to fire whoever had put Dos Passos's book on the reading list. The questions were apparently framed to ascertain whether the teachers were true Texans or "foreigners." Each teacher was asked where he had been born, how long he had taught at the University, where he had got his education, what was his rank in the department, whether he was married, whether he had children, and whether he knew who had put the book on the list.

Fortunately for the professors, no one person could be singled out as the selector of the book; it had been chosen by committee action. However, the regents ordered it removed from the list immediately. A large number of students, eager for adulthood as symbolized by familiarity with the "facts of life," objected strongly to the order.

On October 12, 1944, President Rainey called the faculty together and read them a statement describing sixteen violations of academic freedom and good university government on the part of the regents. Since the case of the economics professors was already widely known, he did not dwell upon it. He neither endorsed nor condemned the Dos Passos book but did mention that it had been "selected within recent weeks as one of the five greatest literary productions of this generation in American literature."

The removal of Mr. Arthur L. Brandon from his position as director of public relations was described in detail. "Without my knowing anything about it," said Rainey, "a member of the board of regents . . . called Mr. William McGill on the telephone the night before the precipitate dismissal of Mr. Brandon occurred and told Mr. McGill that the board was going to change the director of public relations at its meeting the next day and asked Mr. McGill if he would take the position." McGill refused. At its meeting, the board abolished Brandon's job "without bringing a single charge against him and denied his own request for an opportunity to come before the board and be heard."

The abolishment of Brandon's job was subsequently described, by the same board member who had offered it to McGill, as an economy measure. This was Regent Orville Bullington of Wichita Falls, a lifelong, militant Republican. Bullington had been appointed to the board by Governor W. Lee O'Daniel in January 1941.

In addition to official acts of the board as a whole, Rainey enumerated several moves on the part of individual members that he considered harmful to the "free trade in ideas" which is essential in a first-class university. Officials personally unsatisfactory to certain board members had been begged and pressured to resign. One regent had wanted to fire three University-extension officials for enacting an interscholastic-sports rule which rendered his two sons ineligible to play football. Another had "insisted on subjecting all of us to a patriotism test in the form of a questionnaire prepared by himself and to be submitted to every faculty member and employee of the University." When this project failed, he had attempted to abolish the University's rule protecting academic tenure.

Moreover, the board had consistently refused to grant money for social-science research, limiting its grants to the physical sciences. Some board members, instead of striving to get more money for the University, were determined to keep appropriations low and thus mitigate the tax burden of the large corporations with which they were connected.

So ran Rainey's declaration, made to the faculty and published throughout the state. He had first tried to caution and conciliate the regents, but his efforts only minimized their faith in him, a faith that had already been mitigated by the left-wing tone of his public speeches.

While he lost the support of the regents, Rainey was gaining that of the students and faculty. To a majority of these, the contest was not an ordinary trial of strength between two political points of view. It was a fight for survival on the part of intellectual liberty. Rainey represented the American principle of tolerance, whereby all views could compete on their own merits in the open market of public discussion, unhampered by pressures or fears from any quarter; the regents represented a conspiracy against this principle, a movement to use coercive force in stamping out all viewpoints except their own.

As October drew to a close, the regents met in Houston behind closed doors. Fearing that they were going to fire Rainey, the faculty sent a committee there to remonstrate. After deliberating until ten o'clock on the evening of November 1, 1944, the regents adjourned with the announcement that Rainey was no longer president of the University and that Dr. Theophilus Shickle Painter, a member of the faculty's remonstrating committee and a lifelong biologist, had been chosen acting president.

Painter wrote a letter to the faculty, saying: "I want it definitely understood that I am not a candidate for the position of permanent president, and I will not accept it, if it were offered me."

But he said "certain factors" made him feel "duty bound to accept the position temporarily for the general welfare of the University of Texas." He asked the professors what they thought he ought to do. Fearing that a regent-appointed president from outside the faculty might have been worse, the faculty unanimously passed a resolution asking Painter to accept the post for the interim.

The news of Rainey's removal spread gloom throughout the University campus. In the eyes of teachers and pupils, the University had been doomed by the regents to abject ignominy among the world's great educational institutions. The Lone-Star flag hung at half mast before the main building on the hill north of the capitol. The regional wealth displayed by the three-million-dollar University tower, which shoots 307 feet into the sky, honeycombed with offices and crowned with four twelve-foot clocks and a forty-thousand-pound carillon, appeared futile to those who had just heard the news. The inscription on the sprawling central building at the tower's base: "Ye shall know the truth and the truth shall make you free" seemed rather hollow now. Even the dullest office drudges were keenly conscious of the world-wide shame to which they had been condemned.

The students went on strike. Refusing to attend classes until Rainey was reinstated as president, they accumulated on November 3 at a huge rally and moved in mute mourning down the long winding street from the University to the center of town, in step with the slow roll and boom of drums

and the low moan of trombones in the Longhorn Band playing Chopin's Funeral March. At their head moved a long
black coffin, covered with flowers and an explanatory sign:
"ACADEMIC FREEDOM IS DEAD." The youngest participant in the
parade was Lyman Ripperton, just eighteen months old. His
student mother and father pushed him in his baby carriage,
above which hung an interrogatory sign: "WILL I BE EDUCATED
OR INDOCTRINATED?" Another sign, referring to the current governor, Coke Stevenson, asked: "WILL STEVENSON FIDDLE WHILE
THE UNIVERSITY BURNS?" Another read: "RATS AND REGENTS
LEAVE A SINKING SHIP."

City officials, listing the procession as a legitimate funeral,
re-routed buses and cleared the road ahead for the slowly moving coffin and its followers. Their destinations were the capitol
and the governor's mansion, where they stood outside and sang
"The Eyes of Texas Are upon You." The police publicly
complimented the student body, saying that the demonstration was one of the most impressive they had ever seen.

On the following Monday the students returned to their
classes "under protest" and went to work on an organized
"spread the facts" campaign. Letters and telegrams deploring
Rainey's dismissal poured into the University offices. Sixty
per cent of the communications received by Governor Stevenson favored Rainey. Mrs. I. D. Fairchild, from the East Texas
town of Lufkin, being the only regent who had voted against
firing Rainey, was bombarded with praise by wire and mail
and word of mouth. She was hailed as the "dear lady who
dared say the 'no' that was the 'yes' for the University." The
student body sent her two hundred dollars' worth of flowers.
Student President Mac Wallace shouted: "We'll put flowers
all over her house!"

Rainey went to the stadium expecting only to see a football game and hear the pep squad cheer for the University's
team. He saw these things, but he also saw the whole audience

rise to applaud him and heard them sing "The Eyes of Texas" in his honor.

In public statements made for the announced purpose of justifying their action, the regents emphasized the immorality of the Dos Passos book, assuming that Rainey had approved it and that his morals were therefore questionable. They also dwelt at length on ugly tales which gravely damaged the University's reputation.

The controversy soon drew nationwide comment. *Time* magazine described the fight in its terse, picturesque way, averring that the "rangy sons of the Lone-Star State" were "quick to honor a hero, quick to resent a slur. . . ." The *New Republic* said: "The regents sought to perpetuate reaction . . . and Rainey opposed them." The *Daily Californian* could well understand the Texas students' demonstration, for "students have an added incentive for protest since the value of their degrees is at stake." Bernard De Voto wrote a fiery article for *Harper's* magazine, declaring: "The University of Texas can no longer seek the truth, discover the truth, or teach the truth. It has been taken over by a dictatorship." Drew Pearson called attention to the relationship between Senator O'Daniel and the University's regent trouble. Pulitzer-Prize-winning columnist Thomas L. Stokes said that the fight had "national implications." Also, many young Texans whose views were permanently influenced by the Rainey-regent contest have since gone elsewhere to become prominent. Worthy of note among them is John Henry Faulk, radio commentator for the Columbia Broadcasting System, who always introduces himself by saying that he is from Texas.

By the beginning of 1945 the terms of three of the regents had expired and three others had resigned. Governor Stevenson's six new appointees were far more suave than their predecessors. Prior to their approval by the senate, they met in open session and voted to refuse the numerous resolutions from groups throughout the state, including the University faculty, which demanded Rainey's reinstatement. Shortly afterward the Texas senate met behind closed doors and confirmed the governor's appointment of these new regents. Although the entire state was vitally interested in the issue, Texas voters were never allowed to ascertain specifically which senators had supported the confirmation. Yet the regents interpreted the senate's approval as a green light from the people.

On February 16 the new board met and adopted a statement of policies and principles, declaring that "the board is unreservedly in favor of academic freedom at the University of Texas and will afford it complete recognition and protection. It understands academic freedom to mean freedom in research, freedom to proclaim and to teach the results of such research, freedom to teach what the teacher believes to be true, limited only by the recognized decencies and proprieties obtaining among normal human beings." It also announced that an "era of tranquillity" had begun at the University and asked the faculty to appoint a committee to advise the board in selecting a new president. The committee was accordingly appointed, but months passed and Painter continued as acting president.

On July 22, 1945, the Southern Association of Colleges and Secondary Schools placed the University on probation, saying that academic freedom was "reasonably safeguarded" there, but that the "situation in the institution" was "unhealthy." By the fall of this year, however, the new board's mood had grown exceedingly benign. Research funds were approved even for so abstruse a project as the study of Locke and Bacon. Re-employment was offered to those three economics instructors who had been fired for trying to clarify the true nature of the forty-hour-week law at the Dallas mass meeting four years before. Only two of them were interested. They were rehired at higher ranks and salaries.

In the spring of 1946 three events occurred in such rapid

succession that some editorialists suspected direct cause-and-effect connections between them. Rainey announced that he would run for governor, Painter was made permanent president of the University, and the American Association of University Professors blacklisted the University administration. The association based its action on "attempts by a politically dominant group to impose its social and educational views on the University." The administration was kept under censure until 1953.

Painter explained in a long speech why he considered it necessary that he accept the permanent presidency. Outstanding men, recommended by the faculty and approached by the regents, had refused the position, yet somebody had to carry on. He called for an armistice and asked all to join him in the one area where all were of one mind: "building an institution of learning to which all free people can look with pride." Although annoyed at this shift from his former statement that he would not take the job, the faculty assured him of its support "in all measures conducive to the success and sound progress of the University."

Today, after several administrative shifts, including Painter's return to biology, the University faces a future of continuous expansion under President Logan Wilson, a native of Huntsville, Texas. In addition to the Galveston medical school, it now has branches in Houston, El Paso, and Dallas. The Post-Graduate School of Medicine, dedicated to keeping general physicians up to date through short courses given by specialists, is located in Houston and has divisions in Tyler, Corpus Christi, El Paso, Lubbock, Temple, San Antonio, and San Angelo. The Dental Branch and the M. D. Anderson Hospital and Tumor Institute are also at Houston. Texas Western College at El Paso, originally known as the College of Mines and Metallurgy, is also a branch of the University. Among the University's youngest additions is the Southwestern Medical School at Dallas.

The financial report of the entire University for the fiscal year ending August 31, 1953, shows total endowment funds of $202,801,062.35. The main University at Austin now has twelve colleges and schools and nine additional units of instruction. Under the administrative jurisdiction of the main University there are more than fifty units of organized research, including an off-campus research center with a 397-acre tract on the Balcones fault line eight miles north of Austin, an institute of marine science at Port Aransas on the Gulf Coast, and the McDonald Observatory for astronomical research atop Mount Locke, near Fort Davis in West Texas. The observatory is used in co-operation with the University of Chicago. Since 1941 other universities have also used the observatory under special arrangements.

There is also a co-operative program between the University engineering college and the two religious schools, Baylor and Texas Christian University, whereby a student can get his engineering at Texas and his liberal-arts education at either Baylor or T. C. U.

The University of Texas library and archive collection is one of the largest in the country, with volumes and documents numbering in the hundreds of thousands. While it contains rare items from all over the world, with a fine Dryden and Pope collection, it is richest in materials dealing with Texas and Latin American history. Particularly useful in the Texas collection is an alphabetical card file of all individuals whose names appeared in nineteenth-century Texas newspapers, with the names of the papers, the publication dates, the pages, and the columns of all the news items in which they figure. The private papers of numerous illustrious Texans have also been accumulated together with the general archives and all items relating to Texas in the Eugene C. Barker Texas History Center, a long, low building in the shadow of the University tower. The Hispanic collection was begun in 1899, when the 80,795 documents of the Bexar Archives, amassed during

Fondren Science Building at Southern Methodist University, Dallas.

Lamar State College of Technology, Beaumont.

Administration Building at Texas Tech (Texas Technological College), Lubbock.

Texas Southern University, erected for Negroes, Houston.

Texas's long career as a Spanish province, were transferred from San Antonio to the University. The foundation of the book collection is the private library of the famous Mexican historian Genaro García, purchased by the University in 1921. Both the archives and the bookshelves have been vastly expanded by the addition of transcripts from old Spanish government archives and the private libraries of other eminent historians. The papers of many Latin American leaders, mostly Mexican, have also been added to the archives. At present the Latin American collection is strongest in history and weakest in the fine arts, although the Mexican literature section is rich. Geographically, the Latin American coverage is best for Mexico. For South America it is spotted, the largest collections being those that deal with Paraguay and the La Plata region.

The student-teacher ratio at Texas compares favorably with that of parallel institutions in the neighboring states. There are fifteen students for every teacher hired by the University of Texas, whereas the University of Oklahoma has twenty students per teacher and the University of New Mexico hires only one teacher for every twenty-three students. But Texas falls below other large universities in the west and east. On the Berkeley campus of the University of California there are only nine students per teacher. The University of Maryland hires a teacher for every ten students. Yale University has only about five students for each teacher hired. Harvard has only three.

Texas still suffers from an overemphasis on technical training at the expense of the human sciences. For each semester hour of engineering taught in the long session of 1952–3, the University paid $19.11 purely in salaries for faculty and staff. This was for the benefit of only 1,926 specialized individuals. Yet in English, a subject which is essential to all students, only $6.95 was paid in salaries for each semester hour taught. English classes were crowded. Of the 215 English sections taught during the first semester, 177 had more than twenty students each. Meanwhile the engineering school, despite its smaller clientele, gave 232 classes of which only 100 had more than twenty students each. The English department could afford only one advanced class of less than five students, whereas engineering had thirteen such classes. Since small classes are vital to effective instruction in English, these figures tell a sad story. The emphasis on engineering is of course symptomatic of the state's rapid industrial growth, but this should not justify the wholesale production of robot-like technicians with deficient knowledge of the humanities. The situation indicates that, with all its physical expansion, the University has not come a very long way since the dark days of the Rainey fight.

In his race for the governorship, Rainey drummed up enough support to put him in the run-off, where he lost, polling only 361,178 votes while the winner, Beauford H. Jester of Corsicana, got 700,178. As a candidate, Rainey had much in his favor. He was a deeply religious native Texan and a self-made man, having worked his way through school and college. He had a good mind, and he parried the attacks of his opponents with courage and dexterity. But he lacked two important essentials for victory in Texas at this time: the backing of big business and at least a touch of the O'Daniel salesmanship. Instead of protecting business from the taxes that it always feared, he threatened to impose more and heavier duties in the interest of better public institutions and a free university. Large oil, gas, and sulphur interests consequently dreaded his election and exerted their powerful influence against him.

His education, far superior as it was to O'Daniel's, proved more of a liability than an asset in getting Texas votes. Besides identifying him with the type of standardized priesthood which Texans had never appreciated, it gave him the wrong orientation altogether. Heavy with ponderous abstractions, his speeches lacked the lilt, the verve, and the concreteness of the O'Daniel creations.

He did take a few superficial tips from the O'Daniel record. He endeavored to amuse the folk with simple fireside poems and illustrate his points with anecdotal stories. But the poems were gleaned from library shelves, and his recital of them was sadly flat compared to O'Daniel's animated outbursts. The stories, told in Rainey's dignified prosaic tones, never lost their academic smell. When he tried to illustrate his points with metaphors and similes, his style became stiff and schoolmasterish.

Moreover, Rainey's opponents never allowed his listeners to forget that irreligious Dos Passos book which he had supposedly condoned. Candidate Grover Sellers used the book and a series of "men only" meetings to touch one of the deepest and strongest of human instincts: the urge to protect family integrity. After reading a select passage, Sellers would say: "That, gentlemen, is the kind of thing which will help break down the American home, one of the few things we have left. . . . Shotguns have popped all over Texas for far less than that." Rainey no doubt suffered as a result of these meetings, but so did those who thus lambasted him. Naïvely confident though they seemed until election day, they got a mere pittance of votes.

And so the Rainey race reiterated the same lesson that politicians might have learned from O'Daniel's rise and fall: modern Texans do not like mud-slinging. By mud-slinging I mean the effort to besmirch the character of a specific opponent. The method backfires because the victim's friends rush to his rescue. Yet since the world loves a warrior, a champion must have some target to shoot at.

O'Daniel's early success is largely due to the fact that he chose an indefinite straw man to lambast: "professional politicians." In addition to being easily linked with the academi-

cally trained church hierarchy which Texans had learned from
camp-meeting Protestantism to suspect, this scapegoat was
sufficiently vague so that no particular individual could consider himself attacked. Even the lawyers in Austin could point
to their private practice and exonerate themselves, to their
own satisfaction, at least, from the role. Thus the supposed
source of all evil floated from place to place and everybody
could join the flour-salesman in his thrilling pursuit of it.
While it might seem to reside at times in fellow hunters, no
particular Texan had to find it in himself. This became even
more true when O'Daniel went to Congress and reported the
enemy's residence in the safely remote national capital. With
Satan at this great distance, Texans could feel blissfully virtu-
ous and militant.

Thus in his early campaigns O'Daniel awakened the same
warlike response, the same glorious abandon, the same blind
faith that has produced great religious and military movements from time immemorial. This zeal, being inherent in
human habits for thousands of tribal generations, is a sure-fire
hit, especially in that Lone-Star State to which so many restless souls tramped in pioneer days "to fight for their rights."

O'Daniel was all the more invincible because there was
some truth in his contentions. Genuine guilt did exist among
some individuals generally embraced by the scapegoat phrase,
and unscientific minds quickly jumped to the conclusion that
all the world's woes would be cured as soon as their hero
reached Austin—and later Washington—and cleaned up the
mess. It is a flattering sensation to consider onself among the
select few who are wise to the long-hidden source of all un-
happiness. It is a sweet, self-congratulatory thought to consider the world's rejuvenation so close at hand, in one's very
grasp. It gives one a sense of power, of discovery, of unprecedented insight. At the same time, it unifies a man's emotions,
so that he can focus all his anger on one supposed universal
menace. Yet however gratifying to the ego and successful in

politics, this habit of personifying and dramatizing issues can siphon people's energy away from the real causes of their troubles and so prevent progress.

The Rainey campaign also had its scapegoat: "big business." Rainey declared that the people were held "in the chains of powerful business interests which dominate our government, our industries, and our natural resources." Big business was held responsible even for the rivalry between homecoming veterans and organized labor, and for the century-old antagonisms between racial groups! Like O'Daniel's wholesale blaming of "professional politicians," this interpretation was partly true but dangerously oversimplified and therefore generally misleading. Politically, in the Texas of the mid and latter 1940's, it was badly timed, for the state was full of businessmen who hoped to be considered big. Even the poorest farmers and the humblest laborers might suddenly get rich on oil, and they would not endorse a man who condemned either their present or their future.

Jester's battle cry was more in harmony with the times. He issued dramatic threats toward "red labor leaders" who he said were "seeking to impose their will on the people of Texas and make this state one big union under their command." Like O'Daniel, he linked these unidentified goblins with emotion-rousing images: floating flags and silver platters: "This is the crowd whose Communistic leadership think that the Russian Hammer and Sickle should float above the Stars and Stripes. They are the bunch that urges we give the atomic bomb secret to Russia on a silver platter." He could not bear to think of Texas being made into a "spawning ground for alien radicalism." As was the case with Rainey, the dangers which he saw were partly real. The difference was that Texas voters could join Jester with no risk of humiliation to their own egos.

While he refrained from naming names, Jester used some oblique slurs which were obviously aimed at Rainey. "I'm not running for governor to spite somebody, to get revenge, or to

get even," he proclaimed. "I'm one of those fellows who has
got some higher education but hasn't let it ruin him." Again
like O'Daniel, he called attention to his forbearance from personal acrimony: "I'm going to let the other candidates scratch
and fight. I'm talking about my own record. Maybe their
records aren't worth talking about." He said Texas needed
government with "a smile and friendly handshake rather than
government with malice and revenge by a man with a stick in
his hand who wants to use it on a lot of people who could be
of service if they were handled right."

As often happens in a democracy, Rainey's fight was only
superficially a failure. His recommendations for improved education, research facilities, rural roads, sanitary conditions, and
care for the aged and infirm have been accepted since his day,
timidly at first, but with ever increasing momentum and precision as previously opposing forces pooled the fruits of their
divergent points of view in the self-enriching processes of democratic action. One reason for the new movements was the
fact that Jester, in his second campaign for governor, did not
get as much support as he had expected from his former constituents. As a result, he adopted a more liberal policy than
that of his first term. Increased revenue from oil and gas is
another reason for the subsequent adoption of large-scale
development programs originally recommended by Rainey.
The increase came partly from a slight boost of tax rates and
partly from the rising price of oil and gas with the removal
of O.P.A. ceilings. Whereas the state government's income
in fiscal 1944 was only a little over $46,000,000, it rose in 1948
to almost $108,000,000. This sudden bonanza enabled state
officials to initiate building programs that they had previously
considered too expensive.

Rainey had called for extensive new buildings to take care
of post-war needs and a special university for Negroes. In 1947
the Texas State University for Negroes was established at
Houston, and in 1953 its name was changed to Texas Southern

University. A colored A. and M. already existed at Prairie View in Southwest Texas. However, since the opportunities provided by these schools could not equal those available at the older institutions, Negroes have successfully established their right to attend the regular University at Austin.

A huge over-all building program for the fourteen state-supported institutions of higher learning was passed in 1947. The cost was estimated over thirty years at between $60,000,-000 and $70,000,000. Increased funds for general education also began in 1947, the legislative year which followed Rainey's defeat at the polls. One bill required a $2,000-per-year minimum salary for teachers. The appropriation for over-all rural aid was increased from $28,000,000 biennially to $36,000,000 biennially. State institutions of higher learning got a raise to $45,000,000 from their previous appropriation of only $26,000,-000, and the junior colleges got almost three times what they had had in the preceding biennium. Vocational training got $1,000,000 more than ever before, and the sum for teaching handicapped children rose from $300,000 to $700,000. Governor Jester first opposed some of these bills, but later allowed them to become laws without his signature.

Many of the advances desired by Rainey have come about very differently from the way he visualized. The story of the Gilmer-Aikin movement shows how chimerical were both his and O'Daniel's straw men. A desire for better public schools had triumphed in the state legislature of 1947 so decisively that all hope was lost for Jester's no-new-tax program. But if large sums of money were to be spent on public schools, the school system had better be such that none of the funds would be used wastefully.

The traditional Texas school system was sadly encumbered with clumsy administrative growths and lucrative political jobs duplicating one another's duties. On March 11, 1947, Representative Claud Gilmer of Rocksprings, who had voted against the $2,000 minimum teachers' salary, introduced in the house of representatives a resolution to create an interim committee to study the school system and make recommendations for revising it. The resolution passed and was sponsored in the senate by A. M. Aikin of Paris, Texas, who had supported the $2,000 minimum teachers' salary bill. The result was a group of eighteen persons known as the Gilmer-Aikin Committee, who spent eighteen months and $2,500 blueprinting a new streamlined school system for Texas. To obtain a full expression of opinion from all parts of the state, the Gilmer-Aikin Committee set up county committees which canvassed the populace and filed reports at a central office. Thousands of questionnaires and opinion sheets were distributed and filled out. From them came a comprehensive plan for a drastic reorganization of Texas public schools. In the legislature of 1949 it was written into three detailed bills known as the Gilmer-Aikin laws.

Many educators at first looked askance on the project. Conservative elements formerly branded by Rainey as enemies of all progress were represented on the committee. Previous Rainey-backers were convinced that nothing good could come from such quarters. They were mistaken. Since private schools are scarce in Texas, businessmen had as much to gain as anybody else from a truly efficient public-school system. They therefore supported the movement with complete sincerity.

Under the Gilmer-Aikin bills, the schools are run by a state board of education which consists of an elected member from each of the twenty-one Congressional districts in Texas. This board chooses a professional commissioner of education, who in turn appoints a state department of education to serve as his clerical staff. On the commissioner's recommendations, a textbook committee is appointed by the board to nominate textbooks. The commissioner may select texts only from among those nominated by this committee. A complex minimum-salary schedule based on college training and length of service has been adopted for all teachers. Special allotments are made for operating buses in districts of scattered population.

The program is far superior to anything that could have been done by the liberals alone or the business interests alone. It is one of those rare masterpieces which can result only from the combined work of people with widely divergent backgrounds and political opinions operating together in the free air of tolerance. Representatives from such groups as the Texas Manufacturers' Association gave the system a degree of perfection which could have come only from their long experience with business organizations. Classroom teachers brought the benefit of their wisdom regarding the most efficient division of classes and guidance programs. It is doubtful that any individual, however talented, could have lived long enough and achieved a wide enough backlog of knowledge to devise such a system. Nor could it have evolved in any nation or institution where all points of view except one are excluded.

Like any important reform movement, the Gilmer-Aikin program met with bitter opposition from those who had been profiting under the *status quo*. When vilification and filibustering failed, its enemies in the house of representatives decided that they would not be present on the day when the first Gilmer-Aikin bill was to come up for vote. Their absence would prevent its passage, since there would not be a quorum on the floor.

Some of these truant members took airplane rides, thus increasing their appreciation of the beautiful farm-covered hills around Austin. Others, being either of a more frugal bent or imbued with less acumen as fugitives, merely drove out into the wooded highlands to hide in taverns or tourist cottages.

Since they were being paid to attend the legislative session, the law provided that they could be apprehended and carried back to the capitol, at the point of a pistol if necessary. Therefore, Sergeant-at-Arms Bob Murphey went with a couple of deputies to scour the hills and round up the recalcitrant law-

makers. Most of them came quietly, but at one tavern three
of them tried to hide behind the bar. When Murphey and his
helpers rousted them out, one ran through the tavern-owner's
living-quarters, where the lady of the house was trying to get
her baby to sleep. In his haste he awakened the child and
plunged into a clothes closet. Fearful of being trapped there,
he emerged almost at once and rushed, with Murphey close
on his heels, out the back door, through a slough of ankle-deep
mud, and into a creek bed, where he was captured. Another
ran into a clothesline loaded with diapers and had to get a
fresh start. This, plus other obstacles such as scattered logs and
tall wet grass, handicapped him considerably, so that he gave
up and agreed to be present at the legislative session. His vote
would be against the reform measures, but his presence would
make the quorum possible. Thus the baby's diapers also contributed their bit to the improvement of its subsequent education. The third fugitive fell down under a big live-oak tree
where chickens habitually roosted. He had to change his
clothes before he could voice his "nay."

Since the passage of the Gilmer-Aikin bills, the legislature
has further improved the school system with better provisions
for the instruction of backward children. A special session in
1954 placed the minimum salary for beginning teachers at
$2,805 a year, and the entire scale, based on experience and
degrees held, was shifted upward accordingly.

Governor Jester died suddenly on July 11, 1949. His lieutenant governor, Allan Shivers, completed his term and has
since been elected thrice to the governorship. Representing the
same pro-big-business regime which has held the ascendancy
with rare interruptions since O'Daniel's day, Shivers has had
to compromise with strong movements for higher teachers'
salaries. Consistently he has favored better public services such
as highways and hospitals. In the summer of 1954 he almost
lost to Ralph Yarborough, who proposed to break the "one
man rule" and improve the state's facilities for public health,

care of the needy, old-age assistance, and similar services in which it still ranks shamefully low among the forty-eight.

Yarborough's campaign closely resembled the earlier, less successful Rainey movement. He declared that "Texas was once an American free state but has been temporarily captured by millionaires." He promised to make it a "people's state" again. Shivers, he averred, was financed mainly by big gas.

The closeness of the race was partly due to several inconsistencies and unfortunate occurrences in Shivers's record which weakened him personally and made him a tempting target for mud-slinging. His family owns a palatial estate known as Sharyland in the lower Rio Grande Valley. While as governor he maintained the Good Neighbor Commission, wetbacks were being hired at twenty-five cents per hour on Sharyland farms. While his own son was attending a desegregated Catholic school along with Negro children in Austin, he proclaimed that all his "instincts," his "political philosophy," his "experience," and his "common sense" revolted against the Supreme Court decision about segregation.

Until the summer of 1954 several insolvent insurance companies operated in Texas without government interference while one of them—Lloyds of North America—paid $1,000 a month to Shivers's former campaign-manager, John Van Cronkhite. Governor Shivers was informed of the company's insolvency as early as April 1, 1953, but nothing of consequence was done about it as long as Van Cronkhite was getting the $1,000-per-month "public-relations fee." Shortly after the payments stopped, the government interfered. So said Ralph W. Hammonds of Lloyds in a last-ditch fight to save his company, whose liquidation was decreed in June 1954.

Back in 1946, when he was lieutenant governor, Shivers bought from Lloyd Bentsen, Sr., an option on some Rio Grande Valley land for $25,000, agreeing to pay this amount within one year. Six and one half months later he sold this option back to a Bentsen-owned company for $450,000.

Drew Pearson told these embarrassing tales, except for the wetback-hiring, in his nationwide column on July 23, 1954, the eve of the primary election. To the land transaction he added a subtle suggestion and a bit of flattery for Texas voters: "What the lieutenant governor of Texas did in return for this $425,000 handed him on a silver platter was not revealed in the court depositions and has never been explained. But the Bentsens were then anxious to obtain precious water and irrigation rights in order to sell a big land-development scheme. What the deal amounted to was a $425,000 windfall to a very important Texas official, and the voters of Texas, not easily fooled, don't seem to like it." Pearson followed this with a story on August 9, in the heat of the run-off, of how the Times Publishing Company of Mission, much of whose stock belonged to Shivers's relatives, had received large printing jobs from the state government.

Yarborough used the reports with considerable skill, but Shivers countered with some clever variations on the old appeals that had proved reliable from the days of W. Lee O'Daniel. The land deal he described as nothing more than a profitable business transaction. He expressed surprise that Yarborough disapproved of making a profit in business. Thus, without any open accusations, he identified Yarborough with the Communist ideology. Labor unions were described as Communist-inspired and Shivers was pictured as the state's only protection against them. Large billboards along the highways featured Shivers's handsome face beseeching the traveler to "please drive carefully."

Yarborough's chances were further jeopardized by a strike of 400 retail workers against 19 stores in Port Arthur. The strike had been begun without recourse to the established National Labor Relations Board procedures, and two of its early leaders had previously been connected with the Communist Party. This enabled Attorney General John Ben Sheppard, a Shivers man, to state that the strike appeared to be part of "a Communist plot to take over the Gulf oil ports." Other Texas merchants feared that Yarborough's election would encourage organization among retail workers in their own stores and thus force them to raise salaries. The Shivers supporters capitalized on the situation by describing Port Arthur as paralyzed by the strike and assuring all other Texas cities that only Shivers could save them from a similar fate.

According to an article by Stuart Long in the *Reporter* magazine for October 21, 1954, "doctors were told that Yarborough would favor the chiropractors. Chiropractors were told he would favor the M.D.'s. Truckers were told he was friendly with the railroads, and the railroad men were told he wanted to increase the load limit on trucks. Wets were told he was dry, and drys were informed that he was wet." Long adds that anonymous threats and abusive midnight phone calls were used on Yarborough-supporters and that employers discharged employees who put Yarborough stickers on their cars. Meanwhile, Yarborough was handicapped by a comparative lack of funds for travel and broadcasting.

Large cartoons in the leading Texas dailies pictured Shivers standing on a platform built of "higher pay for teachers," "better roads," and similar liberal moves. These made sense because Shivers had called a special session of the legislature at the beginning of the year to get money for such measures, and it is probable that if he had not done so he would have lost the election. His administration, therefore, cannot be correctly described as purely a big-money regime. Big money can safely expect better treatment from him than from the Yarborough people, but he has been kept in power at the cost of important compromises.

The distribution of the returns is very revealing. Shivers's best support came from the regions originally settled by big plantation-owners of the deep south. Yarborough's heaviest vote came from the pious small-farm or agrarian areas of the Red River Valley, North Central Texas, upper East Texas, and the Panhandle. W. Lee O'Daniel, with his hillbilly music, his "old-time religion," and his promise of a "businesslike" government, had made a hit in both the plantation and the agrarian areas, but the high-minded agrarians are not so much impressed with Shivers, who lacks the hillbilly lilt and whose wife is Roman Catholic.

The run-off showed considerable gains for Yarborough in the lower Rio Grande Valley, where his supporters had been active among the Mexican laborers. But Yarborough got his most promising support from labor groups in the big cities. It is promising because with further industrialization, even though petroleum and petrochemistry involve a heavy proportion of trained technicians, it is bound to grow, and the Shivers people will have either to deal with it or to lose control of the state government. Inasmuch as the views of Texas millionaires are far from uniform and many of them have liberal tendencies, the state's future looks bright as well as exciting.

VIII

THE HEART OF TEXAS

◇◇◇

1. Big Money

MOST TEXAS MILLIONAIRES made their money from oil. Their bonanza came suddenly, in a flood. Many of them had hard sledding in their early days and are still strongly imbued with pioneer traditions. Yet they vary so widely that any attempt to put them all in one category must constitute a dangerously erroneous oversimplification. Not even an approach to accuracy could be achieved by their classification into fewer than five types, and even these would leave some of them vacillating from one class to another or hanging in vast limbos between. Respecting their attitudes toward community welfare, however, the following rough classification will help clarify an otherwise unintelligibly complicated picture.

Class One: those who neither give money to public institutions nor attempt to control them beyond voting their own individual tickets and taking their part as citizens in those community organizations which interest them. Class Two: those who undertake to control public institutions without giving them anything other than the taxes they are forced to pay. Class Three: those who keep their money until they die, then leave it to some welfare enterprise. Class Four: those who give money generously but endeavor to control their beneficiaries. Class Five: those who give freely and essay to remove their own influence from the recipients of their gifts.

Members of Class One are generally well thought of. They take pride in putting themselves on a level with their fellow citizens and in attributing whatever positions of consequence they may hold to purely personal virtues. Lack of confidence in governmental agencies, especially during the latter years of the Roosevelt-Truman period, has tended to keep this class small. Texans with large incomes who disapprove of federal domestic policies would rather donate their money to local concerns, where they can see the results, than pay it in taxes to be "squandered by Washington's politicians."

Class Two has often caused ill will. The University of Texas regents are an example. Also, through such organizations as the Texas Manufacturers' Association, tycoons of this class strive for economy in government in the interest of lower taxes.

The most notable members of Class Three are the children of James Stephen Hogg, who have established the Hogg Foundation at the University of Texas, devoted to mental hygiene. An earlier example is William Marsh Rice. He came to Texas in 1837 and collected land on bad debts through the state's nineteenth-century upheavals. When he died in 1900, he left arrangements for the foundation of Rice Institute at Houston, with a ten-million-dollar endowment. Rice was established in 1912, and has since maintained a high reputation as one of the best postgraduate schools in the country.

Hugh Roy Cullen of Houston, although he has given away hundreds of millions with no strings attached, often falls into Class Four. He is the most generous of all Texas philanthropists with both money and advice. Undoubtedly his dollars and his words are exerting a strong and permanent influence on Texas. One embodiment of his philosophy, uttered at the

San Jacinto celebration of 1949, when President Truman still had hopes for the New Deal, seems to convey some prophetic tones. Its sentiment, backed by the Cullen millions, must have won many a Texas vote in the recent Republican victory. "Suppose my grandfather or your grandfather of the Texas Republic should return and stay awhile with us," he said. "What would he think after the novelty wore off? I've wondered what he would say after having the Washington bureaucrats tell him how he must run his affairs, and having to pay a tax every time he turned around, to support the most extravagant and wasteful government on the face of the earth, in all its grand schemes of bottle-feeding the voting population of this country from the cradle to the grave, and grubstaking the rest of the world.

"After a taste of that, I wonder if our grandfathers wouldn't decide it was time for another Texas declaration of independence."

Cullen's principal beneficiary is the University of Houston. He has endowed it with $160,000,000 plus oil lands which provide an ever expanding base. He is chairman of its governing board.

One more example of this type. The Hoblitzelle Foundation, initiated by Karl Hoblitzelle of Dallas, is now distributing large, gilt-edged, fancy prints of the Texas Declaration of Independence. Other gifts of Hoblitzelle are more in the nature of Class Five. The Texas Research Institute at Renner, which is doing much to revitalize the black-land farms, is largely a child of his charity. In 1941, when placed in charge of the Texas Centennial of Statehood Commission, he declared that the best way to commemorate Texas's entrance into the Union was to "rebuild the land and with the land the man and through the man the state." Accordingly, he recommended the establishment of the Texas Rural Development Commission and donated $250,000 for the erection of the Renner laboratories. Other monuments to his generosity are

Radio House at the University of Texas and the Texas School of the Air. He has also dedicated thousands of dollars to Negro education and the improvement of conditions among Negro farmers.

Haroldson Lafayette Hunt of Dallas is also difficult to classify. His money has initiated a large number of nationwide radio and television programs under the names *Facts Forum, State of the Nation, Answers for Americans,* and *Reporter's Roundup.* Charles J. V. Murphy, in his article for *Fortune* magazine (May 1954), describes the *Facts Forum* programs as "highly controversial" and "highly slanted." Hunt insists that they are "trying to get arguments for both sides before the public to encourage the individual to find out more for himself on each subject discussed, from sources of his own choosing, so that he may make his own decisions on controversial issues."

Dan Smoot, commentator for *Facts Forum,* makes out an excellent case for it. In reply to a *Time* magazine statement that it is "used as a political megaphone for oilman Hunt," he asks: "Is *Time* magazine implying that Mr. Hunt—or anyone else, for that matter—could tell Senator Robert Kerr, Senator John Sparkman, Senator Allen Ellender, Senator John Bricker, Senator Everett Dirksen, and scores of other senators, congressmen, cabinet officers, state governors, and distinguished American newspapermen what to say—or not to say—when they appeared on a *Facts Forum* program?"

A more definite example of Class Five is Tom Slick, founder of the Southwest Research Institute, the Foundation for Research and Education, and the Institute of Inventive Research, three thriving establishments devoted wholly to human progress, located on the Essar Ranch near San Antonio. Slick hailed originally from Oklahoma. Son of a lucky oil wildcatter, he got his education at Yale University, then bought four thousand acres of rolling land just west of San

Antonio for experiments in cattle-breeding. Since his goal was scientific research, he named his place Essar: the phonetic rendering of the initials *S. R.* From a humble beginning in 1940, Essar has expanded to embrace all phases of scientific exploration, serving every conceivable kind of industry and drawing investigators from all over the world. Slick has voluntarily divorced himself from the administration of the institutes and placed them in the hands of Dr. Harold Vagtborg.

Vagtborg is a tornado of energy. Born in Copenhagen, brought to America at the age of two, he has directed research on projects ranging from combustion engines to gas technology, water works, and sewage-disposal. To his broad technical knowledge he has added a keen sense of human relations and a finished skill in salesmanship. He has an aggressive bulldog face from which words shoot like bullets from a machine gun, and Essar's rambling lumber ranch house, with its wide windows and galleries, vibrates from his enthusiasm.

Under his leadership, Essar has come to enjoy a number of important advantages over other investigative endeavors in Texas and environs. It is purely a free-enterprise affair, untouched by political upheavals, bound to no church creed. By pooling the energies and tools of inventors and technicians, it avoids the duplication involved in the maintenance of different laboratories and staffs for different individual enterprises. Without the help of Essar, each company would have to keep separate equipment and pay its own research staff even when there were no pressing problems to be solved. Essar makes it possible for any company to obtain the benefit of research when needed and be free of the expense when there are no questions requiring immediate answers. The concentration of inquiries in one place also enables the various scientific fields —physics, chemistry, biology, etc.—to supply one another constantly with new interpretations and viewpoints. Essar also removes the advantage which large companies have over small ones. Enterprises that could not otherwise afford laboratory equipment have the same opportunities which are open to the wealthier concerns.

Of the three organizations operating on the Essar ranch, the Southwest Research Institute is the largest. It undertakes specific research projects by contract for any client who wishes to obtain its services. The exact results of the research are confidential and usually belong exclusively to the contracting parties, but the general experience gained redounds to the benefit of all. All research projects are undertaken at cost; the Institute charges its clients only enough to cover operating expenses.

The second organization at Essar, the Institute of Inventive Research, enables individual inventors to derive full benefit from their inventions without being inhibited by the expense of materials and patents. Any person with a new idea can bring it to this institute, where it will be examined for feasibility by experts. If it shows possibilities, a contract is made with the inventor and the invention is developed at the Institute's expense. Subsequent sales reimburse the Institute, and the profits accrue to the inventor.

The applied science of the Southwest Research Institute and the Institute of Inventive Research is supplemented and enriched by the fundamental science of the Foundation for Research and Education. Instead of engaging in immediately requested projects for client industries or individuals, the Foundation undertakes to broaden the horizons of knowledge and, as Vagtborg puts it, "develop new correlations among previously known facts." It is a haven for the pure scientist, where long-term pursuits may be undertaken without interruption from the fluctuations of immediate need to which the other two institutions are subject. Even the economic structure of the Essar organizations assures the Foundation against the contingencies of changing times. It owns the land and buildings on the Essar Ranch and derives its support from rental paid it by its two sister institutes. Thus its investigators are insured a steady income throughout booms and depressions.

Slick's original endowment is supplemented by generous donations from business concerns which appreciate the importance of Essar. Vagtborg keeps these concerns awake by holding weekly dinners in the wide front room of the Essar ranch house, where he describes the most recent achievements of the three organizations and has informal discussions of regional and world-wide research needs. Each dinner is followed by a tour of the grounds, where the work in progress is observed. Each week, usually on Thursday, a different group of businessmen and leaders enjoys the dinner and tour. On Friday each member of the recently entertained groups is visited by a solicitor from Essar and invited to contribute regularly anywhere from $30,000 to $50,000 a year. No specific limits are set to the contributions, but they usually range in the neighborhood of $30,000 or $40,000.

Essar's division of oceanography shows how well Vagtborg's vision is sparked with imagination yet balanced by systematized knowledge. This division has made a number of expeditions into the Gulf of Mexico. With a base in Houston and initial co-operation from Rice Institute and the University of Houston, it has several boats on the Gulf: floating laboratories to study water currents and marine biology. Vagtborg can foresee a time when hurricanes can be predicted far in advance and their cause possibly cut off in early stages. Fish ranches, where fish can be cross-bred and fed for larger size and quality of meat, just as beef cattle are cross-bred and fed today, may fill the Gulf. Invisible oceanic fences may be made by projecting radio waves through the water, certain frequencies being repugnant to fish. "One acre of Gulf bottom," says Vagtborg, "will produce two and a half times as much protein as the best farm land, and all minerals are present in sea water."

According to Vagtborg, preoccupation with oil is one of Texas's chief present-day drawbacks. Texans have so much oil on the brain that they can think of nothing else, and they are therefore missing many other fruitful opportunities. He sees one glaring evidence of this in the ceramic tile and white-ware industry. This industry was attracted to Texas by such inducements as cheap fuel, and three big plants are operating in San Antonio, Houston, and Dallas. The Texas earth is full of clays which may be exactly the kind needed to feed these industries, but everybody is too busy looking for oil to supply them.

By far the greatest of the Texas millionaires is E. L. De Golyer of Dallas. In addition to being the world's most widely known oil geologist, he has become a recognized authority on literature, with a large private library of southwestern lore and an excellent collection of books on Spanish colonial America. The *Saturday Review* owes its continued existence to his investments and leadership, for it was on the verge of bankruptcy before he rescued it, and a little over a year after he became its publisher it was making money. With all his world-wide interests, De Golyer finds time to write frequent book reviews for the *Dallas Morning News*.

All told, more than one hundred and thirty foundations, trust funds, and benevolent institutions have been established in Texas by wealthy Texans. Dr. Robert L. Sutherland, of the Hogg Foundation at the University of Texas, has been instrumental in bringing them together for an annual conference whose purpose is to keep them informed about the work of their neighbors and thus prevent too much duplication of effort. The pooling of experience also helps eliminate the multiplication of errors among these numerous independent projects.

2. Big Brains

THE HUMAN SCIENCES, creative writing, and the fine arts have also been stimulated by the wealth of Texas. The Texas Institute of Letters, consisting of the state's leading writers and literary critics, meets annually and gives a series of awards which, supplemented and criticized, may be taken as what Texans consider their best literary products.* Supplementing is necessary because several outstanding books may appear in a single year, yet only a limited number can get the top awards. Others, though worthy of attention, are excluded. In dry years, when no literature of merit is published, the awards must be given just the same, so that mediocre works get on the lists.

Among the award-winners are the state's two leading historians, Eugene Campbell Barker and Walter Prescott Webb. Barker and Webb are both fine scholars, widely known and highly regarded, but they differ as night and day. Barker is a fact-finder, a careful operator within a narrow field: pre-revolutionary Texas and the career of Stephen F. Austin. The award he received, in fact, did not result from a selection on the part of the Texas Institute of Letters membership, but from a group of historians connected with the Institute by special agreement. Since he limits himself to one small area, his generalizations are few and relatively inconsequential.

Webb has gone to the opposite extreme. In *The Great Plains* (1936) he describes how the exigencies of the dry, treeless, uncivilized western plains evoked the widespread use of three new tools: the water-pumping windmill, the barbed-wire fence, and the Colt revolver. Once adopted, these three de-

---

* The Institute's awards are listed in the appendix.

vices had a molding effect on the plains society. *The Great
Plains* marks the climax of Webb's greatness as a historian. In
it, his faculty for generalization has carried him just far
enough to reveal some formerly unrecognized truths about the
interplay of influences between men and their habitat in the
American west. It has not yet led him far enough to distort his
view.

His subsequent work is also instructive, but in a different
way. It demonstrates that this fine generalizing faculty is like
fire. Kept within reasonable bounds, it can be useful and enlightening; given too much scope, it can prove destructive. Its
conclusions can canker into prejudices, blind their author to
the most obvious facts, and lure him into the same sort of
wild-goose chase that we have seen at work in Texas politics.
In *Divided We Stand* (1937) Webb began showing symp-
toms of the same nostalgia for pioneer life that bothers Hugh
Roy Cullen of Houston. The only difference is, Cullen sees the
federal government as the source of all evil, the destroyer of his
lost Eden, whereas for Webb the big eastern corporation is
the iniquitous villain. Both men are romantics at heart and,
like all romantics, they personify and oversimplify the forces
with which they deal in the same way that hero and villain are
oversimplified in melodrama.

In his Institute award-winning book, *The Great Frontier*
(1953), Webb's idealization of the pioneer environment leads
him into a long, wearisome series of absurdities. Imagining
that the land frontier is the only possible one, he refuses to
recognize the new frontiers that are constantly being opened
up: in oil, in the ocean, in chemistry, in atomic power, in outer
space. Determined to condemn modern civilization's en-
croachment on his romantic dream, he adopts the old leftist
notion that the profit motive is necessarily opposed to production for use and views the modern corporation as a despotism
as absolute as the most autocratic of pre-American European
tyrannies. Supposing that the degree of freedom enjoyed by

individuals is inversely proportional to the density of population, he concludes that modern Texans, with their smooth-motored, fast-moving, oil-driven vehicles, their unprecedented vocational opportunities, and their vastly varied social life, have less freedom than did such mosquito-hounded, fear-driven, earthbound settlers as John Rabb. Closing his eyes to the many panics and famines of the last four centuries, he assumes that from the discovery of America and other virgin islands until the close of the frontier in 1900, the world experienced a four-hundred-year boom. He then defines a boom as being "abnormal" and accordingly prophesies an inevitable return to a "normality" of congestion and group control!

Except for the Institute award and a few local eulogies, the reception of *The Great Frontier* was largely negative. Says De Golyer, reviewing the book for the *Dallas Morning News*: "Professor Webb charges the eroded fields, the slashed forests, the fouled streams, and the depleted mineral resources of the earth to applied science; to technology. This is an unreal and unacceptable disavowal of normal human responsibilities. One might as well charge Lucrezia Borgia's crimes to the inventor of the poison or all revolver murders to Samuel Colt." About Webb's boom theory De Golyer asks: ". . . Why . . . was [there] so little change relatively during the first three centuries and so great a change during the last one?"

Reviewing the book for *The Nation*, Oscar Handlin said: ". . . The very concept of the frontier as a uniform and constant phenomenon is untenable. . . . The influence of Peru upon the old world was more analogous to that of Japan than that of Massachusetts. And the frontier did not produce the same political and social institutions in Connecticut as in Canada."

Besides the books of Webb and Barker, several biographies have received awards from the Texas Institute of Letters. Among the best are Joe B. Frantz's *Gail Borden*, which describes the East Texan who invented condensed milk, and

Herbert Gambrell's story of Texas's pioneer president, *Anson Jones*. In addition, Texas has produced many other fine informative books. The general field of history and biography has been systematically cultivated by the Texas State Historical Association. A monumental achievement of this group, under the editorship of H. Bailey Carroll, is *The Handbook of Texas*, a two-volume encyclopedia of essential historical information. Since it deals mostly with the past, it should be supplemented with *The Texas Almanac*, compiled by Stuart McGregor and published by the *Dallas Morning News*. The *Almanac* was begun in 1857 and issued annually, except for 1886, until 1873. In 1904 it was revived and published spasmodically until 1925, when it became a steady biennial. It assembles under one cover all important statistics relating to Texas. Its only weakness is that, like too many other present-day Texas institutions, it is heavily weighted on the side of technology at the expense of the humanities. While it gives full figures on Texas resources, industry, commerce, and government, the 1952–3 issue devoted only three of its 670 pages to "developments in Drama and Music" and in the 1954–5 number even these were omitted.

Among recent instructive Texas books, *Free and Unequal*, by Roger John Williams, stands supreme. While its import is universal, it owes much to the unbounded personal freedom of inquiry, ample research facilities, and political upheavals of Texas. Roger Williams is a bio-chemist, internationally famous for having ferreted out the chemical formulas of vitamins. When the Rainey-regent controversy burst into the open at the University of Texas, he had strong feelings about it. As a leading faculty member, he had long been a close friend of Rainey, but the latter's sweeping statements about race and the welfare state disturbed him. His extended observation of living organisms had convinced him that such abstract concepts as "the average man," "the common man," "the individual," and "society" were dangerous modern myths.

In the midst of the Rainey fight, therefore, while these phrases were being bandied back and forth by his colleagues, Roger Williams rolled up his sleeves and went to work. He explored every possible source of evidence bearing on the question of human equality and human rights. He instituted and implemented a new approach to the problem which he called the science of "humanics," announcing its method in a preliminary book, *The Human Frontier*. It wiped the slate clean of all preconceived notions about mankind, and trained the light of objective inquiry on individuals. The result, after ten years of careful study, is *Free and Unequal*, a tentative statement.

Williams sees the idea of freedom as a direct result not of human sameness, but of human variability. "If we were all alike," he says, "there would seem to be no reason for wanting freedom; 'living my own life' would be an empty, meaningless expression. True, we are all alike as *human beings* and have a common role to play in the world, but among the infinite number of ways to play the role, we crave the liberty of our own choices. . . . I believe these ideals [the principles of freedom and human worth] came into being because people are *what they are*—creatures possessing high variability—and that therefore the ideals are impregnable." It is difficult to understand why *Free and Unequal*, which expresses some of the most profound thoughts coming from events in twentieth-century Texas, did not get an Institute award.

Fiction has been the most frequent award-winner in the Texas Institute of Letters. Of the many prize novels, two are based on Texas Mexican life. One of these is my own first novel, *The Magic of Limping John*, which tells how a skeptic is forced by his credulous neighbors to accept the role of faith healer. The other is *Wetback*, by Claud Garner. It follows the difficulties and personal development of a young half-breed Mexican who gets into Texas without a passport. Garner's second novel, *Cornbread Aristocrat*, shows him to be one of the state's most skillful writers. It is a stirring story with delightfully human characters, but it got no Institute award.

Although farm life offers less romance than ranch life, it figures frequently in Texas fiction. Laura Krey's *And Tell of Time* expresses beautifully the nostalgia of the old south's plantation life in Texas. It antedates the Institute, but it enjoyed wide circulation both in America and in Great Britain. One of the early Institute award-winners is George Sessions Perry's *Hold Autumn in Your Hand,* a profoundly moving story of Brazos bottom family life among the poor of Franklin D. Roosevelt's day.

Ranching was first put into really good Texas literature by Andy Adams, who spent eight years on the trail and produced a series of highly authentic novels and tales of trail life. These were published in the first decade of the twentieth century: thirty years before the Texas Institute of Letters came into existence. Since then, the cowboy has been widely diffused as a pulp hero, but no purely ranch novel has received the Institute award. However, Elithe Hamilton Kirkland's *Divine Average* contains the most penetrating portrayals of the Texas range man's life and outlook that I have ever read. It is a powerful book which combines the many elements of early Texas society with a universally significant philosophical theme.

Two of the Institute's fiction awards have been nationwide best-sellers. They are Tom Lea's *The Brave Bulls* and Fred Gipson's *Hound-Dog Man,* both published in 1949. The former is a gripping tale of Mexican bullfights: one of the few convincing apologies for this bloody custom to come out in the English-speaking world. The latter is thoroughly Texan in tone and content. Told in the first person by a boy who practically worships an otherwise unglamorous coon-hunter, it possesses a rich Mark Twain quality.

These masterpieces were followed in 1950 by William Goyen's highly experimental *The House of Breath,* an impressionistic picture of life in and around a typical Texas village called Charity. More thought-provoking though not more artistic is George Williams's *The Blind Bull*, fiction award-winner for 1952. It gives, through reminiscent flashes, the story of Major Clement Sweeny, who lies wounded on Saipan. Suspense is maintained by the fear that Sweeny may succumb to his lung injury because of gloomy memories which come to him from his past life in Texas, this life having developed in him a highly romantic, pessimistic philosophy. In the end, he gets well to please the doctor who has worked so hard to cure him. It is unlikely that this masterpiece, with its manifold problems and implications, will reach many Texas readers. Its treatment of sex is flagrantly frank, and its cast of characters is heavily packed with illicit females. Those who condemned Dos Passos are not apt to profit from *The Blind Bull's* positive values.

The same may be said for John Howard Griffin's highly artistic but heavily gloom-laden novel, *The Devil Rides Outside*. Unlike *The Blind Bull*, it got no Institute award, but it was published in Texas and subsequently became a national seller. Another important Texas writer, not yet recognized by the Institute, is Lula Grace Erdman, of whom the Panhandle is proud. Her novels, dealing primarily with life on the high plains, have been widely successful.

Supreme in my opinion among Texas fictioneers is Dillon Anderson, a successful young Houston lawyer who has begun a brilliant literary career with *I and Claudie*. I have never met any fictitious characters that strike me as being more genuine, more moving, or more delightful than Anderson's Clint Hightower and Claudie Hughes. Clint is a worldly vagabond with some knowledge of scripture and an inventive mind. He calls himself "the mental type." Claudie is a big, heavy-boned, gangly Alabaman, abysmally green and irresistibly lovable. Together they come to Texas, and their adventures, besides being packed with high suspense and warm humor, tell a lot about the state that you don't get from the Chambers of Commerce.

In Texas, says Clint, "it's a great deal like it was in Old Testament stories. They haven't all learned to love new neighbors yet in Texas: they don't always turn the other cheek." Among the threads that enter the story plots are the camp-meeting spirit of Texas's country folk and the hillbilly music of her politicians. That Anderson fully deserved the Institute's fiction award, which he received in 1951, there can be no question.

The most frequent individual recipient of awards from the Texas Institute of Letters is J. Frank Dobie. Drawing on all phases of pioneer life while maintaining a broad knowledge of present-day affairs, Dobie has grown to be Texas's greatest living man of letters. His books are of three types, each unique in the literary world and peculiar to Dobie. One of these is the creative biography, which combines an individual with the broad currents of endeavor which dominate his existence. Notable among books of this type are *A Vaquero of the Brush Country* and *The Ben Lily Legend*. Then there is the type which takes some important animal of the American southwest, outlines its career, and recounts the most interesting episodes connected with it: *The Voice of the Coyote, The Longhorns, The Mustangs*. The third type is the book of tales gathered from wide travels, selected with fine artistic taste, and exquisitely told. My favorites among these are the two which deal with buried or lost treasure: *Coronado's Children* and *Apache Gold and Yaqui Silver*. Because they touch a universal urge for mysteriously concealed treasures, they need no injection of sex to make them interesting. Because they belong to the land, they are molded by their content rather than by preconceived literary forms. This makes them thoroughly Texan and gives them universal value at the same time. Unique among Dobie's books is *A Texan in England*, written when he was visiting professor at Cambridge University in 1943. It describes with amusing but moving simplicity how he mingled with Britain's best and what he thought about them.

Besides his outstanding literary contributions, Dobie has done more than any other one man for the Texas Folklore Society. Organized in 1909, supported by wealthy patrons and a statewide membership, this group publishes an annual volume of collected tales, songs, folk proverbs, and remedies. In addition to Dobie, three nationally known folklorists have been connected with the Texas Folklore Society. These are Stith Thompson, the late John Avery Lomax, and the Negro folklorist from the Brazos bottoms, John Mason Brewer.

Another important group, more creative than scientific, is the By-Liners of Corpus Christi. Under the leadership of Dee Woods, they hold a yearly writers' conference, usually in the opening days of June, devoted generally to keeping up an interest in good literature. Writers and publishers of note come there to address the public and display their wares. Successful authors are surrounded by admiring eyes and featured at autographing parties. Manuscripts in all genres are submitted and prizes are awarded by a board of able critics. It is an excellent contact point for publishers, talent scouts, and aspiring writers.

The man who is now doing most to keep Texas awake to the best current literature is Professor Lon Tinkle of Southern Methodist University. Assisted by a large staff of reviewers, he edits the *Dallas Morning News* book page. Tinkle is more than a mere critic. He is an excellent public-relations man. Much of his contribution to Texas literature consists in advising, helping, and inspiring the state's leading writers. Two other good critics, more devoted to the printed word than to the prospective author, are Gerald Ashford of San Antonio and Margaret Page of Houston. On music and theatrical entertainment, John Rosenfield of Dallas is the best-known authority in Texas. Like the literary critics, he ranges far both in geography and in subject matter, drawing broad but accurate generalizations about the problems of the stage and movie industries in America and Europe.

Texas is further served by conscientious observers contributing to approximately 100 daily newspapers, 26 semi-weeklies, some 560 weeklies, and 300 other periodicals. Among the dailies, the *Fort Worth Star Telegram* has the largest circulation, with more than 200,000 copies going out to both a morning and an evening audience. Its coverage is good and its editorial policy is well balanced. Dallas has two excellent dailies, the *Morning News* and the evening *Times-Herald*. San Antonio and Houston both have several dailies each, the best coverage at present being provided by the *San Antonio Express* and the *Houston Post*. Among the most dynamic of the state's newspapermen is Carl Victor Little, columnist for the *Houston Press*. He is a man of rare insight, enthusiastically optimistic about the future of Texas. He foresees triumphs in petrochemistry which surpass the powers of the imagination, and in her human relations Texas strikes him as being capable of immediate changes for the better. Important reforms, he says, have taken place in Houston, and the people are not nearly as disturbed as they would have been a few years ago about the betterment of conditions among minority groups.

Supplementing the newspapers are almost three hundred radio and television stations, making Texas the leader of the forty-eight states in broadcasting. Book-making also has become a highly developed art in Texas, her best-known typographer being Carl Hertzog of El Paso. His production of *The Typical Texan*, a folkloristic study by Joseph Leach, received the Texas Institute of Letters award for typography in 1952.

These publications and observers deal mainly in prose and drama of the entire nation. Poetry, from Texas or elsewhere, seldom gets their attention. It is particularly fortunate, therefore, that the Texas Institute of Letters gives awards for Texas poetry books. Supreme among the winners of poetry awards is

Main Building of the University of Texas, Austin.

Walter Prescott Webb

J. Frank Dobie

Whitney Montgomery. His long devotion to the muse and his masterful handling of the ballad form make him the dean of Texas poets in my opinion. Born at Eureka, near Corsicana, in 1877, he moved with his wife, Vaida Stewart, also a poet, to Dallas in 1929, where the couple has since been publishing *Kaleidograph*, a monthly magazine of verse. Kaleidograph Press, owned and run by Whitney and Vaida, has also published books of verse featuring poets throughout the country.

But the three classic Texas poems, on the lips of school children in declamation contests long before the Institute began giving poetry awards, are "Song of the Forerunners," by Karle Wilson Baker, "Cattle," by Berta Hart Nance, and "Planter's Charm," by Fay M. Yauger. The first of these, as its name implies, eulogizes the "men who made Texas":

> Old men and young men, little men and tall,
> Bad men and good men—but strong men, all.

and the "women who bore Texas":

> Stern women, laughing women, women stout or small,
> Bronzed women, broken women—brave women, all.

The second expresses, better than any other poem, the strong bond between Texas and cattle. Two stanzas will suffice to give the general idea of the piece:

> Other states were carved or born,
> Texas grew from hide and horn.
>
> . . .
>
> Other soil is full of stones,
> Texans plow up cattle bones.

"Planter's Charm" features the widow Nan, planting corn, thinking of her husband, herself, and their two sons. They are like four grains of corn, only one of which may take root and thrive. Her husband, with his "cheating ways and words," has

been shot long ago. Her first son has wandered away. She herself is doomed to wither at her work. But her second son has
hopes,

> For his chin is firm, and his mouth is grave,
> And the look in his eye is bright and brave,
>
> And she, remembering farm-hand talk:
> "You lose three seeds to get one stalk,"
>
> Stands tall and proud and her pale cheeks glow
> As she drops a kernel: "One to grow!"
>
> Slowly Nan the widow moves
> Up and down the furrowed grooves,
>
> Peace in her heart and a smile on her lips
> As the kernels fall from her finger-tips:
>
> *"One for the buzzard—*
> *One for the crow—*
> *One to rot—and—*
> *One to grow!"*

Texas poetry also receives some stimulus from the Texas
Poetry Society, which meets annually and gives awards for
poems by members. In addition, there are many amateur
poetry groups scattered over the state. Border Poets, begun at
the South Texas town of Kingsville in 1933, has a system
which other such groups would do well to emulate. Each
member submits a poem monthly. These poems are mimeographed or duplicated anonymously into a small magazine.
One copy of this magazine is sent to a professional critic or
outstanding poet for rating and criticism. The other copies are
distributed among the members at the monthly meeting. Since
no member knows who are the authors of the poems other

than his own, criticisms at the meeting are entirely objective. After the poems are read orally by an expert interpreter, they are discussed and rated by vote. Then the comments and rating of the professional critic are read and compared with the popular evaluations. Finally, the names of the authors are revealed. Thus each poem is made to stand on its own feet, with no help from the previous prestige of its author or the personal feelings of his fellow members. The critic, a different expert of nationwide fame chosen each month and paid to criticize, keeps the standards of the group in tune with national literary tastes. Border Poets also publishes a yearly anthology of the best poems by its members. The organization has become so popular that stringent entrance requirements have been set up to keep the membership workably small and select. Outstanding among its pioneer members is Frances Alexander, whose *Time at the Window* won the Texas Institute of Letters's poetry award for 1949.

Most Texas versifiers are still too busy being poets to write good poetry. Anxious to excel in the literary world's critical eyes, they adopt the classic poet's manner without capturing his fire. They follow his metrical rules without fully feeling the rhythmic needs which provoked them. They spend all their powers shying from clichés and baying the moon in accepted bardian style. They think they have to speak in terms of Greek mythology and cosmic dreams, treating the seasons as if they were lovelorn spirits and the heavenly bodies as if they were rational creatures. The task of expressing these trite ideas without using the trite words which have traditionally conveyed them is too much for the average Texas poetaster, as it would be for anyone else. He hence emerges with little more than a few lame lines in slender books printed at his own expense.

In music, the College of Fine Arts at the University of Texas is doing a good job despite limited funds. Clifton Williams, a young composer from Arkansas, at present Assistant

Professor of Theory and Composition, has organized a yearly symposium for the threefold purpose of keeping the public interested in fine music, encouraging new composers, and building a native American art. The symposium lasts three or four days in March or April and features unpublished compositions by Americans. Williams also edits the *Southwestern Composers' Journal*, a University of Texas publication.

The symphony orchestras of San Antonio, Houston, and Dallas have attained major status and are soon to be rivaled by rapidly developing orchestras in Corpus Christi, Austin, El Paso, Lubbock, Amarillo, Wichita Falls, and Tyler. The Dallas Grand Opera Association provides $250,000 for underwriting Metropolitan Opera tours to Texas. The New York Association gives four performances each year in Dallas and two in Houston. San Antonio and Fort Worth have their own opera companies.

In the graphic arts, the Contemporary Arts Association in Houston embodies a spirit of functionalism which the state's writers and musicians would do well to adopt. Begun in 1949, this group has done much to take art out of the museums and make it useful as it was in the days of Michelangelo. It condemns "art for art's sake" and strives to make Texas art serve educational, religious, commercial, residential, and other ends. So thoroughgoing is its functionalism that it seeks to promote the best not only in painting and sculpture but also in architecture, industrial design, furniture, and interior decoration. Besides seeking to make modern art more understandable through exhibits, educational activities, and the enlistment of local talent, it aims to stimulate artistic interest in such fields as photography, advertisement, ceramics, fabrics, and jewelry. Such objectives fit well into Texas's cultural focus on industrial development.

Outstanding in Texas fine art is Tom Lea of El Paso. With an intimate and sympathetic knowledge of West Texas life he combines a finished technical education obtained at the Art

Institute of Chicago in the latter 1920's, four months abroad in 1930, and experience as war artist for *Life* magazine during World War II. In 1937 he met J. Frank Dobie, and he has since illustrated several of the latter's best books. Much of Lea's finest work has gone into the writing and illustration of brief local books in limited editions printed by Carl Hertzog. Many of the important public buildings of El Paso, including the new library, are adorned with Lea's murals, and he is now engaged with Hertzog on a book about the King Ranch. The vigor, the leathery toughness, and the steel-like sinews of West Texas range men are rife in both his drawing and his writing, though he has temporarily departed from this local setting in his best-selling novel *The Brave Bulls*.

❖❖❖❖❖❖❖❖❖❖❖❖❖❖❖❖❖❖❖❖❖❖❖❖❖❖❖❖❖❖❖❖❖❖❖❖❖❖❖

3. *Lone Star in the Ascendancy*

TEXAS IS A PLACE where things happen fast and furiously. Like the cracking of the earth along the Balcones fault line, life in Texas has long been a series of crises: sudden jumps and upheavals. The revolution against Mexico, the emancipation of the slaves, and the opening of the cattle trails to Kansas all came through relatively intense climaxes. Even the iron horse, having already been gradually developed elsewhere, hit Texas with a bang, and the Spindletop gusher, greatest climax of all, set off a whole chain of social explosions. The camp-meeting movement, like the railroads, got its growth in the older states and struck Texas with the impact of a finished technique. Once admitted into the republic after its independence from Catholic-dominated Mexico, romantic Protestants aspired to make mass conversions accompanied by high emotional excitement.

Only in labor relations has Texas been relatively quiet. As has been shown, this is because the nation's big labor fights had all been fought and their issues decided before the state became industrialized. Consequently, there is less rancor between employer and employee in Texas than elsewhere, and the most successful politicians are those who can make the most noise without actually upsetting industrial tranquillity: who can create the biggest semblance of drastic change without threatening the moral and governmental *status quo*.

The free press, the radio, and television have of course done much to sharpen the critical eyes of Texas. Old associations and loyalties are fast being broken and lost in a cumulative process of shifts and readjustments. Predominantly Protestant, she embraces a Roman Catholic McCarthy because he looks like a better bulwark against Communism than the State Department diplomats whom she customarily mistrusts. Traditionally wedded to the Democratic Party, she endorses the Republican presidential candidate by a landslide vote. Together with the rest of the country, Texas is rapidly developing the ability to disregard previous ties and throw her support to any individual who has earned her confidence.

To be sure, an important item in Texas's dramatic shift to the Republican side in the national election of 1952 was the fact that Dwight D. Eisenhower had been born in the North Texas town of Denison. The same sentiment which prevents the state's dividing itself was thus enlisted on behalf of the Republicans. It lent conviction to the motto, spread on posters throughout the state during the campaign: "A vote for Ike is a vote for Texas." Another important item was the tidelands oil question. The Democrats maintained that the immense oil reserves beneath the Gulf of Mexico belonged to the entire United States, but Eisenhower maintained that it should be considered the property of the coastal states alone. Texas, with her long coast line, had everything to gain and apparently nothing to lose by taking Eisenhower's side on this issue.

The tidelands fight shows that the old trick of manipulating Texas local pride for a political purpose, used so flagrantly by O'Daniel in his steps toward the senatorship, still gets results. Most Texans consider the tidelands bill a victory for them. Few realize that it is also an important victory for big oil. Oil companies have to pay the federal government a 37.5-per-cent royalty on the exploitation of all nationally owned public lands. Now that Texas is the legal owner of the petroleum under the tidelands, oil companies will have to pay only a 12.5-per-cent royalty for the privilege of extracting it. Also, the state government, being easier to influence than the federal government, makes a far more desirable landlord from the oil company's point of view. These facts were not brought out in the bulk of the political speeches. The debates posed only the welfare of Texas school children against that of children in other states. Property rights were invoked. Much was made of the annexation contract, which reserved the underwater lands for Texas. Texas stood on her treaty rights, as any independent nation would, and Texas bosoms swelled. So did the volume of Eisenhower votes in Texas ballot boxes. And so did the volume of votes for Governor Allan Shivers, who supported Eisenhower.

The strength of Texas's patriotism is in evidence every day along her highways. The Ford Motor Company may ship its cars and trucks ready-made to other states, but not to Texas. It has an assembly plant in Dallas. Fords are shipped there in unfinished form and put together within the state. Thereupon they are labeled "Built in Texas by Texans." This gives Fords an important advantage over other makes on the Texas market. In 1954 General Motors opened a similar assembly plant at Arlington, midway between Dallas and Fort Worth, so that such well-known makes as Buicks, Oldsmobiles, Pontiacs, Cadillacs, and Chevrolets can now bear the same commendatory label.

To those who know Texas intimately and sympathetically,

the five simple words of that label tell a tale of pioneer triumphs and primitive aspirations, of exploitation rationalized
by bigotry, of bitter opposition against foreign tyranny, of the
Alamo's voluntary victims, of Sam Houston's warlike cunning,
of Jim Hogg's heroic defense against monopoly, of W. Lee
O'Daniel's cry for economic self-sufficiency, of misused power
and angry mourners. It is an epic tale, pitiful and exhilarating
at the same time. Texans will not be permitted to forget it
soon, for the Alamo looms unmoved amid San Antonio's noisy
novelties. The San Jacinto Monument stands firm among the
Gulf-born clouds of the Texas sky and the slow-moving vessels
of the Houston Ship Channel. Pecan and walnut trees grow
tall in the Texas wind. The universities and the cities are growing islands of culture, but hillbilly bands continue to agitate
the Texas ether waves.

APPENDIX

Yearly Awards of the Texas Institute of Letters, and Winners

1. $1,000 for the best Texas book of the year. Donor: Carr P. Collins.

J. Frank Dobie	*Apache Gold and Yaqui Silver*	1939
Dora Neill Raymond	*Captain Lee Hall of Texas*	1940
George Sessions Perry	*Hold Autumn in Your Hand*	1941
Edwin Lanham	*Thunder in the Earth*	1942
Fayette Copeland	*Kendall of the Pickayune*	1943
Frank Goodwyn	*The Magic of Limping John*	1944
J. Frank Dobie	*A Texan in England*	1945
Green Peyton	*San Antonio, City in the Sun*	1946
John A. Lomax	*Adventures of a Ballad Hunter*	1947
Herbert Gambrell	*Anson Jones*	1948
Tom Lea	*The Brave Bulls*	1949
Roy Bedicheck	*Karánkaway Country*	1950
Joe B. Frantz	*Gail Borden*	1951
J. Frank Dobie	*The Mustangs*	1952
Walter Prescott Webb	*The Great Frontier*	1953
Paul Horgan	*Great River*	1954

2. $100 for the best book of verse. Various donors.

David Russell	*Sing with Me Now*	1945
Whitney Montgomery	*Joseph's Coat*	1946
Arthur Sampley	*Of the Strong and the Fleet*	1947

Vaida Stewart Montgomery	Hail for Rain	1948
Frances Alexander	Time at the Window	1949
Mary Poole	Being in Night	1950
Arthur Sampley	Furrow with Blackbirds	1951
William D. Barney	Kneel for the Stone	1952
Robert Lee Brothers	The Hidden Harp	1953
William Burford	Man Now	1954

3. $250 for the best first book of fiction. Donor: McMurray Book Shop, Dallas.

Claud Garner	Wetback	1947
David Westheimer	Summer on the Water	1948
Fred Gipson	Hound-Dog Man	1949
William Goyen	The House of Breath	1950
Dillon Anderson	I and Claudie	1951
George Williams	The Blind Bull	1952
Madison Cooper	Sironia, Texas	1953
Wililam A. Owens	Walking on Borrowed Land	1954

4. $500 for the best regional descriptive book. Donor: *The Dallas Morning News.*

| Vance K. Johnson | Heaven's Tableland | 1948 |
| Carl Coke Rister | Oil! Titan of the Southwest | 1949 |

5. $50 for the best juvenile. Donor: Cokesbury Book Store, Dallas.

Elizabeth Baker	Sonny-Boy Sim	1949
Carol Hoff	Johnny Texas	1950
John Latham	Lonesome Longhorn	1951
Siddie Joe Johnson	A Month of Christmases	1952
Charlotte Baker	Magic for Mary M.	1953
Irmengarde Eberle	Lone-Star Fight	1954

6. $25 for the best book design. Donor: Dallas Museum of Fine Arts.

Carl Hertzog	*The Journey of Fray Marcos de Niza*	1950
Texas U. Press	Garcilaso de la Vega's *Florida of the Inca*	1951
S.M.U. Press	Joseph Leach's *The Typical Texan*	1952
Texas U. Press	J. Evetts Haley's *Life on the Texas Range*, with photos by Erwin Smith	1953

7. $1,000 Sons of the Republic of Texas award. Summerfield G. Roberts, donor. Book chosen by historians' group rather than by members of the Texas Institute of Letters.

Eugene Campbell Barker	*The Life of Stephen F. Austin*	1951
J. Evetts Haley	*Fort Concho and the Texas Frontier*	1952
Chris Emmett	*Shanghai Pierce*	1953
Llerena B. Friend	*Sam Houston, the Great Designer*	1954

8. Special award for scholarship.

| Ernest Mossner | *Life of David Hume* | 1954 |

ACKNOWLEDGMENTS

FOR THE CONTENTS of this book I am heavily indebted to my Texas friends, too numerous to name, who have given generously of their time and energy discussing the project with me, supplying me with information, putting me in touch with key persons, entertaining me in their homes, reading and criticizing my manuscript, and educating me in the details of their widely varied specialties. Supreme among my mentors throughout the two years of research and writing was my wife, Elizabeth Goodwyn, who, in addition to undertaking numerous research assignments and making many useful suggestions regarding research procedure, has read the manuscript several times in its sundry forms as it progressed toward perfection. Among the many others whose observations opened new paths of inquiry, the following were particularly influential: Horace Ainsworth, Marihelen McDuff, and John Rosenfield of Dallas; Tom Sutherland and John R. Stockton of Austin; Harold Vagtborg and G. J. Sutton of San Antonio; and John C. McMann of Weslaco. Without the long talks I had with these unusually keen observers, the book would have been considerably different from, and far inferior to, what it is.

Equally penetrating and useful, though limited to more specialized areas, were the observations made by Walter Freytag of La Grange, M. K. Brown of Pampa, Gerald Ashford of San Antonio, J. L. Baughman of Rockport, R. W. Foy and Stuart McGregor of Dallas, George L. Brotherton of Temple, F. D. Wood of Royce City, and Stanley Caufield of Corpus Christi. My brother Finley Goodwyn gave me a good general description of the chicken-raising business in Texas, and J. P. Nystel spared no pains in acquainting me with the Lubbock area. My brother Robert C. Goodwyn showed me through the Celanese plant in Pampa, and I enjoyed tours with detailed explanations from G. Z. Koenig, F. H. Fredricks, Hamilton McGruder, Sam Cantey, M. G. Hassler, and Jim Pringle, through industrial plants, seaports, and social establishments. William F. Keys of the University of Texas, Howard Thompson of Rice, and Charles F. Hiller of the University of Houston provided the most enlightening and thought-provoking of the numerous interviews I held with educational leaders.

Amy Jo Long and Adrian Vaughan of the University of Texas introduced me to many of that institution's leading scholars, and other important contacts were made for me by Lon Tinkle, William H. Kittrell, and Elizabeth Ann McMurray of Dallas, Florence Rosengren and the Maury Mavericks, Jr. and Sr., of San Antonio, Margaret Young of Houston, Hawley Richeson of El Paso, and Clifford Whitney of Pampa.

As I traveled through the state, I enjoyed the hospitality of many Texans, my longest and most fruitful visits being at the homes of Mrs. J. R. Miller at Stowell, Mr. and Mrs. J. W. Chesser in Houston, Kenneth Travis, Ethel Monroe, and Mrs. Nellie McKinney in Dallas, Mrs. J. E. Wiltshire in San Antonio, Dr. J. C. Cross in Lubbock, Mr. and Mrs. Tom Sutherland on their farm near Austin, and Mr. and Mrs. R. L. Goodwyn in the Rio Grande Valley.

One device in my research was a mimeographed questionnaire sent to all Texas towns of one thousand population or more, addressed to the Chamber of Commerce or postmaster. I received hundreds of replies, only the most detailed and helpful of which may be mentioned here. Extremely gratifying response came from the Rio Grande Valley, with particularly detailed information from Betty Weisenhaus of Port Isabel, Sam S. Moody of Mercedes, John McMann of Weslaco, Ralph W. Anderson of San Juan, Lari Kendrick of Pharr, Paul T. Vickers of McAllen, Mrs. Warren Hutt of Rocksprings, and Harvey Seymour of Eagle Pass. The best answers on West Texas came from T. M. White of Grandfalls and Kit Moore of Fort Stockton. From the Lubbock area came large amounts of valuable material from J. P. Nystel of Abernathy, and Nick P. Craig introduced me to Dalhart in the northern edge of the Panhandle. The Red River Valley was aggressively helpful, with the fullest replies coming from Don Swick of Henrietta, Ernest E. Hayley of Saint Jo, and Mrs. Elwyn Sealy of Whitesboro. North Central Texas supplied excellent coverage from John E. Davis of Mesquite, C. L. McCuiston of Forney, and the writers' club, under the leadership of Ruth Stone, at Ennis. The best information from Central Texas I owe to Mrs. Winnie Braden of Hondo, Almond Kirchoff of Fredericksburg, Alfred Wacker of Bartlett, Robert H. Womble of Belton, A. L. Bronstad of Clifton, and Rex Jennings of Brownwood. In East Texas I am particularly indebted to M. V. Watson of Daingerfield, Herman Brown of Lufkin, Wilber H. Propes of Arp, and W. S. Block of Nederland. Much fine information also came from the coastal plain, the best being that supplied by Margaret Webster of Smithville and W. D. Doughty of Robstown. All the larger cities kept me well posted by correspondence and personal assistance throughout the period of research. Especially informative was my correspondence with Mrs. Dorothy Jennings of San Antonio.

To check the accuracy of my statements, I distributed sections of the book among Texans who had specialized in the respective fields of emphasis which I had treated. J. Frank Dobie, who read my sections on Texas literature and range life, was particularly critical and hence particularly helpful. Arthur L. Carnahan, statistician for the Texas Railroad Commission, gave my section on railroads a thorough criticism. Ed Idar of Austin did the same for my section on the Latin American situation and the G.I. Forum. Stuart Long read the two long sections on Texas politics. Hank S. Brown and Robert C. Eckhardt helped me remold and perfect my description of Texas labor laws and conditions. Stanley A. Arbingast of the Bureau of Business Research at the University of Texas read and made some excellent suggestions for my sections dealing with Texas industrial development. Other experts, whose names are too numerous to print, checked briefer portions of the manuscript.

The most complete over-all criticism of the entire book, prior to publication in this final form, came from Herbert Weinstock of Alfred A. Knopf, Incorporated. By discussing it with me, paragraph by paragraph, he has helped me perfect it to a degree far beyond anything I could have done alone. I am also grateful to my agent, James Oliver Brown, for his invaluable contributions both as critic and general counselor.

My published sources are so numerous that a complete set of references is out of the question. Allen Maxwell of the Southern Methodist University Press and Frank Wardlaw of the University of Texas Press have kept me well supplied with complimentary copies of their publications. Stuart Long's *Austin Report* kept me intimately informed of Texas political developments throughout the period of research. Lloyd Glover's *The Pharr Press* and the yearbook published by Mr. and Mrs. Sid Hooper of Donna gave me an equally continuous view of developments in the lower Rio Grande Valley.

The Handbook of Texas, edited by H. Bailey Carroll of the University of Texas, and Stuart McGregor's *Texas Almanac* were indispensable reference tools. For the descriptions of the Texas cattle business I drew heavily on J. Frank Dobie's books and Joseph G. McCoy's *Historic Sketches of the Cattle Trade*, though much of my information came from newspapers of the early days. My description of the Spindletop discovery, while based largely on accounts by Anthony F. Lucas and other eyewitnesses, owes much to James A. Clark and Michel T. Halbouty's *Spindletop*. The story of O'Daniel relies on a combination of newspaper coverage and two book-length biographies, one by C. L. Douglas and Francis Miller, published just after O'Daniel's first election as governor in 1938, and the other by Seth Shepard McKay of Texas Tech, published after the flour-salesman's final election as senator. C. L. Sonnichsen's delightful biography of Roy Bean was an opportunity that I am glad I did not miss. S. G. Reed's exhaustive *History of*

Texas Railroads was the chief source for my narrative of the iron horse, and rich details were gleaned from the plethora of Texas county histories. Among the hundreds of scientific articles and books consulted, those of Elmer H. Johnson, dealing with the petroleum industries and petrochemistry, stand out as being most provocative to me, although the more specialized studies have furnished me more corroboration for my own remarks.

I should like also to express my gratitude to Drew Pearson and Stuart Long for permission to quote them and to Little, Brown and Company, Rinehart and Company, the University of Texas Press, and Kaleidograph Press for permission to quote from books published by them. The *Reporter* magazine has also kindly permitted me to quote from its pages.

Index

A NOTE ON THE TYPE

This book is set in Electra, a Linotype face designed by W. A. Dwiggins. This face cannot be classified as either modern or old-style. It is not based on any historical model, nor does it echo any particular period or style. It avoids the extreme contrast between thick and thin elements that marks most modern faces, and attempts to give a feeling of fluidity, power, and speed.

The book was composed, printed, and bound by Kingsport Press, Inc., Kingsport, Tennessee. Paper manufactured by S. D. Warren Company, Boston. Typography and binding design by Charles E. Skaggs.